THE WOODS

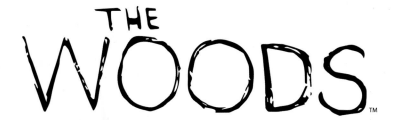

JAMES **TYNION IV** • MICHAEL **DIALYNAS** • JOSAN **GONZALEZ**

VOL. 3
NEW LONDON

BOOM!
STUDIOS

BOOM! STUDIOS

THE WOODS Volume Three, December 2015. Published by BOOM! Studios, a division of Boom Entertainment, Inc. The Woods is ™ & © 2015 James Tynion IV. Originally published in single magazine form as THE WOODS No. 9-12. ™ & © 2014, 2015 James Tynion IV. All rights reserved. BOOM! Studios™ and the BOOM! Studios logo are trademarks of Boom Entertainment, Inc., registered in various countries and categories. All characters, events, and institutions depicted herein are fictional. Any similarity between any of the names, characters, persons, events, and/or institutions in this publication to actual names, characters, and persons, whether living or dead, events, and/or institutions is unintended and purely coincidental. BOOM! Studios does not read or accept unsolicited submissions of ideas, stories, or artwork.

A catalog record of this book is available from OCLC and from the BOOM! Studios website, www.boom-studios.com, on the Librarians page.

BOOM! Studios, 5670 Wilshire Boulevard, Suite 450, Los Angeles, CA 90036-5679. Printed in China. First Printing.

ISBN: 978-1-60886-773-8, eISBN: 978-1-61398-444-4

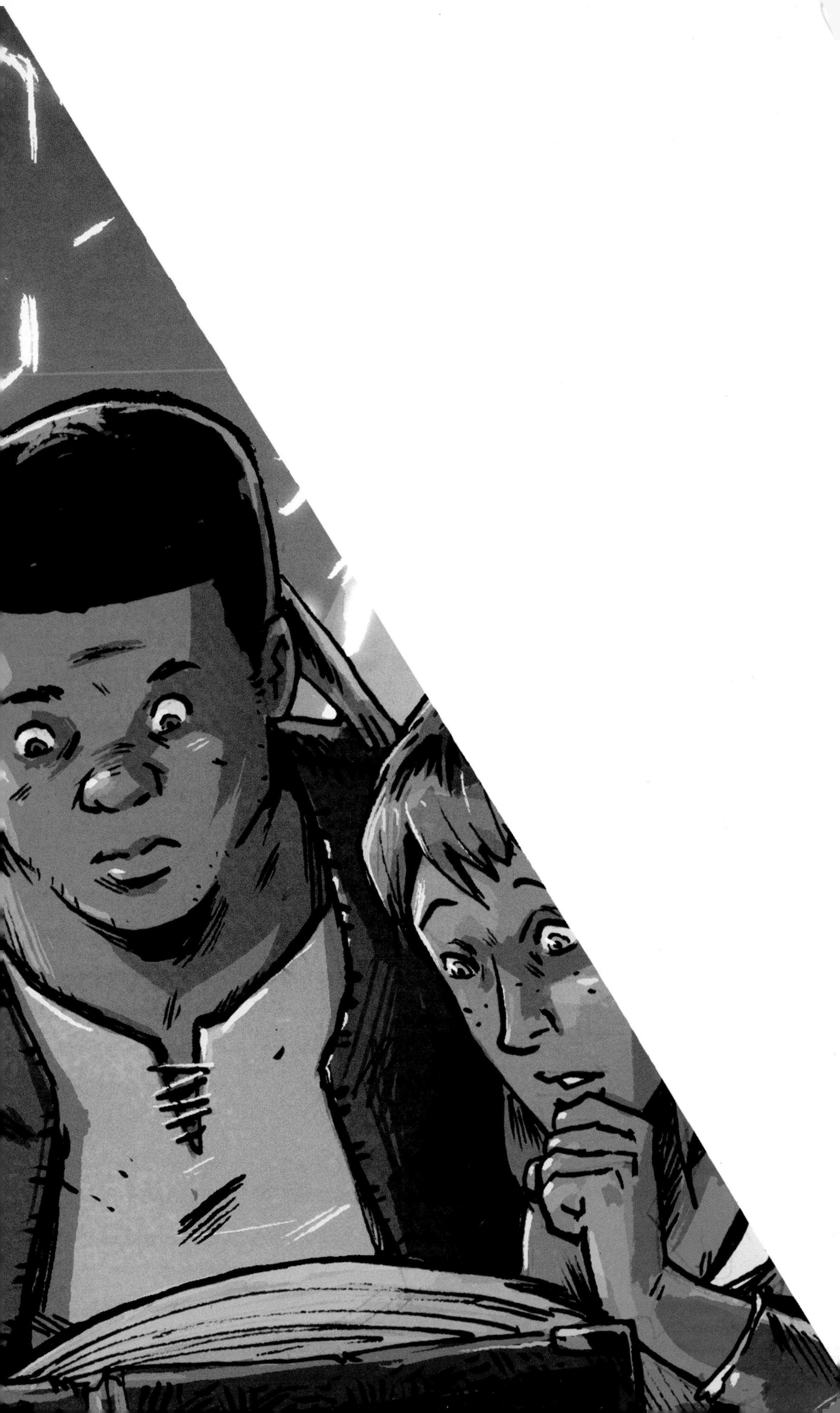

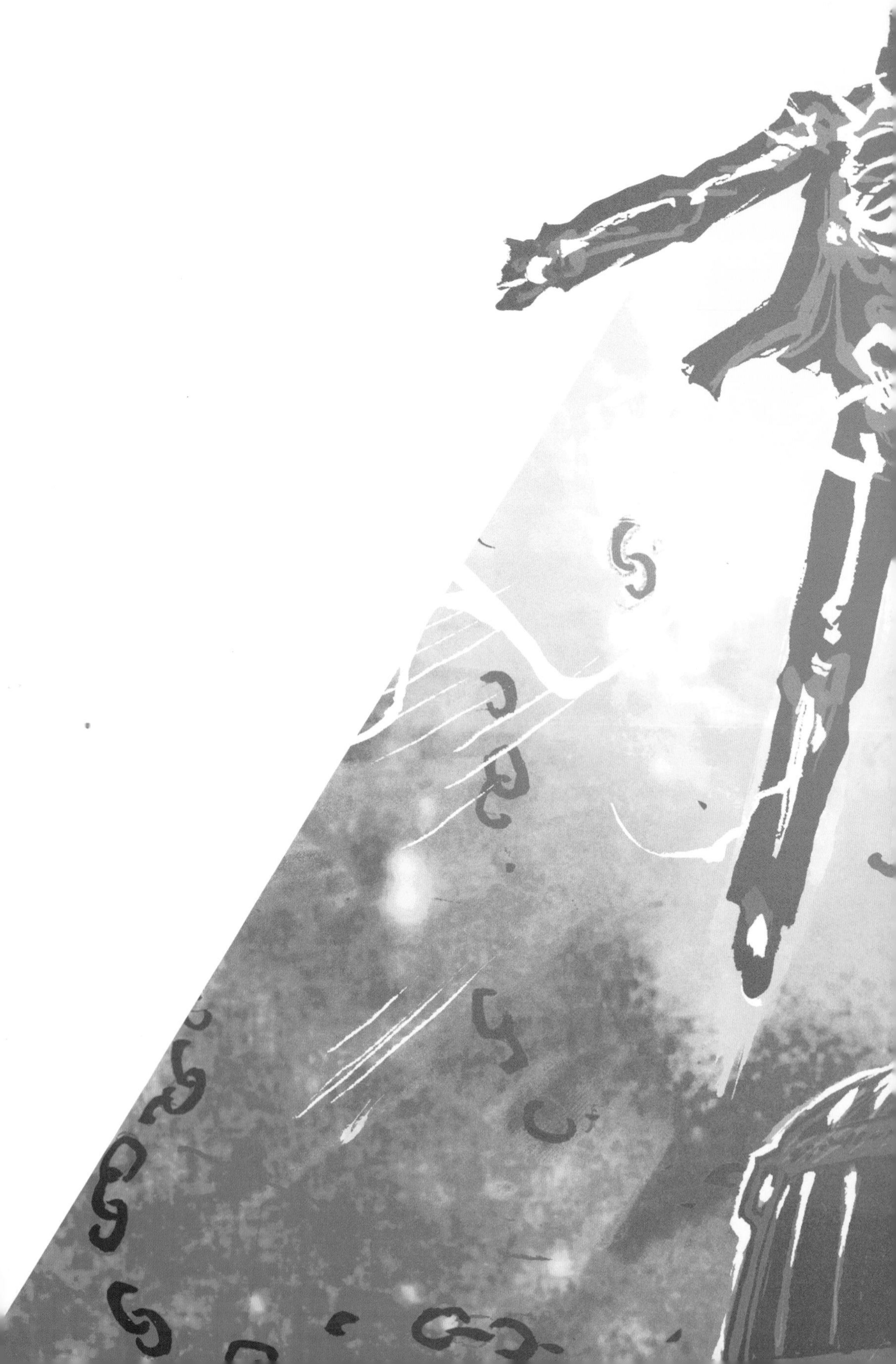

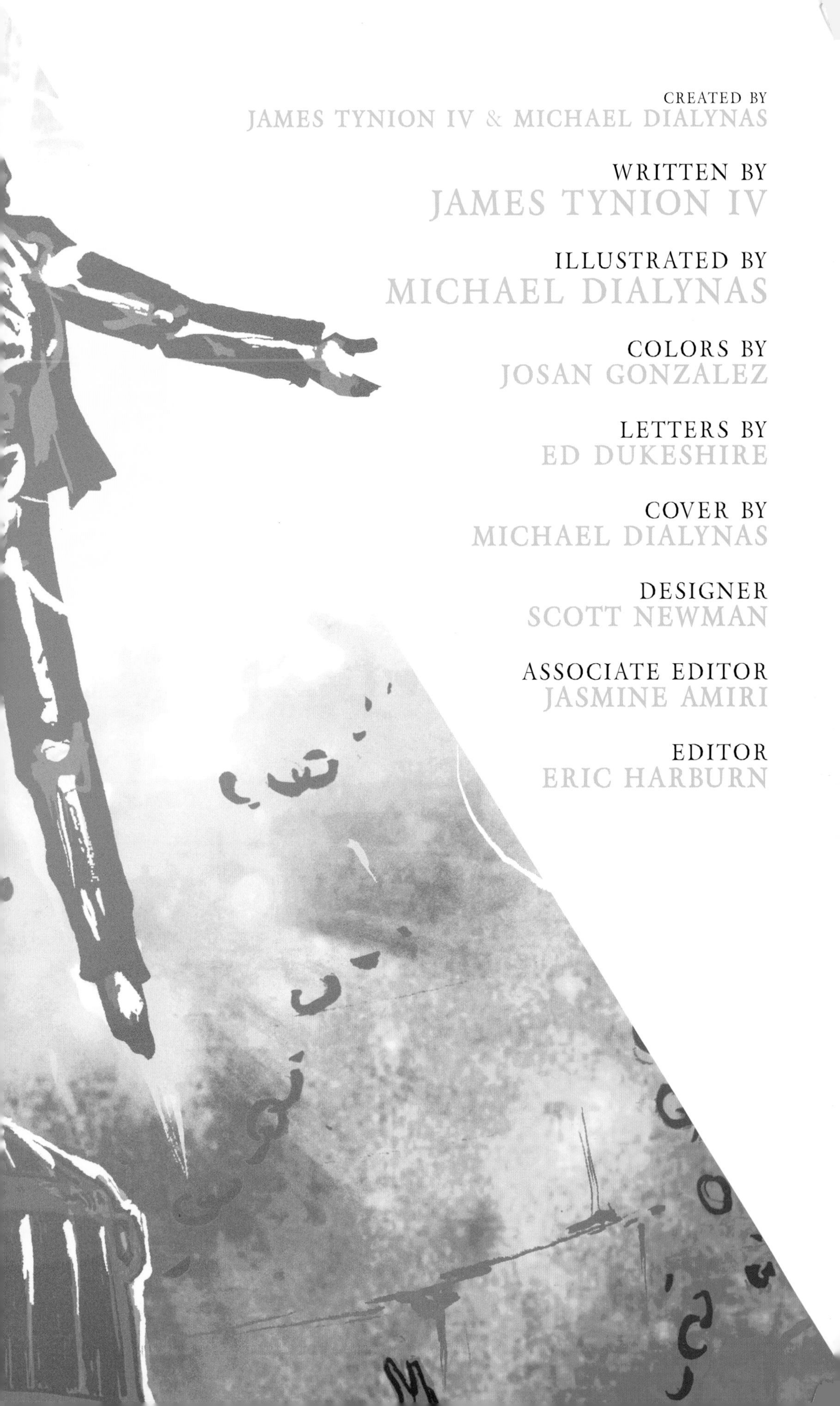

CREATED BY
JAMES TYNION IV & MICHAEL DIALYNAS

WRITTEN BY
JAMES TYNION IV

ILLUSTRATED BY
MICHAEL DIALYNAS

COLORS BY
JOSAN GONZALEZ

LETTERS BY
ED DUKESHIRE

COVER BY
MICHAEL DIALYNAS

DESIGNER
SCOTT NEWMAN

ASSOCIATE EDITOR
JASMINE AMIRI

EDITOR
ERIC HARBURN

CHAPTER NINE

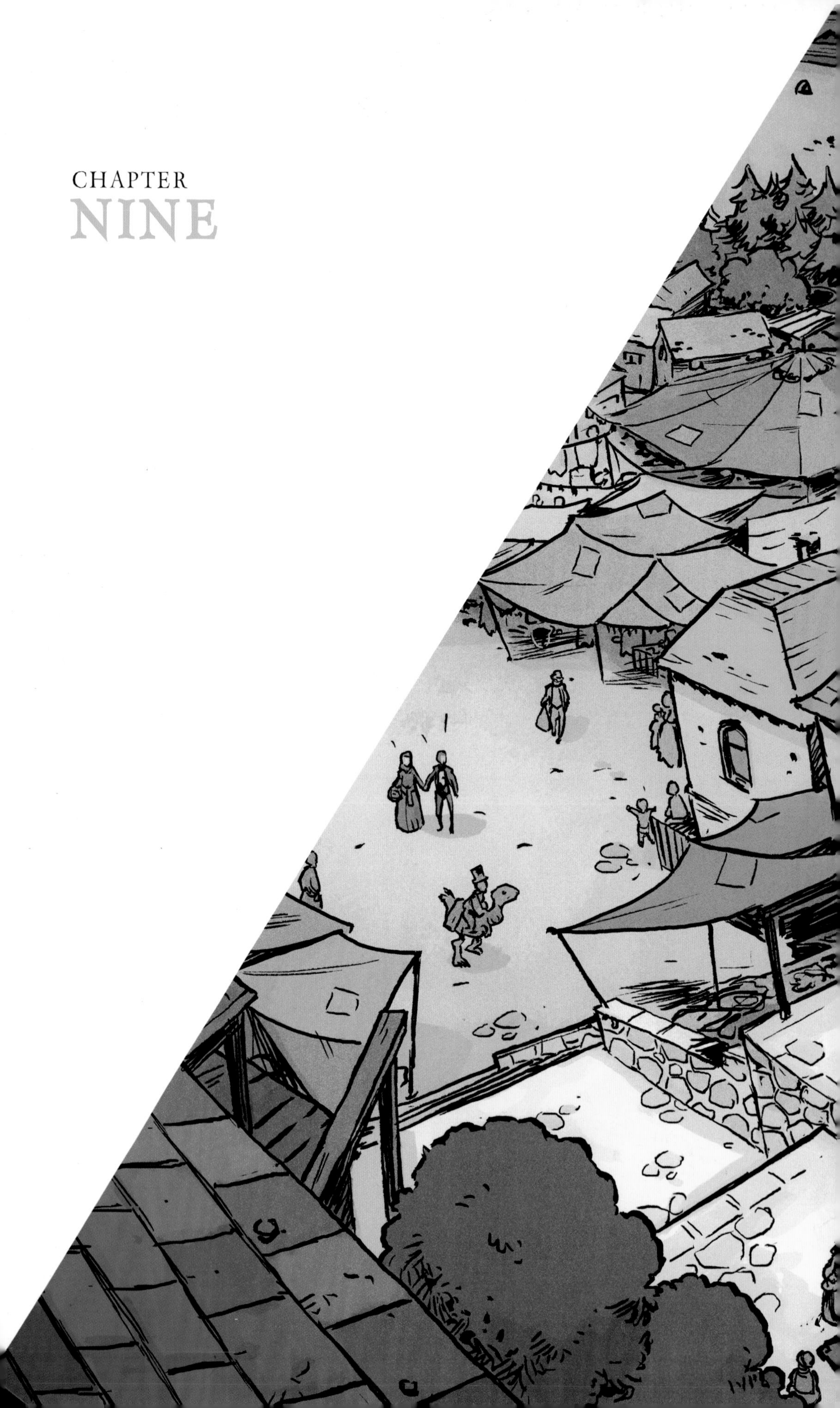

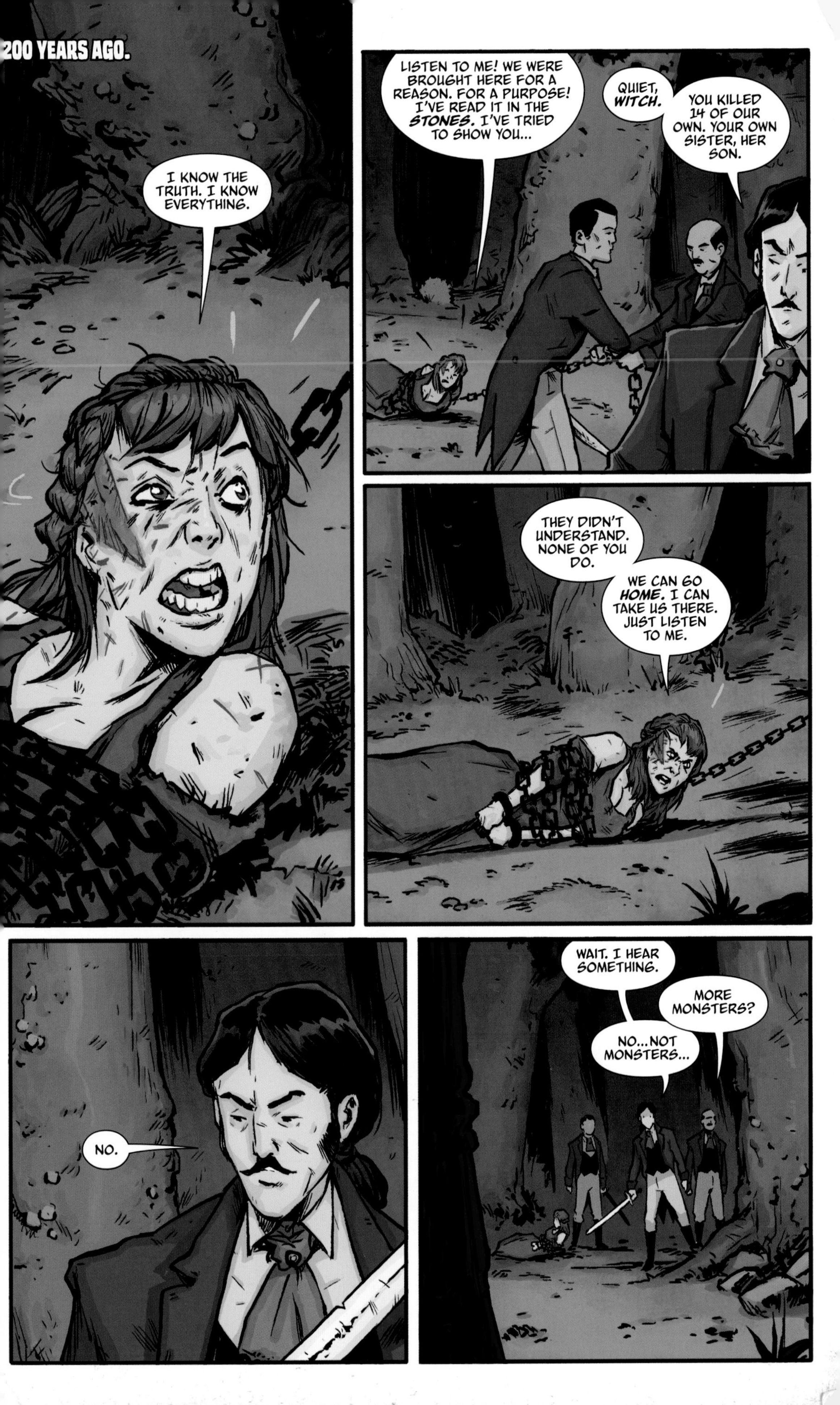
200 YEARS AGO.
I KNOW THE TRUTH. I KNOW EVERYTHING.
LISTEN TO ME! WE WERE BROUGHT HERE FOR A REASON. FOR A PURPOSE! I'VE READ IT IN THE STONES. I'VE TRIED TO SHOW YOU...
QUIET, WITCH.
YOU KILLED 14 OF OUR OWN. YOUR OWN SISTER, HER SON.
THEY DIDN'T UNDERSTAND. NONE OF YOU DO.
WE CAN GO HOME. I CAN TAKE US THERE. JUST LISTEN TO ME.
NO.
WAIT. I HEAR SOMETHING.
MORE MONSTERS?
NO...NOT MONSTERS...

MY GOD. MORE *AFRICANS?*

PERHAPS. BUT YOU KNOW THE LAWS OF INCORPORATION.

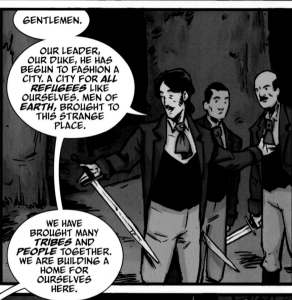

GENTLEMEN.

OUR LEADER, OUR *DUKE*, HE HAS BEGUN TO FASHION A CITY. A CITY FOR *ALL REFUGEES* LIKE OURSELVES. MEN OF *EARTH*, BROUGHT TO THIS STRANGE PLACE.

WE HAVE BROUGHT MANY *TRIBES* AND *PEOPLE* TOGETHER. WE ARE BUILDING A HOME FOR OURSELVES HERE.

COME JOIN US. JOIN US IN *NEW LONDON.* LET US STAND TOGETHER AGAINST THE HORDE.

HER NAME IS *LYDIA COLE*... SHE IS A KILLER, AND A WITCH...SHE DID UNNATURAL THINGS WITH THE *BLACK STONES* IN THREE CAMPS ALREADY.

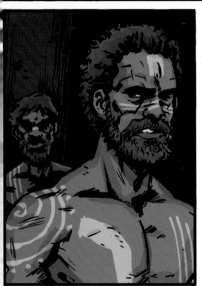

WHERE...
WHERE DID
THEY GO?

THEY'VE BEEN HERE FOR
NEARLY A THOUSAND YEARS.
THE ROCKS TOLD ME. THEY
KNOW WHEN NOT TO
INTERFERE.

NO! THE
LIGHT!

KILL HER,
QUICK.

YOU'VE LOST YOUR CHANCE FOR THAT.

YOU WON'T STOP US.

YOU'RE ALL ALONE OUT HERE...

AM I?

THIS WORLD IS A *WEAPON*, SEEKING SOMEONE TO WIELD IT.

AND WIELD IT, I SHALL.

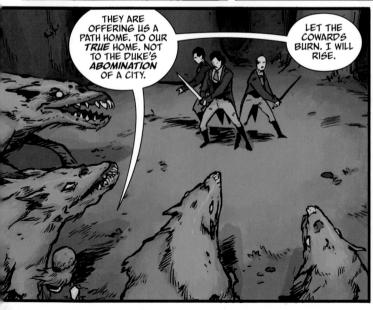

THEY ARE OFFERING US A PATH HOME. TO OUR *TRUE* HOME. NOT TO THE DUKE'S *ABOMINATION* OF A CITY.

LET THE COWARDS BURN. I WILL RISE.

AND BECOME SOMETHING FINER THAN YOU CAN COMPREHEND.

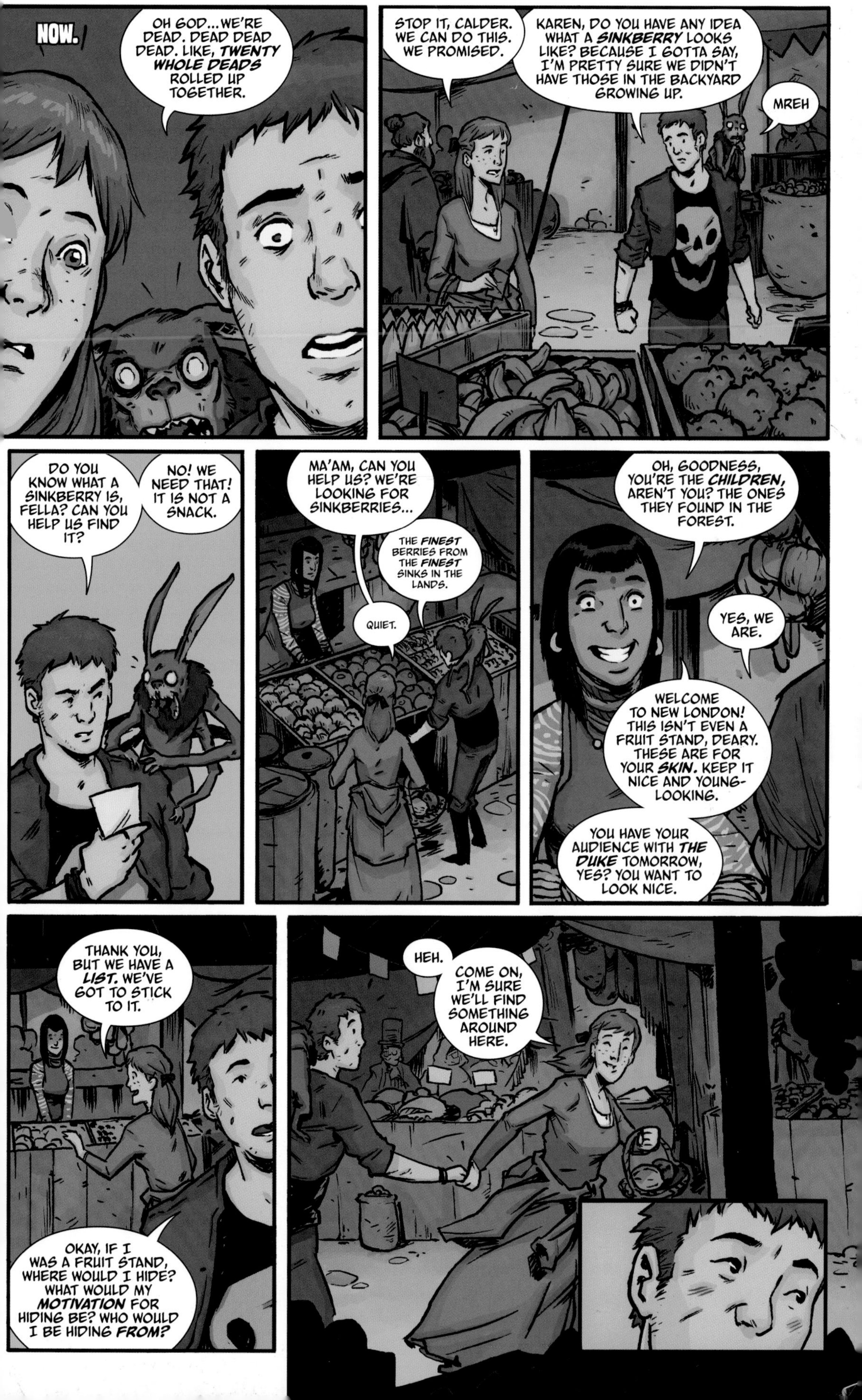
NOW.
OH GOD...WE'RE DEAD. DEAD DEAD DEAD. LIKE, TWENTY WHOLE DEADS ROLLED UP TOGETHER.
STOP IT, CALDER. WE CAN DO THIS. WE PROMISED.
KAREN, DO YOU HAVE ANY IDEA WHAT A SINKBERRY LOOKS LIKE? BECAUSE I GOTTA SAY, I'M PRETTY SURE WE DIDN'T HAVE THOSE IN THE BACKYARD GROWING UP.
MREH
DO YOU KNOW WHAT A SINKBERRY IS, FELLA? CAN YOU HELP US FIND IT?
NO! WE NEED THAT! IT IS NOT A SNACK.
MA'AM, CAN YOU HELP US? WE'RE LOOKING FOR SINKBERRIES...
THE FINEST BERRIES FROM THE FINEST SINKS IN THE LANDS.
QUIET.
OH, GOODNESS, YOU'RE THE CHILDREN, AREN'T YOU? THE ONES THEY FOUND IN THE FOREST.
YES, WE ARE.
WELCOME TO NEW LONDON! THIS ISN'T EVEN A FRUIT STAND, DEARY. THESE ARE FOR YOUR SKIN. KEEP IT NICE AND YOUNG-LOOKING.
YOU HAVE YOUR AUDIENCE WITH THE DUKE TOMORROW, YES? YOU WANT TO LOOK NICE.
THANK YOU, BUT WE HAVE A LIST. WE'VE GOT TO STICK TO IT.
OKAY, IF I WAS A FRUIT STAND, WHERE WOULD I HIDE? WHAT WOULD MY MOTIVATION FOR HIDING BE? WHO WOULD I BE HIDING FROM?
HEH.
COME ON, I'M SURE WE'LL FIND SOMETHING AROUND HERE.

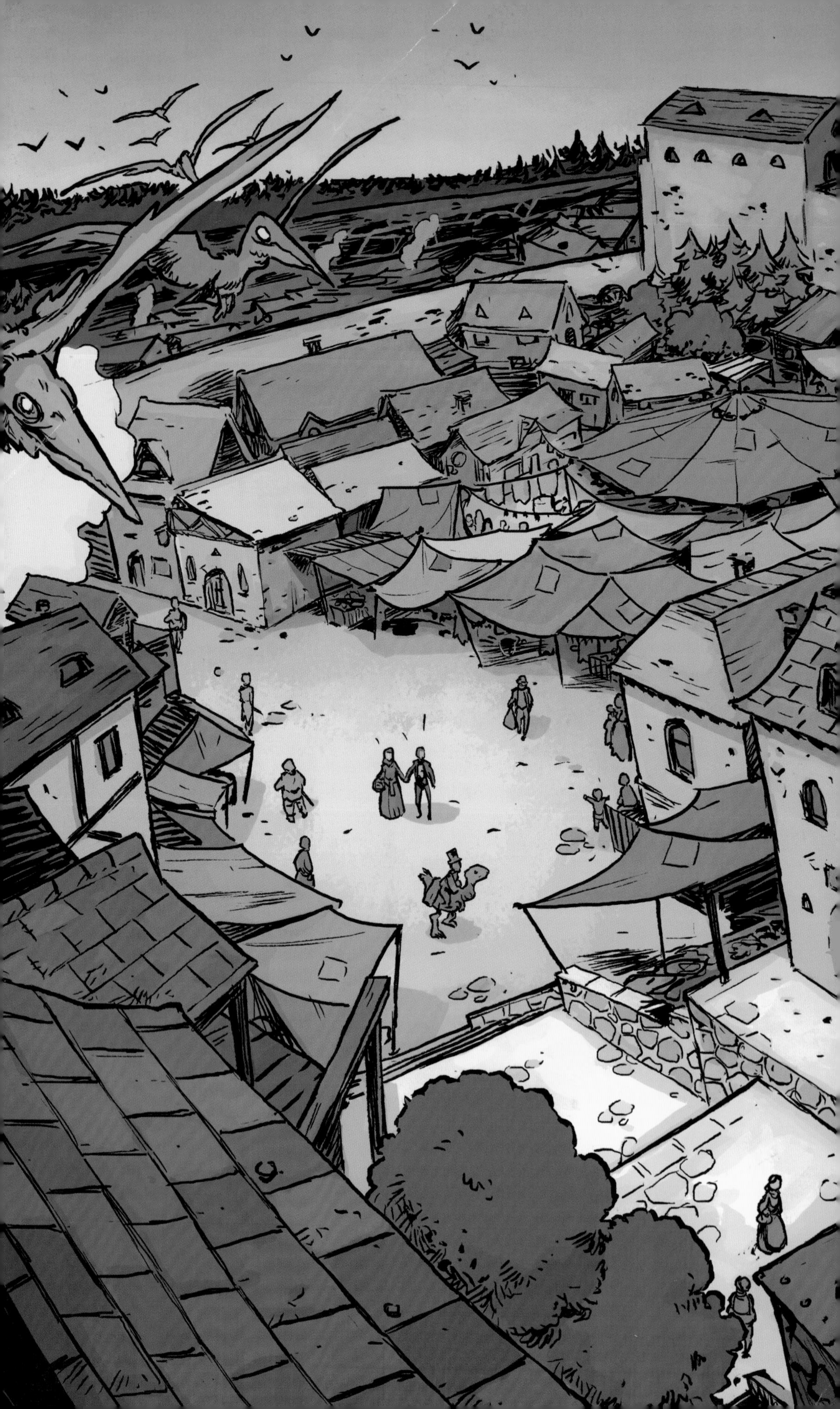

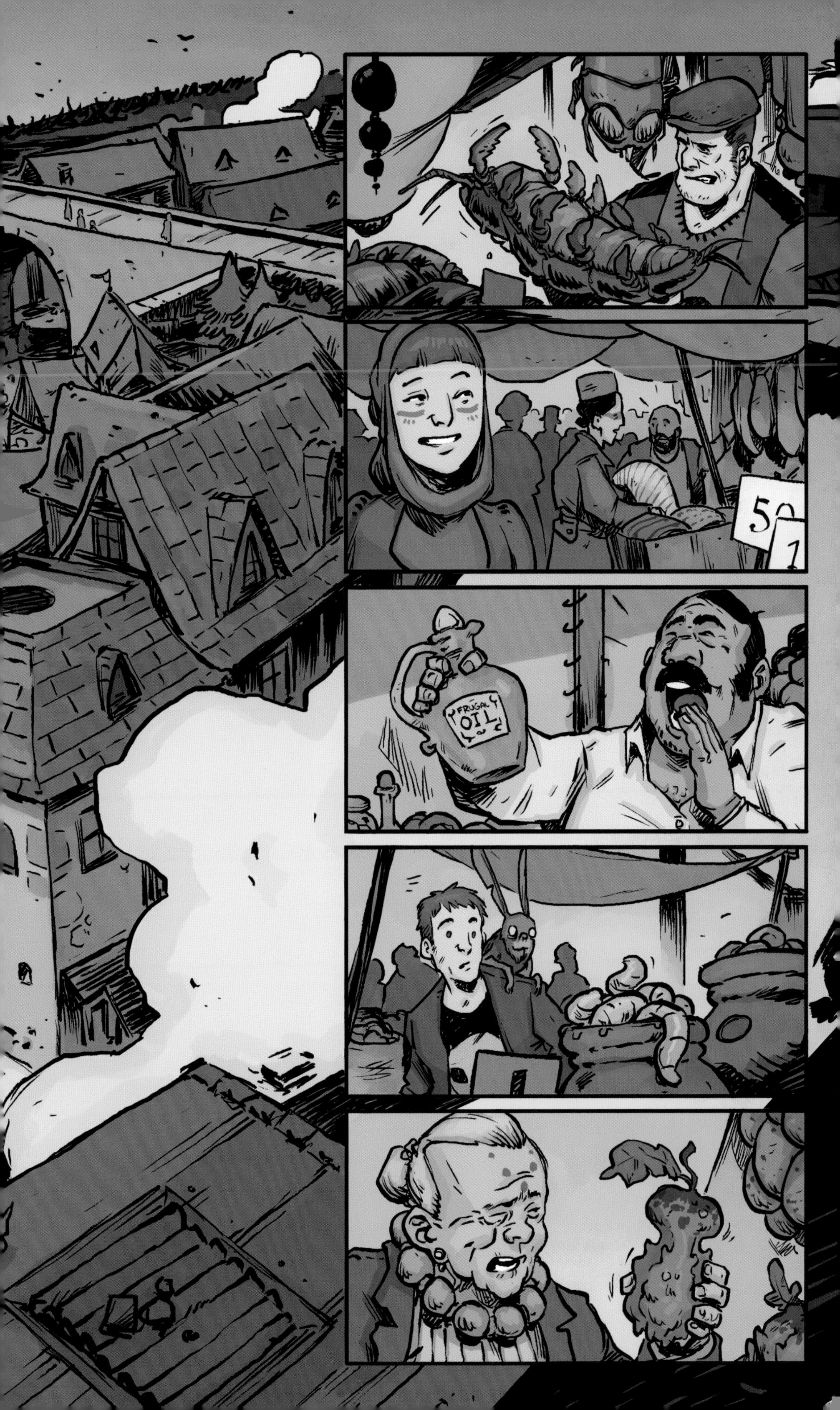
FRUGAL
OIL

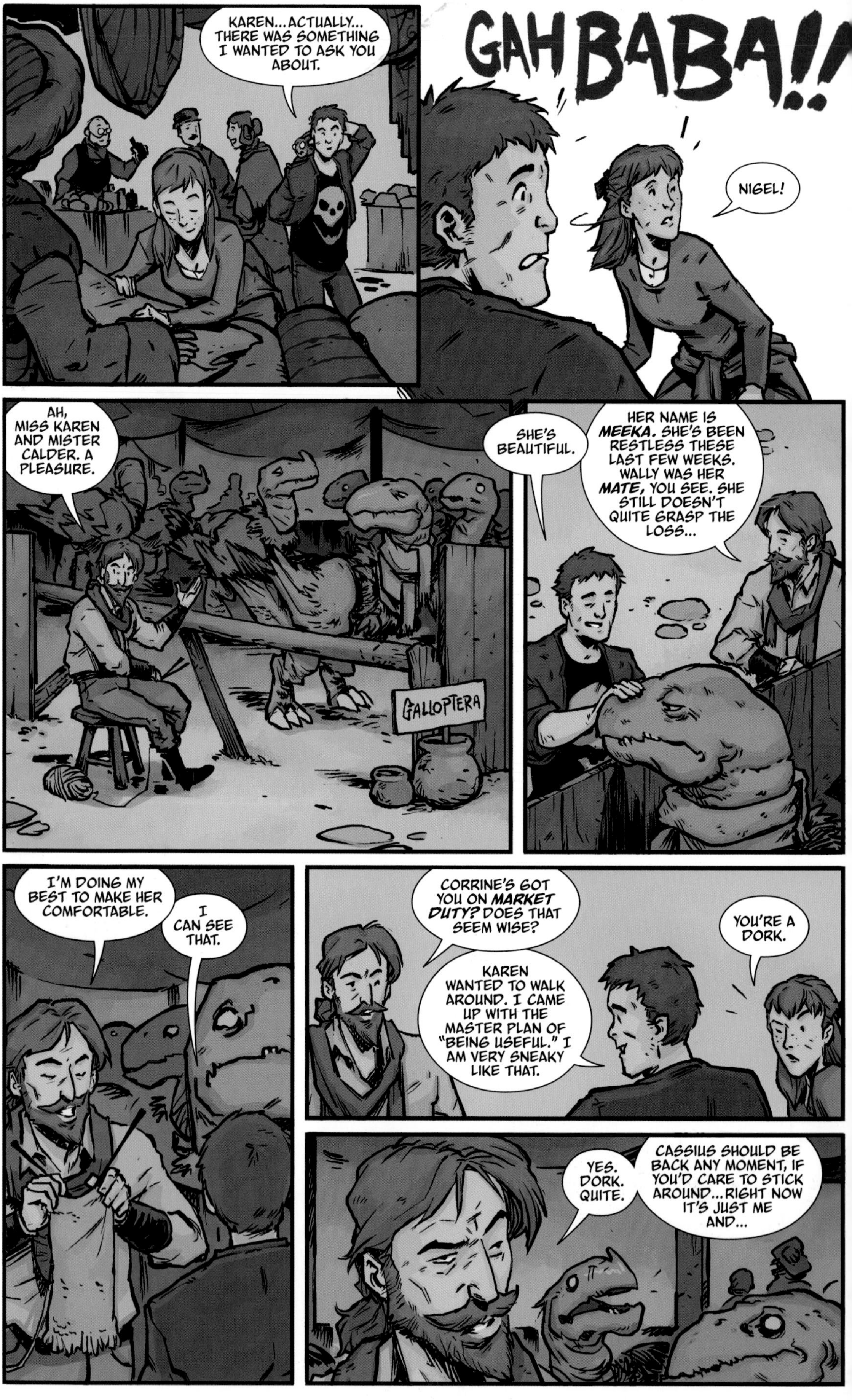
KAREN...ACTUALLY... THERE WAS SOMETHING I WANTED TO ASK YOU ABOUT.
GAH BABA!!
NIGEL!
AH, MISS KAREN AND MISTER CALDER. A PLEASURE.
GALLOPTERA
SHE'S BEAUTIFUL.
HER NAME IS MEEKA. SHE'S BEEN RESTLESS THESE LAST FEW WEEKS. WALLY WAS HER MATE, YOU SEE. SHE STILL DOESN'T QUITE GRASP THE LOSS...
I'M DOING MY BEST TO MAKE HER COMFORTABLE.
I CAN SEE THAT.
CORRINE'S GOT YOU ON MARKET DUTY? DOES THAT SEEM WISE?
KAREN WANTED TO WALK AROUND. I CAME UP WITH THE MASTER PLAN OF "BEING USEFUL." I AM VERY SNEAKY LIKE THAT.
YOU'RE A DORK.
YES. DORK. QUITE.
CASSIUS SHOULD BE BACK ANY MOMENT, IF YOU'D CARE TO STICK AROUND...RIGHT NOW IT'S JUST ME AND...

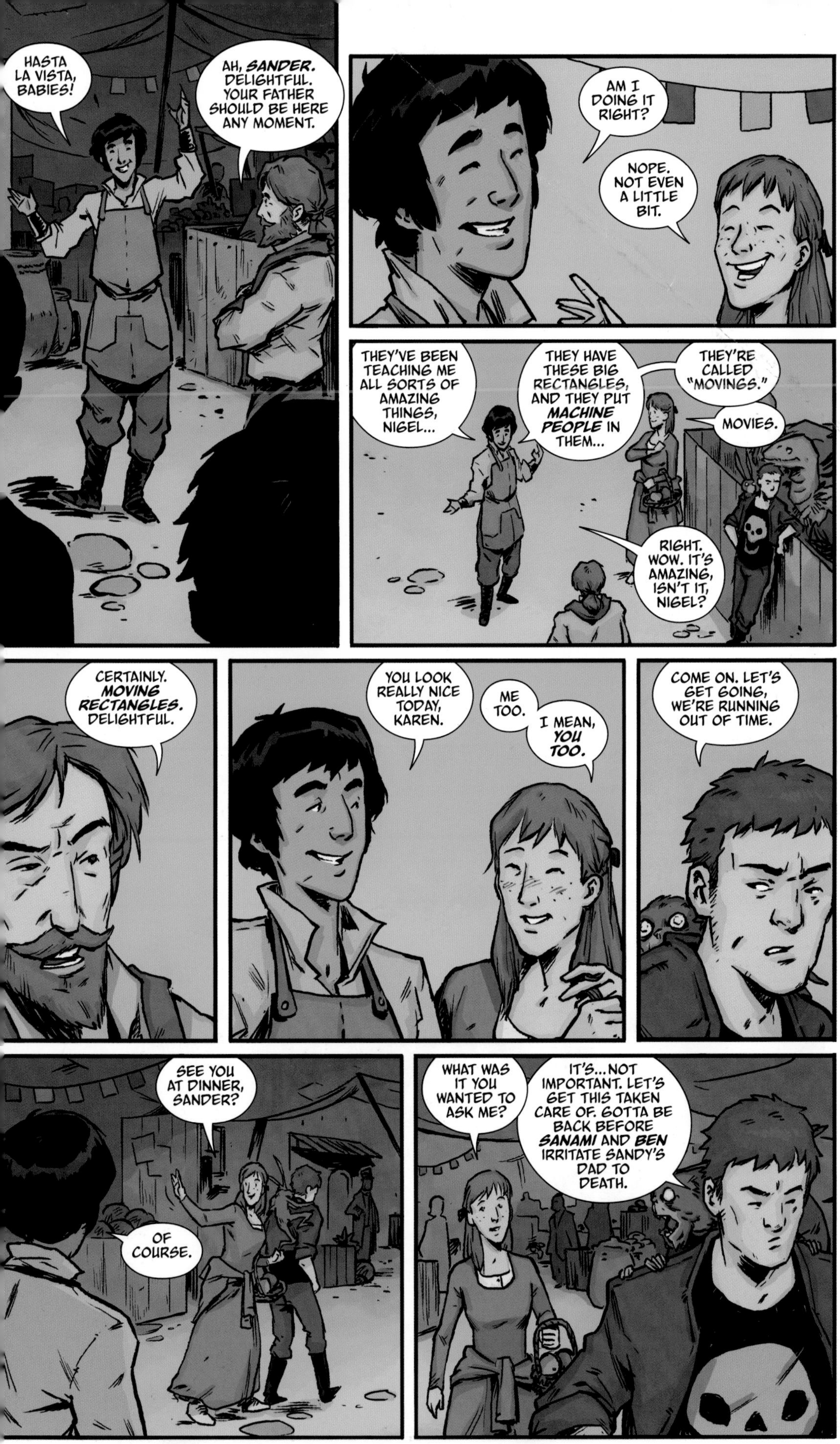
HASTA LA VISTA, BABIES!
AH, *SANDER.* DELIGHTFUL. YOUR FATHER SHOULD BE HERE ANY MOMENT.
AM I DOING IT RIGHT?
NOPE. NOT EVEN A LITTLE BIT.
THEY'VE BEEN TEACHING ME ALL SORTS OF AMAZING THINGS, NIGEL...
THEY HAVE THESE BIG RECTANGLES, AND THEY PUT *MACHINE PEOPLE* IN THEM...
THEY'RE CALLED "MOVINGS."
MOVIES.
RIGHT. WOW. IT'S AMAZING, ISN'T IT, NIGEL?
CERTAINLY. *MOVING RECTANGLES.* DELIGHTFUL.
YOU LOOK REALLY NICE TODAY, KAREN.
ME TOO.
I MEAN, *YOU TOO.*
COME ON. LET'S GET GOING, WE'RE RUNNING OUT OF TIME.
SEE YOU AT DINNER, SANDER?
OF COURSE.
WHAT WAS IT YOU WANTED TO ASK ME?
IT'S...NOT IMPORTANT. LET'S GET THIS TAKEN CARE OF. GOTTA BE BACK BEFORE *SANAMI* AND *BEN* IRRITATE SANDY'S DAD TO DEATH.

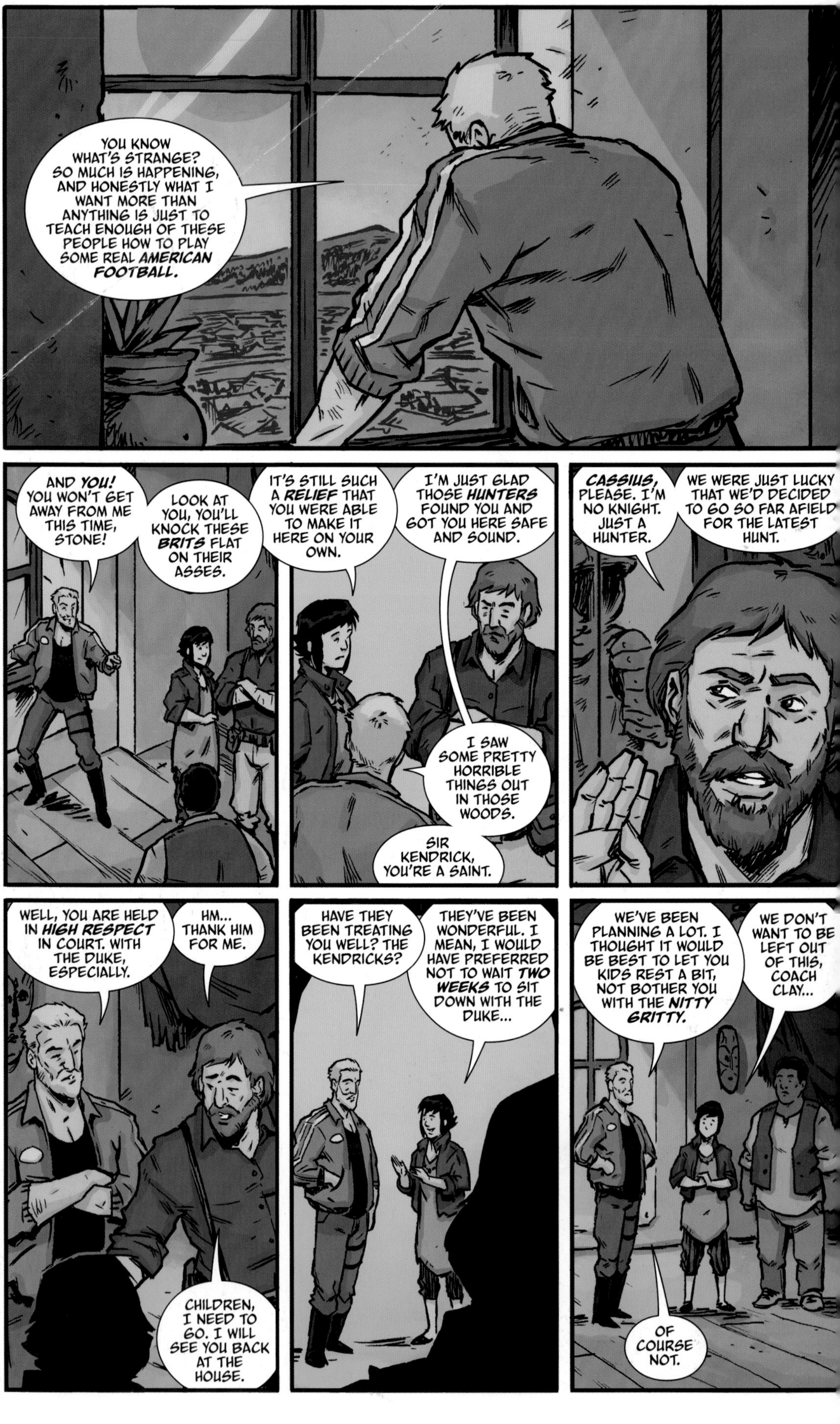

YOU KNOW WHAT'S STRANGE? SO MUCH IS HAPPENING, AND HONESTLY WHAT I WANT MORE THAN ANYTHING IS JUST TO TEACH ENOUGH OF THESE PEOPLE HOW TO PLAY SOME REAL *AMERICAN FOOTBALL.*
AND *YOU!* YOU WON'T GET AWAY FROM ME THIS TIME, STONE!
LOOK AT YOU, YOU'LL KNOCK THESE *BRITS* FLAT ON THEIR ASSES.
IT'S STILL SUCH A *RELIEF* THAT YOU WERE ABLE TO MAKE IT HERE ON YOUR OWN.
I'M JUST GLAD THOSE *HUNTERS* FOUND YOU AND GOT YOU HERE SAFE AND SOUND.
I SAW SOME PRETTY HORRIBLE THINGS OUT IN THOSE WOODS.
SIR KENDRICK, YOU'RE A SAINT.
CASSIUS, PLEASE. I'M NO KNIGHT. JUST A HUNTER.
WE WERE JUST LUCKY THAT WE'D DECIDED TO GO SO FAR AFIELD FOR THE LATEST HUNT.
WELL, YOU ARE HELD IN *HIGH RESPECT* IN COURT. WITH THE DUKE, ESPECIALLY.
HM... THANK HIM FOR ME.
CHILDREN, I NEED TO GO. I WILL SEE YOU BACK AT THE HOUSE.
HAVE THEY BEEN TREATING YOU WELL? THE KENDRICKS?
THEY'VE BEEN WONDERFUL. I MEAN, I WOULD HAVE PREFERRED NOT TO WAIT *TWO WEEKS* TO SIT DOWN WITH THE DUKE...
WE'VE BEEN PLANNING A LOT. I THOUGHT IT WOULD BE BEST TO LET YOU KIDS REST A BIT, NOT BOTHER YOU WITH THE *NITTY GRITTY.*
WE DON'T WANT TO BE LEFT OUT OF THIS, COACH CLAY...
OF COURSE NOT.

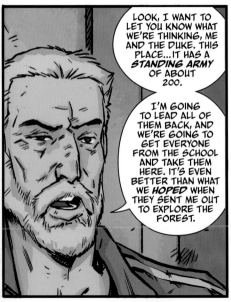

LOOK, I WANT TO LET YOU KNOW WHAT WE'RE THINKING, ME AND THE DUKE. THIS PLACE...IT HAS A **STANDING ARMY** OF ABOUT 200.

I'M GOING TO LEAD ALL OF THEM BACK, AND WE'RE GOING TO GET EVERYONE FROM THE SCHOOL AND TAKE THEM HERE. IT'S EVEN BETTER THAN WHAT WE **HOPED** WHEN THEY SENT ME OUT TO EXPLORE THE FOREST.

LOOK AT THIS PLACE...LOOK AT ALL THEY'VE MANAGED TO ACCOMPLISH.

200 YEARS AGO A **SMALL VILLAGE** WAS BEAMED UP, JUST THE SAME AS US, AND THEY SAW THE OPPORTUNITY TO BUILD A NEW LIFE. A **REAL** LIFE.

IT SEEMS LIKE THERE'S BEEN A BATCH OF HUMANS ONCE A **CENTURY**, GOING BACK AS FAR AS ANYONE REMEMBERS. NEW LONDON, IT'S A PLACE OF **UNITY**. A PLACE WHERE WE CAN ACTUALLY LIVE SOMETHING CLOSE TO A **NORMAL** LIFE.

AND JUST THINK, IN OUR LIBRARY WE HAVE BOOKS ON **ELECTRICITY, BASIC MECHANICS**...WE COULD HELP BRING A WHOLE NEW WAY OF LIFE HERE. A **MODERN** LIFE.

IT SOUNDS INCREDIBLE.

YEAH. IT SOUNDS GREAT.

GOD, I CAN'T WAIT TO SEE THEM ALL AGAIN...I CAN ONLY IMAGINE THE KIND OF **HEADACHES** MARIA IS GIVING PRINCIPAL BEAUMONT.

...

SHE'S A REAL PAIN IN THE BUTT, THAT'S FOR SURE.

WHERE'S YOUR FRIEND? I THOUGHT THAT LITTLE **STAGE CREW KID** WAS SUPPOSED TO COME WITH YOU?

ISAAC?

HE'S...

HE'S **COPING.**

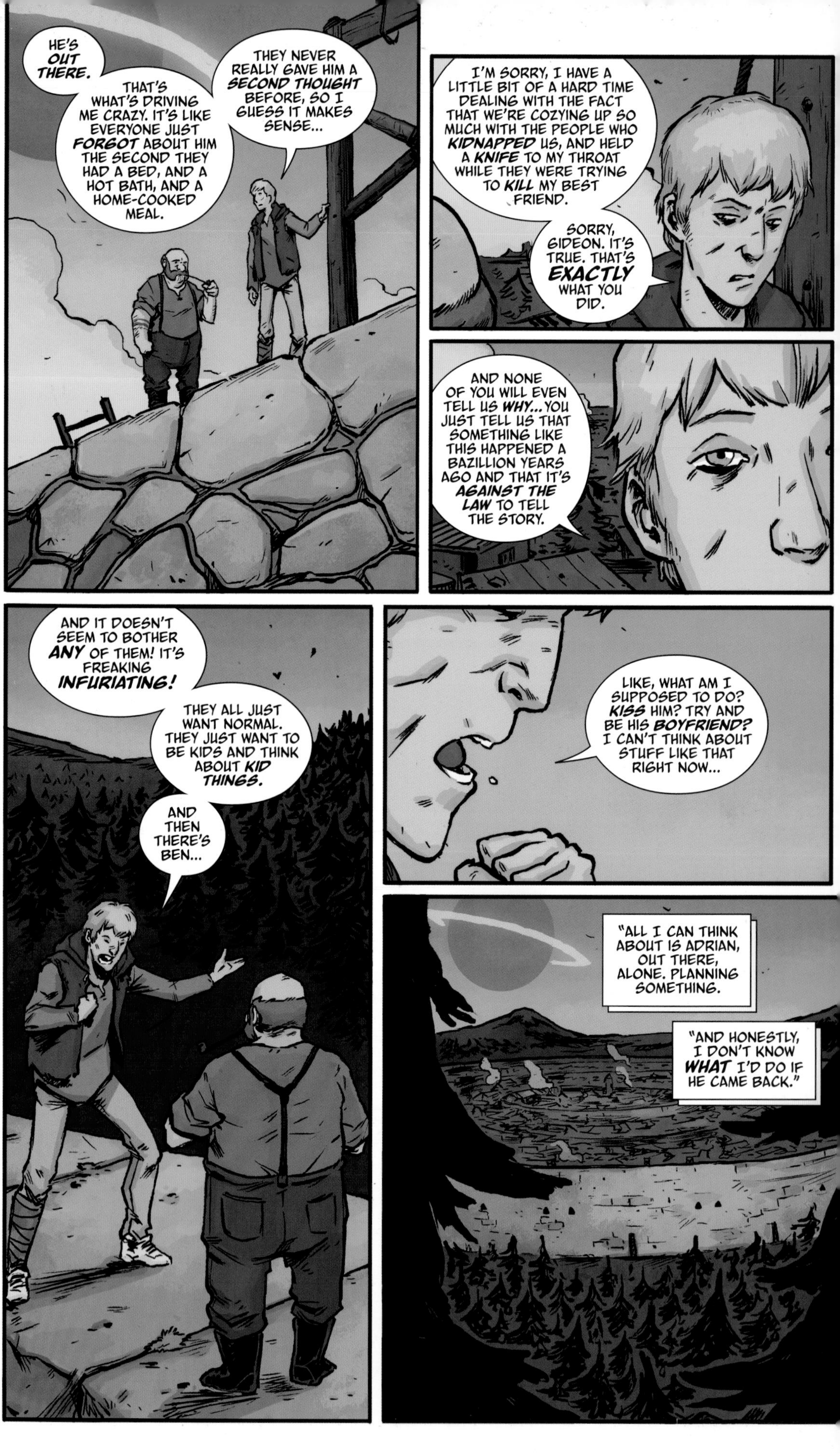

HE'S OUT THERE.
THAT'S WHAT'S DRIVING ME CRAZY. IT'S LIKE EVERYONE JUST FORGOT ABOUT HIM THE SECOND THEY HAD A BED, AND A HOT BATH, AND A HOME-COOKED MEAL.
THEY NEVER REALLY GAVE HIM A SECOND THOUGHT BEFORE, SO I GUESS IT MAKES SENSE...
I'M SORRY, I HAVE A LITTLE BIT OF A HARD TIME DEALING WITH THE FACT THAT WE'RE COZYING UP SO MUCH WITH THE PEOPLE WHO KIDNAPPED US, AND HELD A KNIFE TO MY THROAT WHILE THEY WERE TRYING TO KILL MY BEST FRIEND.
SORRY, GIDEON. IT'S TRUE. THAT'S EXACTLY WHAT YOU DID.
AND NONE OF YOU WILL EVEN TELL US WHY... YOU JUST TELL US THAT SOMETHING LIKE THIS HAPPENED A BAZILLION YEARS AGO AND THAT IT'S AGAINST THE LAW TO TELL THE STORY.
AND IT DOESN'T SEEM TO BOTHER ANY OF THEM! IT'S FREAKING INFURIATING!
THEY ALL JUST WANT NORMAL. THEY JUST WANT TO BE KIDS AND THINK ABOUT KID THINGS.
AND THEN THERE'S BEN...
LIKE, WHAT AM I SUPPOSED TO DO? KISS HIM? TRY AND BE HIS BOYFRIEND? I CAN'T THINK ABOUT STUFF LIKE THAT RIGHT NOW...
"ALL I CAN THINK ABOUT IS ADRIAN, OUT THERE, ALONE. PLANNING SOMETHING.
"AND HONESTLY, I DON'T KNOW WHAT I'D DO IF HE CAME BACK."

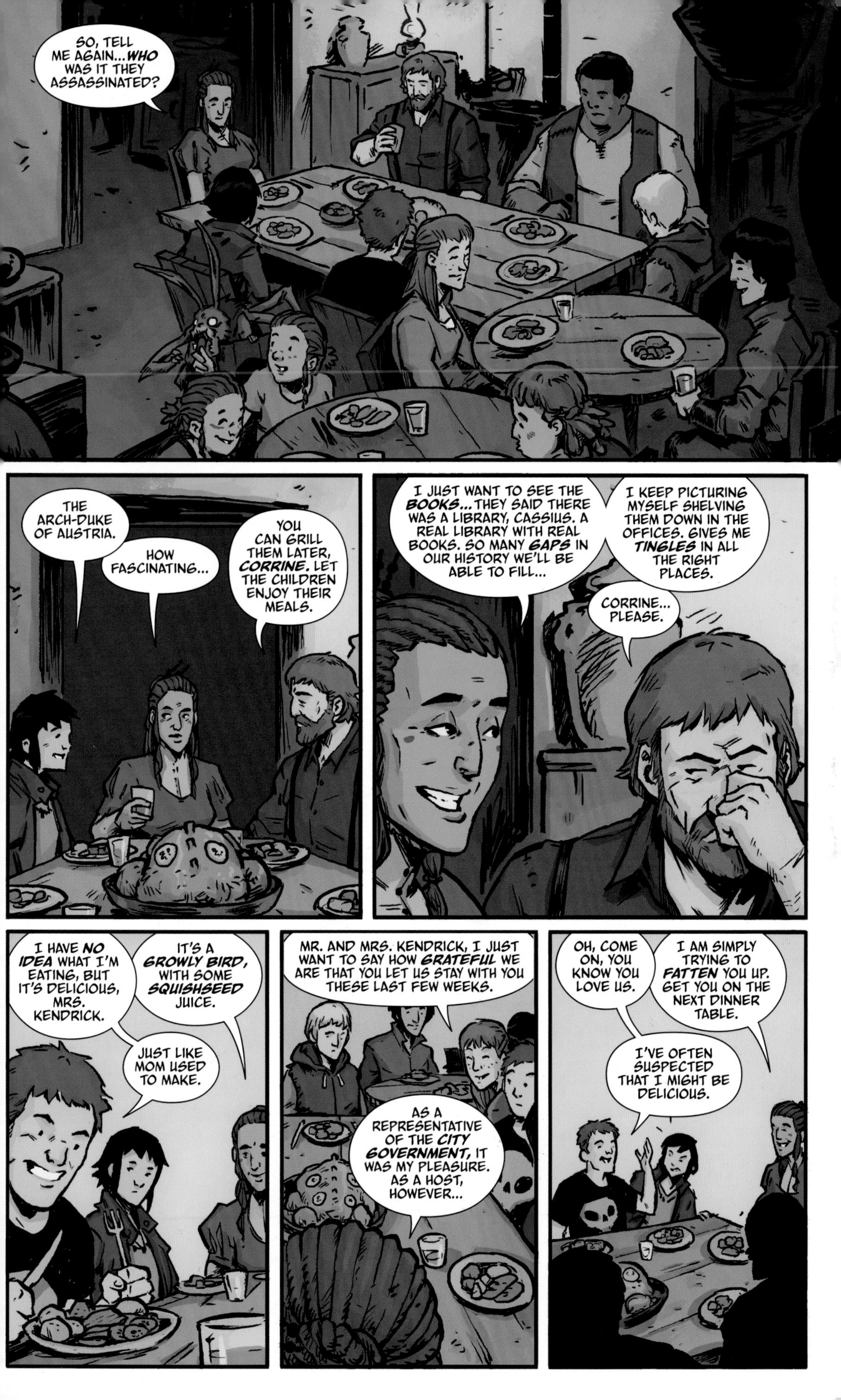
SO, TELL ME AGAIN...WHO WAS IT THEY ASSASSINATED?
THE ARCH-DUKE OF AUSTRIA.
HOW FASCINATING...
YOU CAN GRILL THEM LATER, CORRINE. LET THE CHILDREN ENJOY THEIR MEALS.
I JUST WANT TO SEE THE BOOKS... THEY SAID THERE WAS A LIBRARY, CASSIUS. A REAL LIBRARY WITH REAL BOOKS. SO MANY GAPS IN OUR HISTORY WE'LL BE ABLE TO FILL...
I KEEP PICTURING MYSELF SHELVING THEM DOWN IN THE OFFICES. GIVES ME TINGLES IN ALL THE RIGHT PLACES.
CORRINE... PLEASE.
I HAVE NO IDEA WHAT I'M EATING, BUT IT'S DELICIOUS, MRS. KENDRICK.
IT'S A GROWLY BIRD, WITH SOME SQUISHSEED JUICE.
JUST LIKE MOM USED TO MAKE.
MR. AND MRS. KENDRICK, I JUST WANT TO SAY HOW GRATEFUL WE ARE THAT YOU LET US STAY WITH YOU THESE LAST FEW WEEKS.
AS A REPRESENTATIVE OF THE CITY GOVERNMENT, IT WAS MY PLEASURE. AS A HOST, HOWEVER...
OH, COME ON, YOU KNOW YOU LOVE US.
I AM SIMPLY TRYING TO FATTEN YOU UP. GET YOU ON THE NEXT DINNER TABLE.
I'VE OFTEN SUSPECTED THAT I MIGHT BE DELICIOUS.

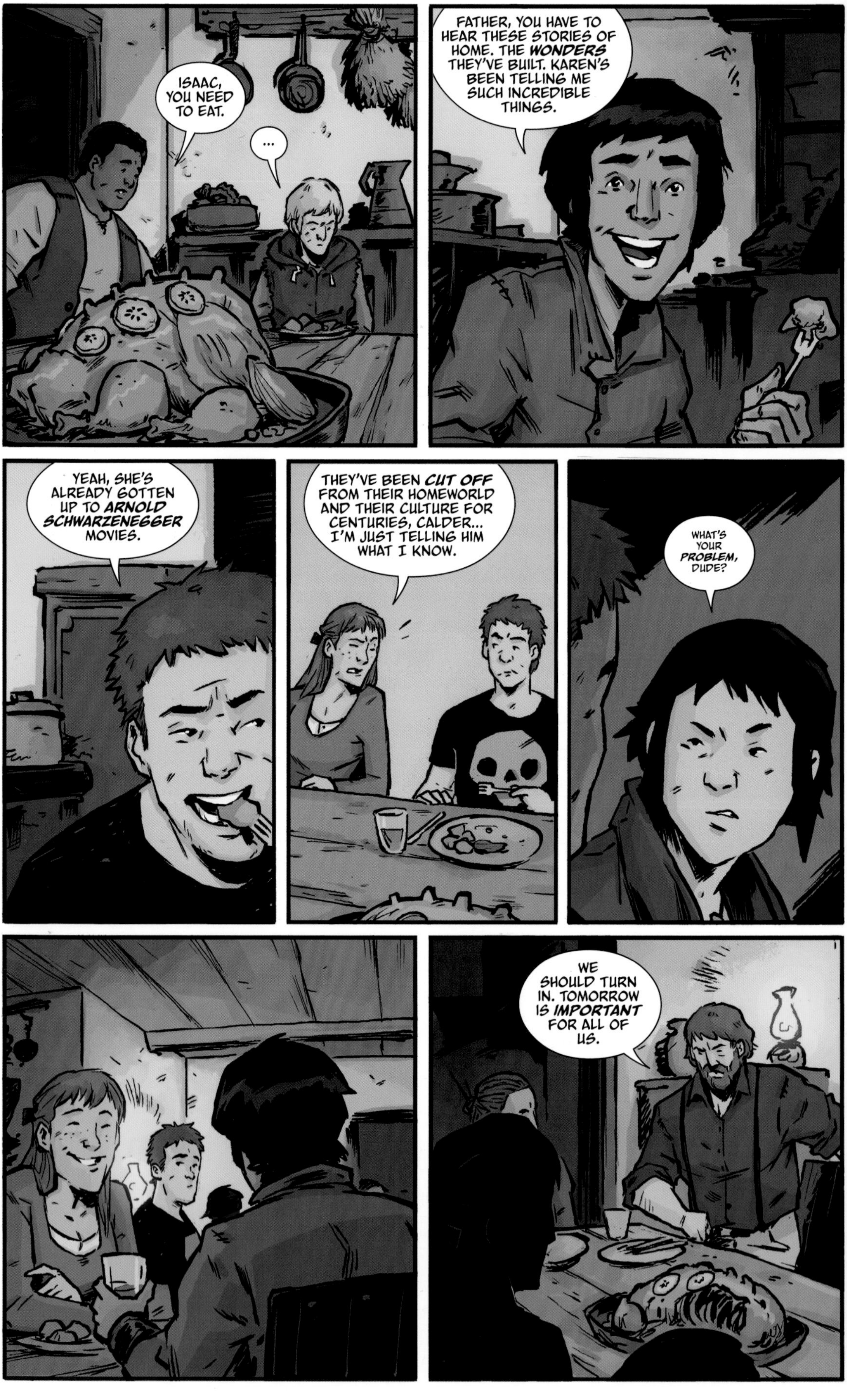
ISAAC, YOU NEED TO EAT.
...
FATHER, YOU HAVE TO HEAR THESE STORIES OF HOME. THE WONDERS THEY'VE BUILT. KAREN'S BEEN TELLING ME SUCH INCREDIBLE THINGS.
YEAH, SHE'S ALREADY GOTTEN UP TO ARNOLD SCHWARZENEGGER MOVIES.
THEY'VE BEEN CUT OFF FROM THEIR HOMEWORLD AND THEIR CULTURE FOR CENTURIES, CALDER... I'M JUST TELLING HIM WHAT I KNOW.
WHAT'S YOUR PROBLEM, DUDE?
WE SHOULD TURN IN. TOMORROW IS IMPORTANT FOR ALL OF US.

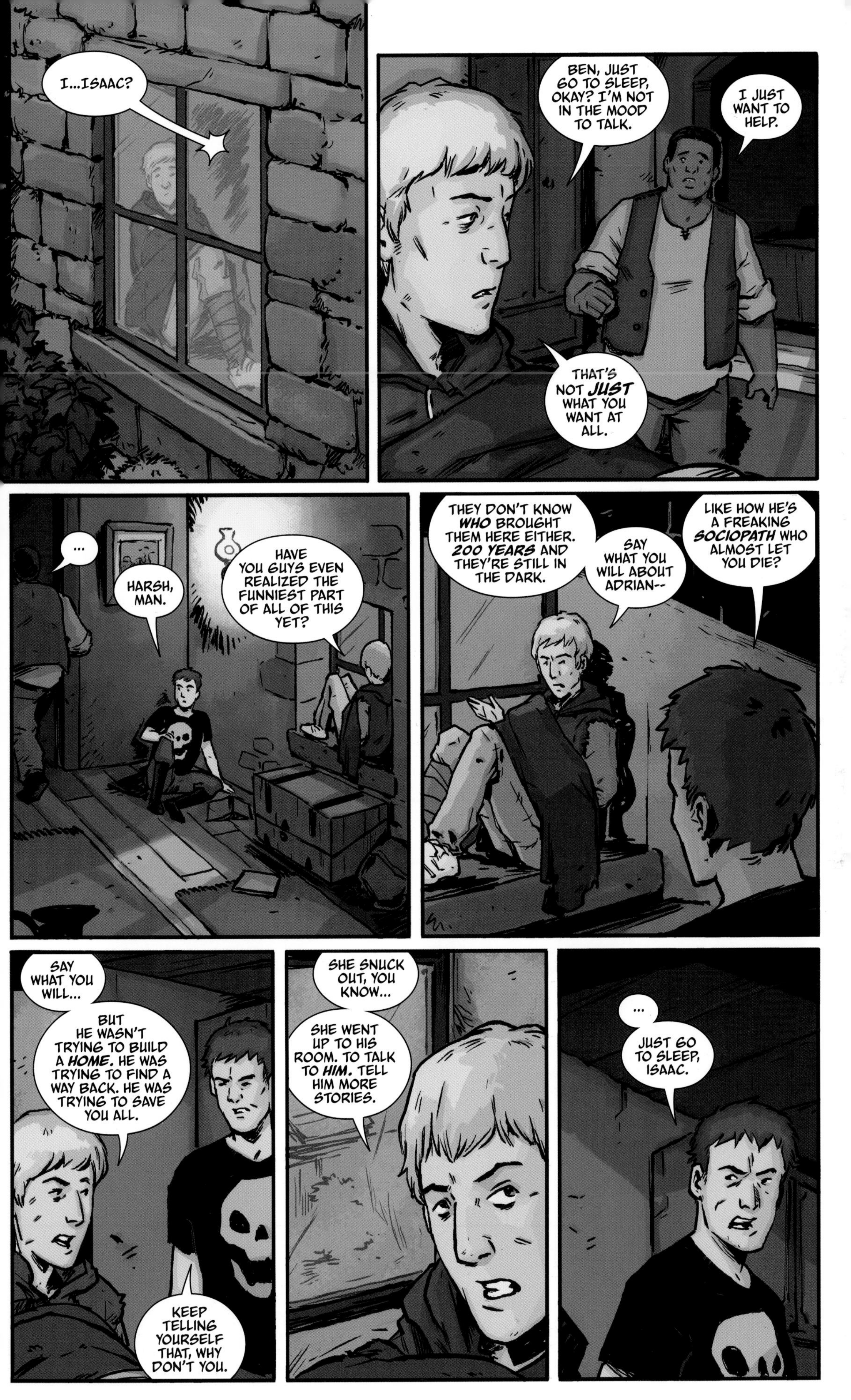
I...ISAAC?
BEN, JUST GO TO SLEEP, OKAY? I'M NOT IN THE MOOD TO TALK.
I JUST WANT TO HELP.
THAT'S NOT *JUST* WHAT YOU WANT AT ALL.
...
HARSH, MAN.
HAVE YOU GUYS EVEN REALIZED THE FUNNIEST PART OF ALL OF THIS YET?
THEY DON'T KNOW *WHO* BROUGHT THEM HERE EITHER. *200 YEARS* AND THEY'RE STILL IN THE DARK.
SAY WHAT YOU WILL ABOUT ADRIAN--
LIKE HOW HE'S A FREAKING *SOCIOPATH* WHO ALMOST LET YOU DIE?
SAY WHAT YOU WILL...
BUT HE WASN'T TRYING TO BUILD A *HOME*. HE WAS TRYING TO FIND A WAY BACK. HE WAS TRYING TO SAVE YOU ALL.
KEEP TELLING YOURSELF THAT, WHY DON'T YOU.
SHE SNUCK OUT, YOU KNOW...
SHE WENT UP TO HIS ROOM. TO TALK TO *HIM*. TELL HIM MORE STORIES.
...
JUST GO TO SLEEP, ISAAC.

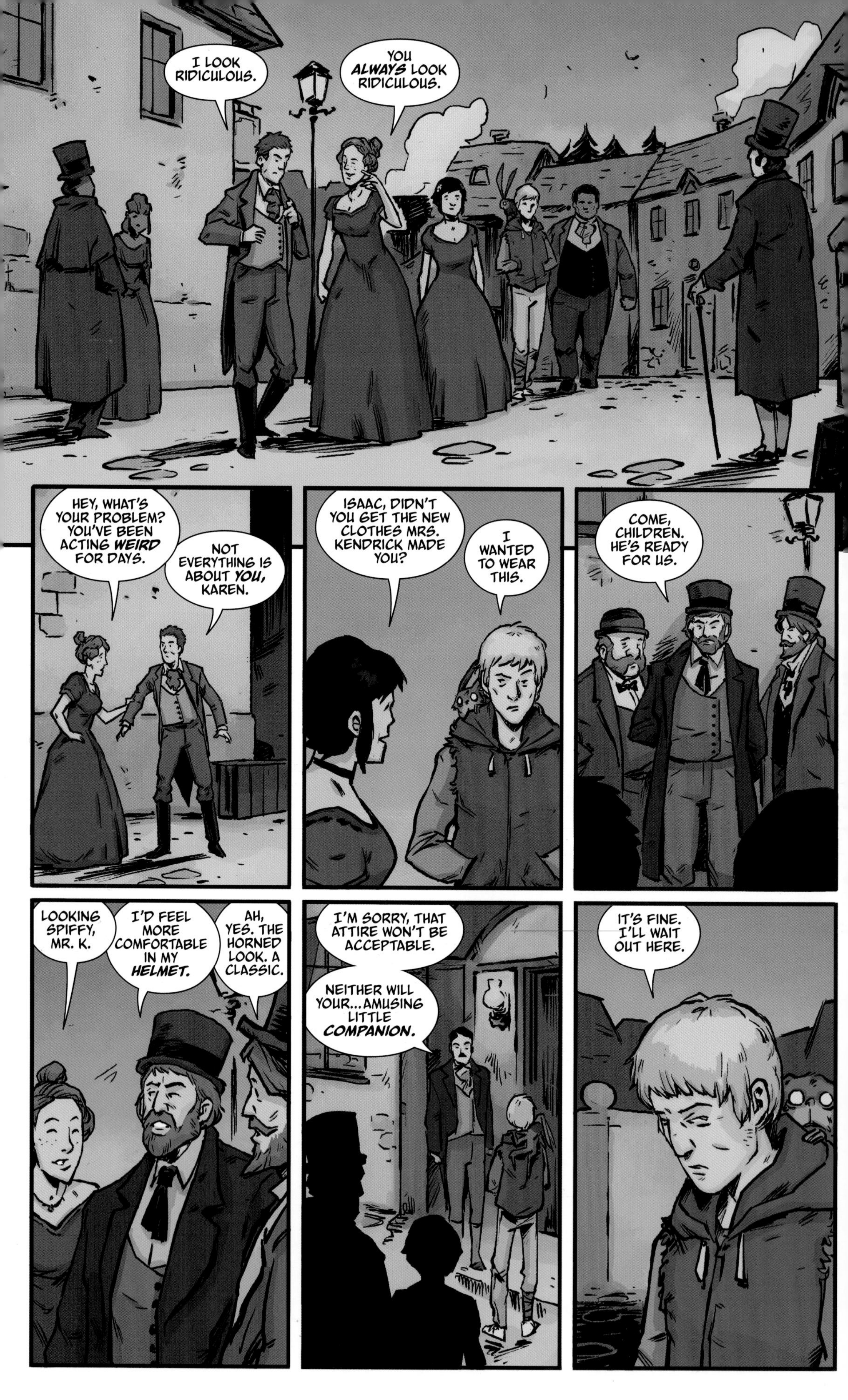
I LOOK RIDICULOUS.
YOU ALWAYS LOOK RIDICULOUS.
HEY, WHAT'S YOUR PROBLEM? YOU'VE BEEN ACTING WEIRD FOR DAYS.
NOT EVERYTHING IS ABOUT YOU, KAREN.
ISAAC, DIDN'T YOU GET THE NEW CLOTHES MRS. KENDRICK MADE YOU?
I WANTED TO WEAR THIS.
COME, CHILDREN. HE'S READY FOR US.
LOOKING SPIFFY, MR. K.
I'D FEEL MORE COMFORTABLE IN MY HELMET.
AH, YES. THE HORNED LOOK. A CLASSIC.
I'M SORRY, THAT ATTIRE WON'T BE ACCEPTABLE.
NEITHER WILL YOUR...AMUSING LITTLE COMPANION.
IT'S FINE. I'LL WAIT OUT HERE.

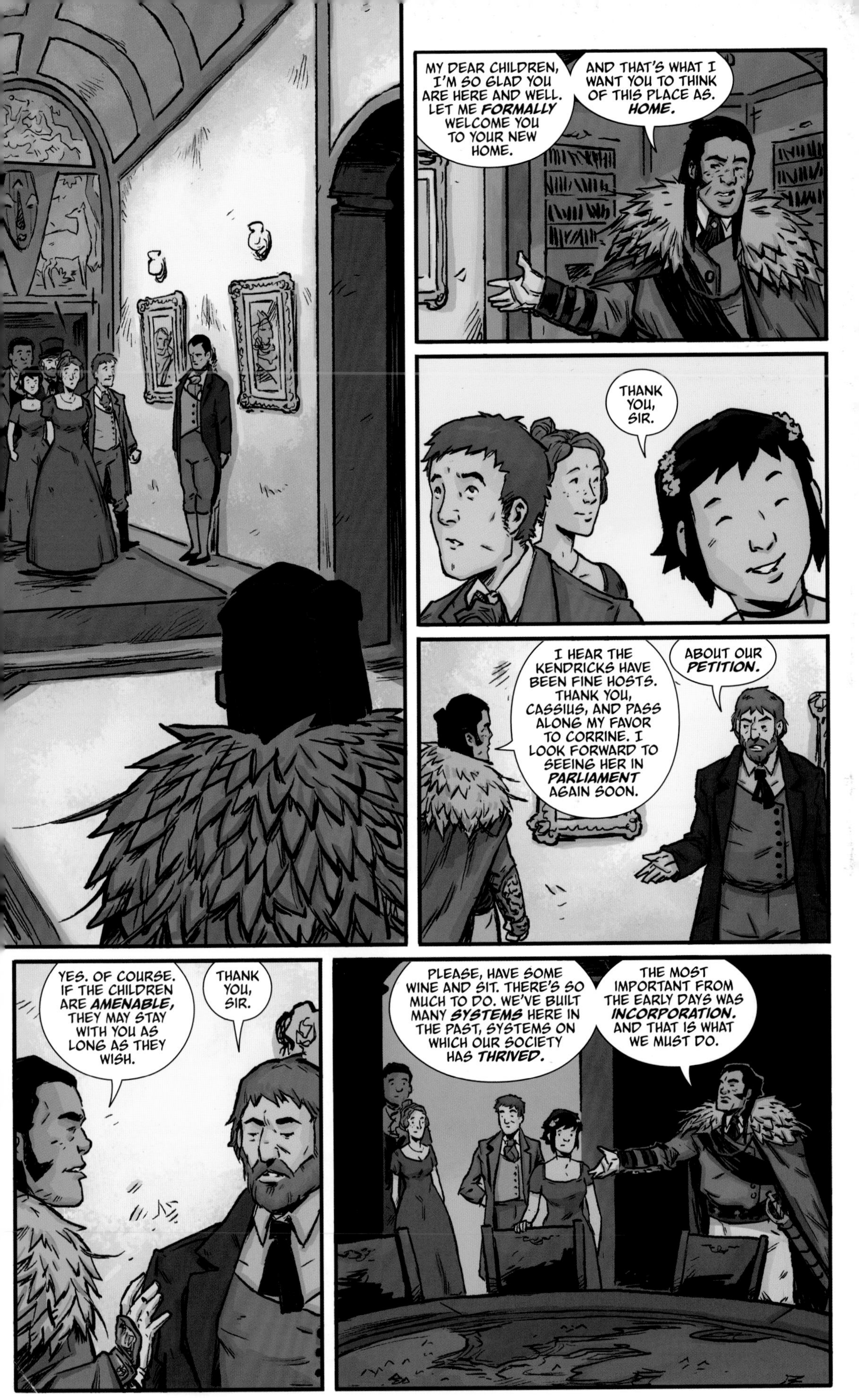

MY DEAR CHILDREN, I'M SO GLAD YOU ARE HERE AND WELL. LET ME FORMALLY WELCOME YOU TO YOUR NEW HOME.
AND THAT'S WHAT I WANT YOU TO THINK OF THIS PLACE AS. HOME.
THANK YOU, SIR.
I HEAR THE KENDRICKS HAVE BEEN FINE HOSTS. THANK YOU, CASSIUS, AND PASS ALONG MY FAVOR TO CORRINE. I LOOK FORWARD TO SEEING HER IN PARLIAMENT AGAIN SOON.
ABOUT OUR PETITION.
YES. OF COURSE. IF THE CHILDREN ARE AMENABLE, THEY MAY STAY WITH YOU AS LONG AS THEY WISH.
THANK YOU, SIR.
PLEASE, HAVE SOME WINE AND SIT. THERE'S SO MUCH TO DO. WE'VE BUILT MANY SYSTEMS HERE IN THE PAST, SYSTEMS ON WHICH OUR SOCIETY HAS THRIVED.
THE MOST IMPORTANT FROM THE EARLY DAYS WAS INCORPORATION. AND THAT IS WHAT WE MUST DO.

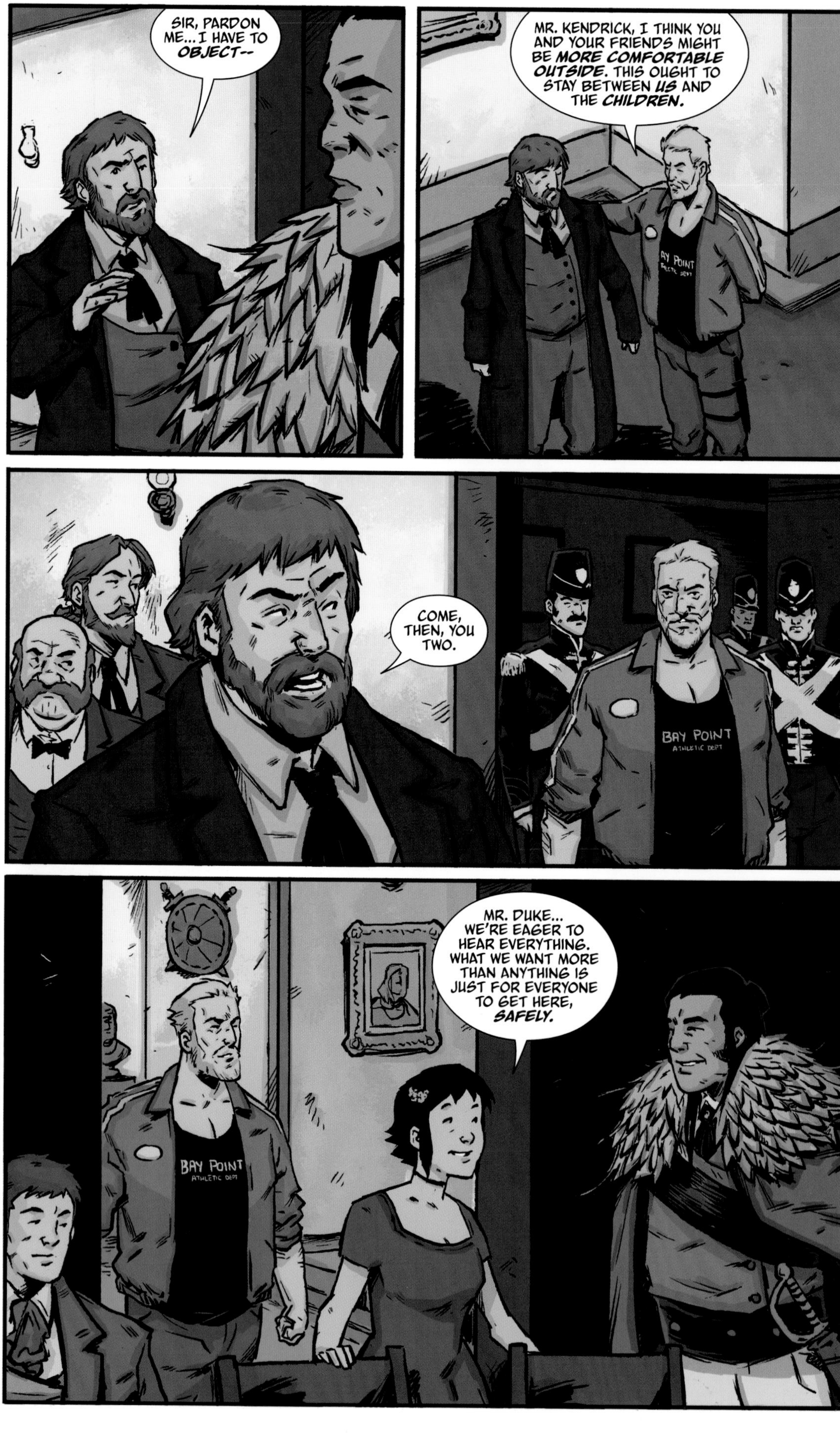
SIR, PARDON ME... I HAVE TO OBJECT--
MR. KENDRICK, I THINK YOU AND YOUR FRIENDS MIGHT BE MORE COMFORTABLE OUTSIDE. THIS OUGHT TO STAY BETWEEN US AND THE CHILDREN.
BAY POINT ATHLETIC DEPT
COME, THEN, YOU TWO.
BAY POINT ATHLETIC DEPT
MR. DUKE... WE'RE EAGER TO HEAR EVERYTHING. WHAT WE WANT MORE THAN ANYTHING IS JUST FOR EVERYONE TO GET HERE, SAFELY.
BAY POINT ATHLETIC DEPT

INCORPORATION, NIGEL. DID YOU HEAR THAT?

BLOODY *INCORPORATION*.

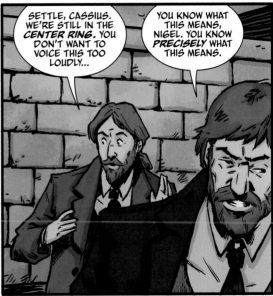

SETTLE, CASSIUS. WE'RE STILL IN THE *CENTER RING.* YOU DON'T WANT TO VOICE THIS TOO LOUDLY...

YOU KNOW WHAT THIS MEANS, NIGEL. YOU KNOW *PRECISELY* WHAT THIS MEANS.

ENSLAVEMENT.

ALL THOSE CHILDREN... THEY'LL BE *CONSCRIPTED* TO WAR AGAINST THE HORDE. AND THOSE WHO CAN'T FIGHT WILL BUILD THEIR *WEAPONS.*

WHAT KIND OF LIFE IS THAT?

IF THEY TRIED IT WITH *SANDER,* I DON'T KNOW WHAT I'D DO.

CASSIUS. CALM YOURSELF.

THESE CHILDREN ARE SAFE. IF THEY LEARN WHAT THE DUKE IS PLANNING, WHO *KNOWS* WHAT THEY'LL DO.

WHAT IF THEY ATTEMPT TO BRING THEIR *FRIEND* BACK INTO PLAY? WE ALL SAW WHAT HE WAS ON THE PATH TO BECOMING. THERE'S NO ROUTE BACK FOR HIM...

AND IF THEY TRY, *ALL* OF NEW LONDON MIGHT BURN.

THEY HAVE A CHANCE AT *NORMALCY* NOW. THEIR PEERS MIGHT NOT, NOT AT FIRST...BUT WHAT HOPE IS THERE TO FIGHT BACK?

YOU KNOW WE NEED TO KEEP THIS SECRET. LET THEM LIVE THEIR LIVES.

MREH.

NO, DOCTOR ROBOT. NOT NOW.

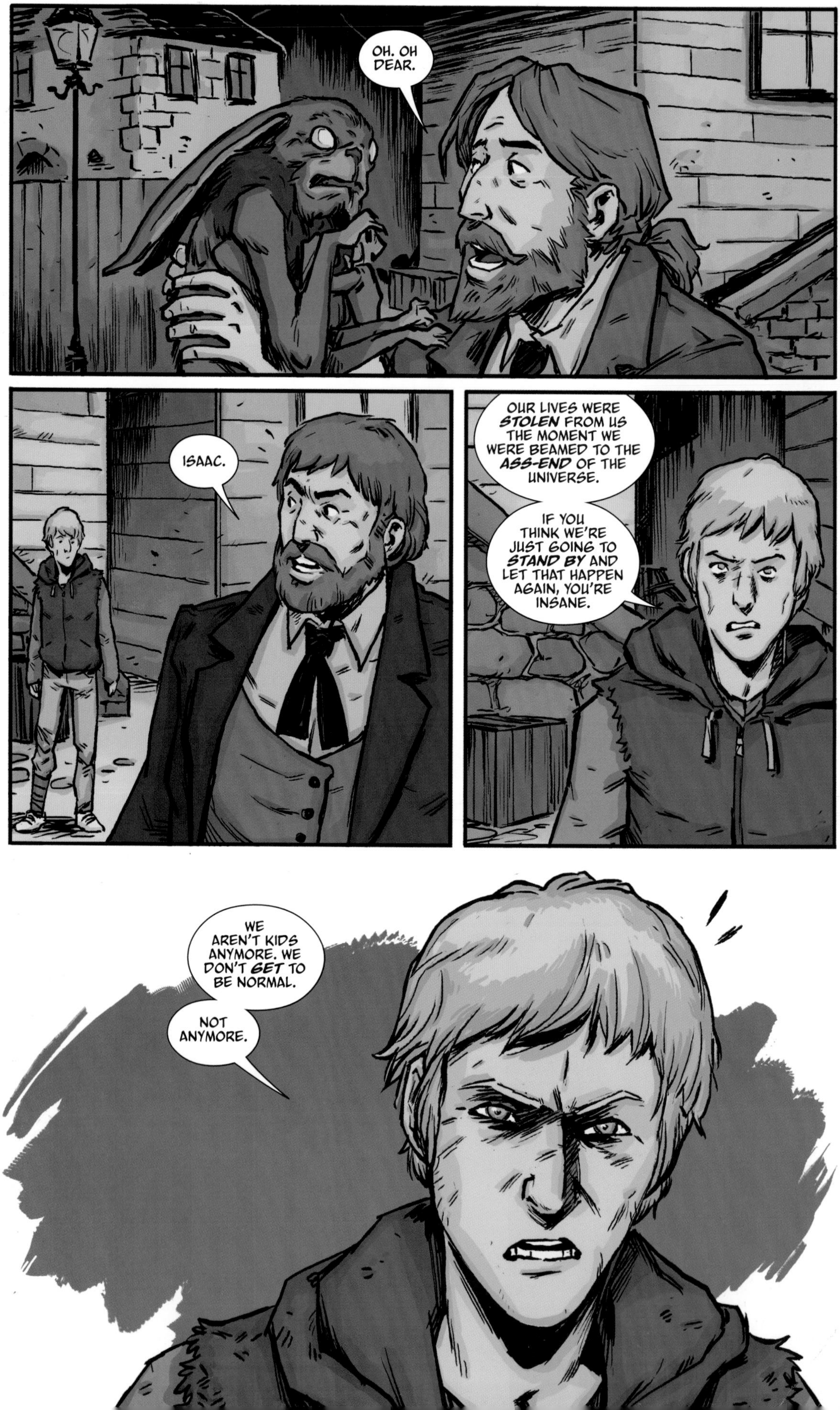
OH. OH DEAR.
ISAAC.
OUR LIVES WERE STOLEN FROM US THE MOMENT WE WERE BEAMED TO THE ASS-END OF THE UNIVERSE.
IF YOU THINK WE'RE JUST GOING TO STAND BY AND LET THAT HAPPEN AGAIN, YOU'RE INSANE.
WE AREN'T KIDS ANYMORE. WE DON'T GET TO BE NORMAL.
NOT ANYMORE.

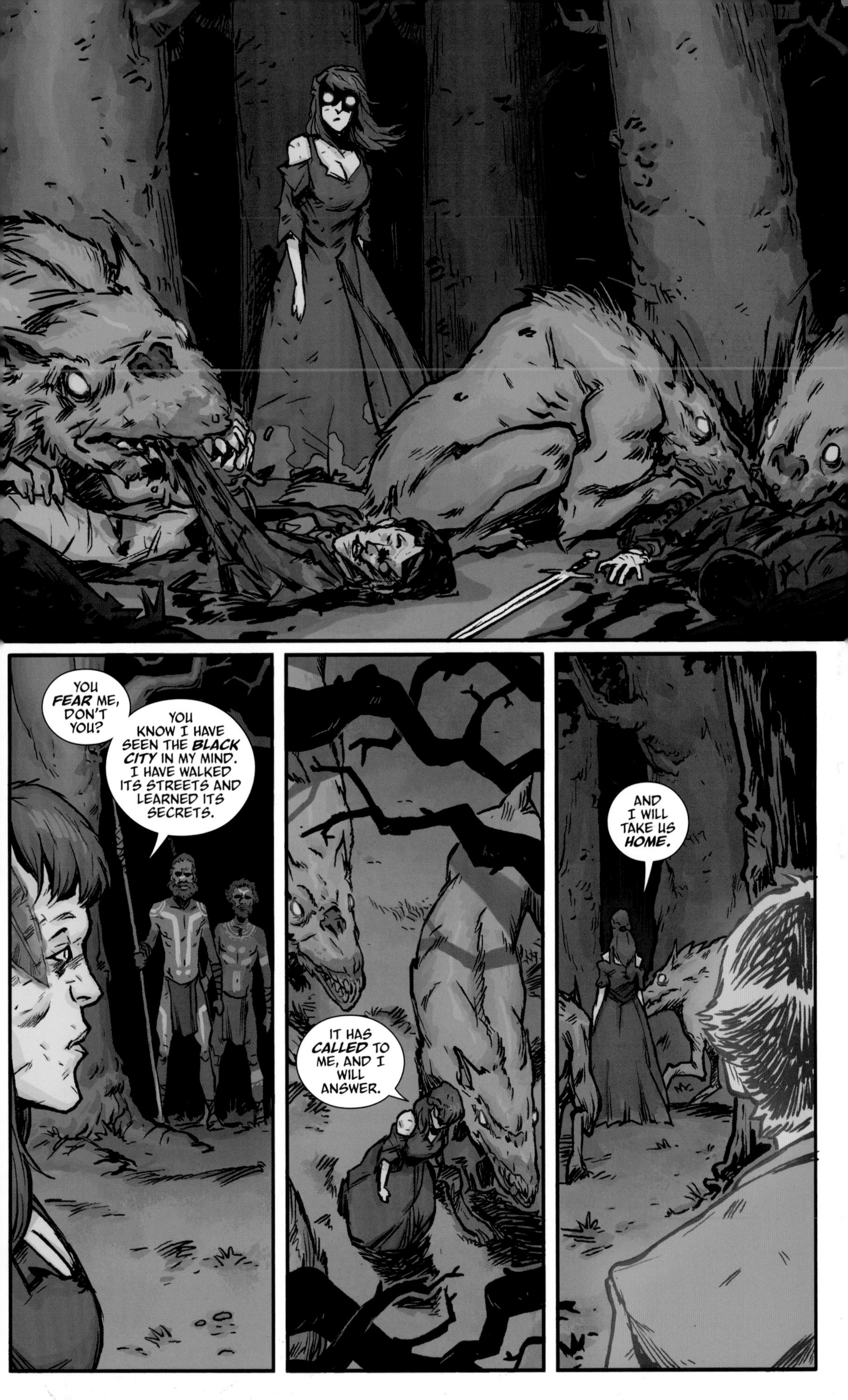
YOU FEAR ME, DON'T YOU?
YOU KNOW I HAVE SEEN THE BLACK CITY IN MY MIND. I HAVE WALKED ITS STREETS AND LEARNED ITS SECRETS.
IT HAS CALLED TO ME, AND I WILL ANSWER.
AND I WILL TAKE US HOME.

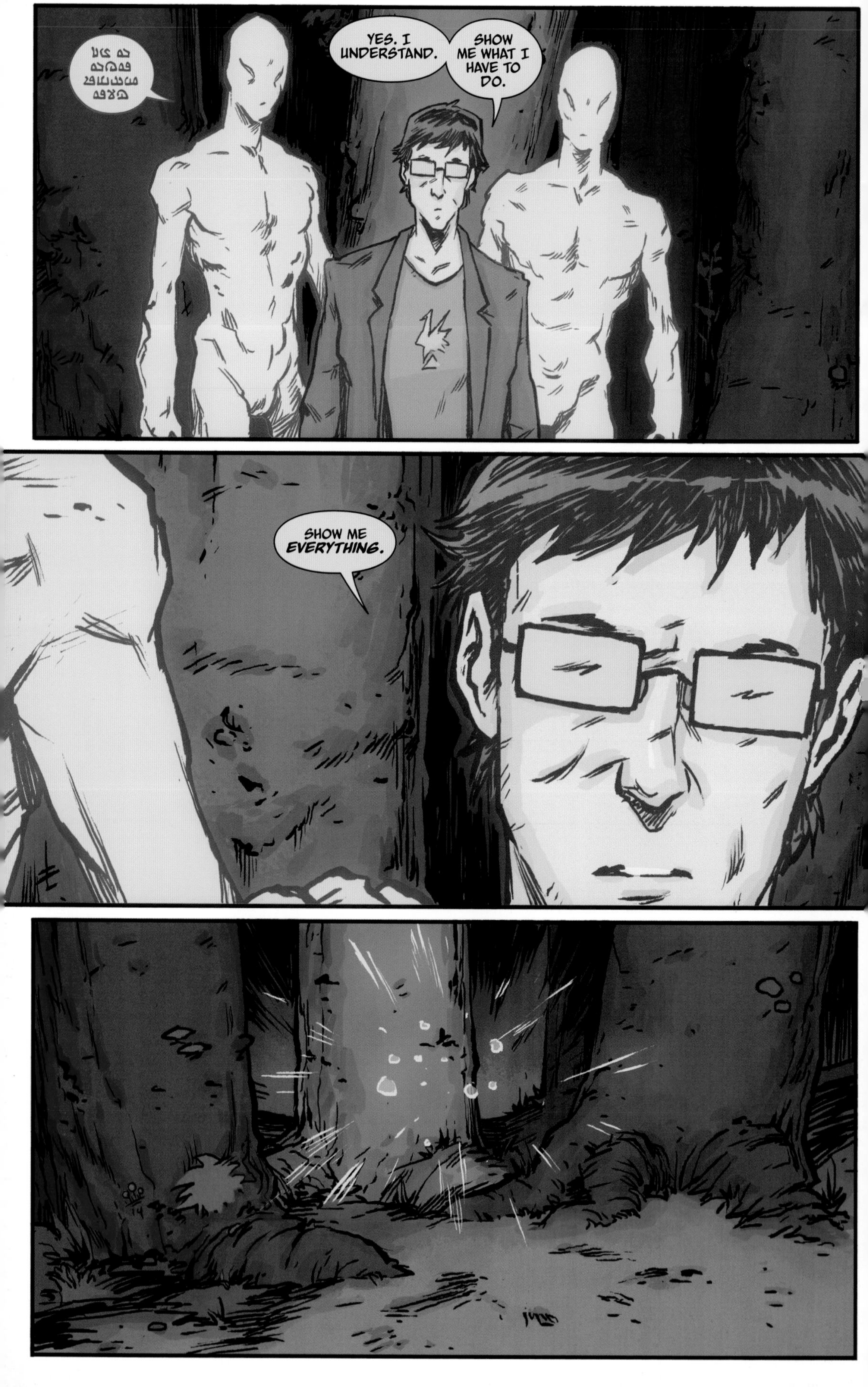
YES. I UNDERSTAND.
SHOW ME WHAT I HAVE TO DO.
SHOW ME *EVERYTHING.*

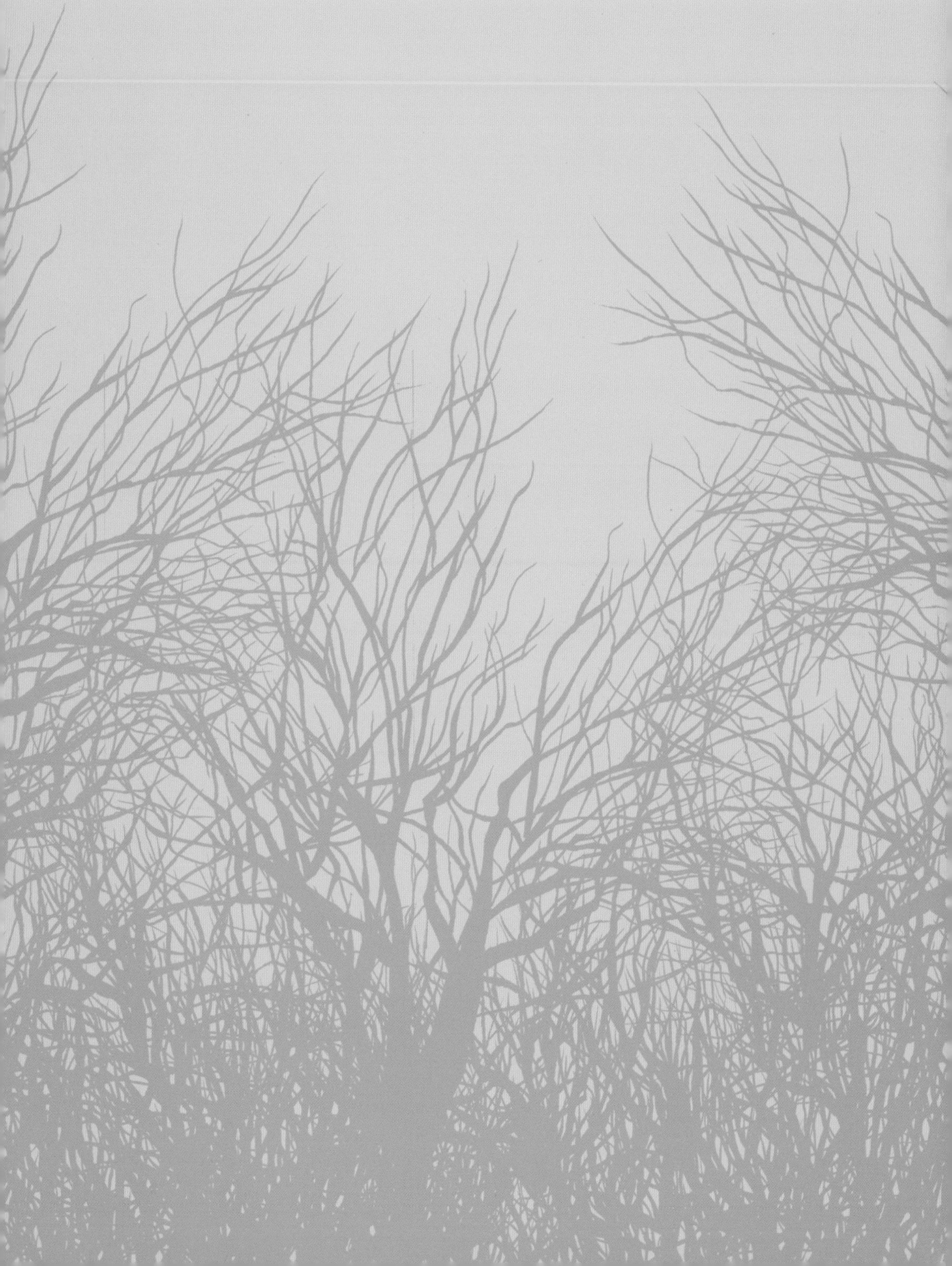

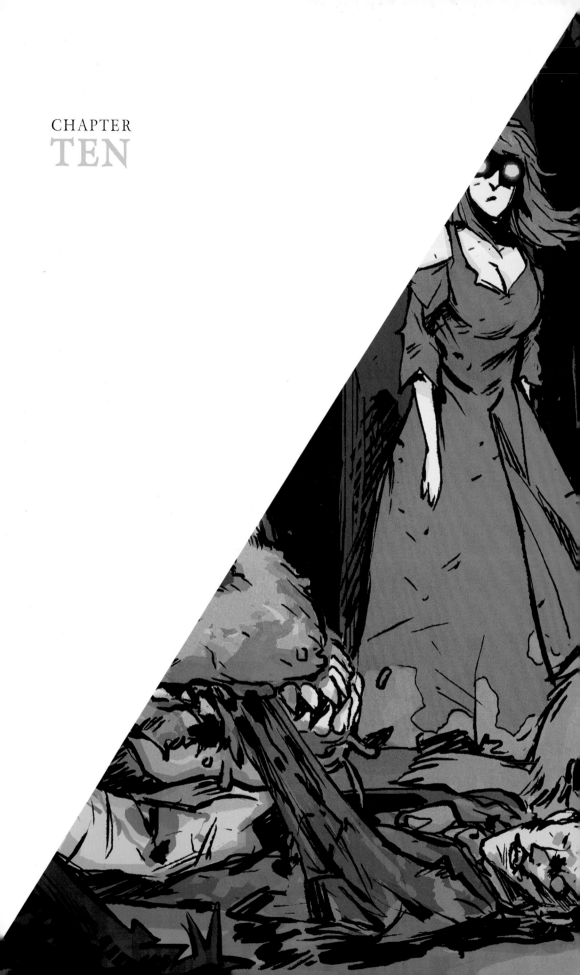

CHAPTER TEN

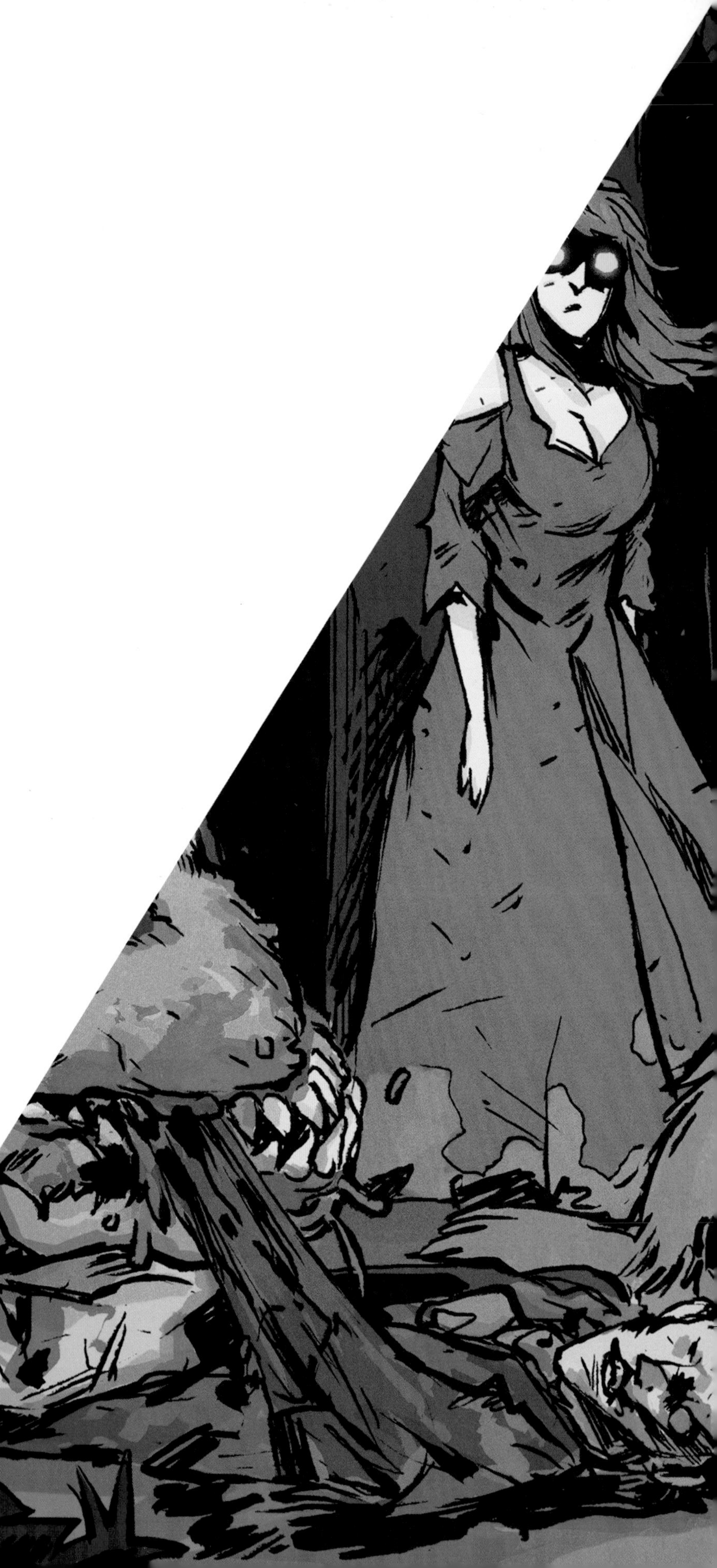

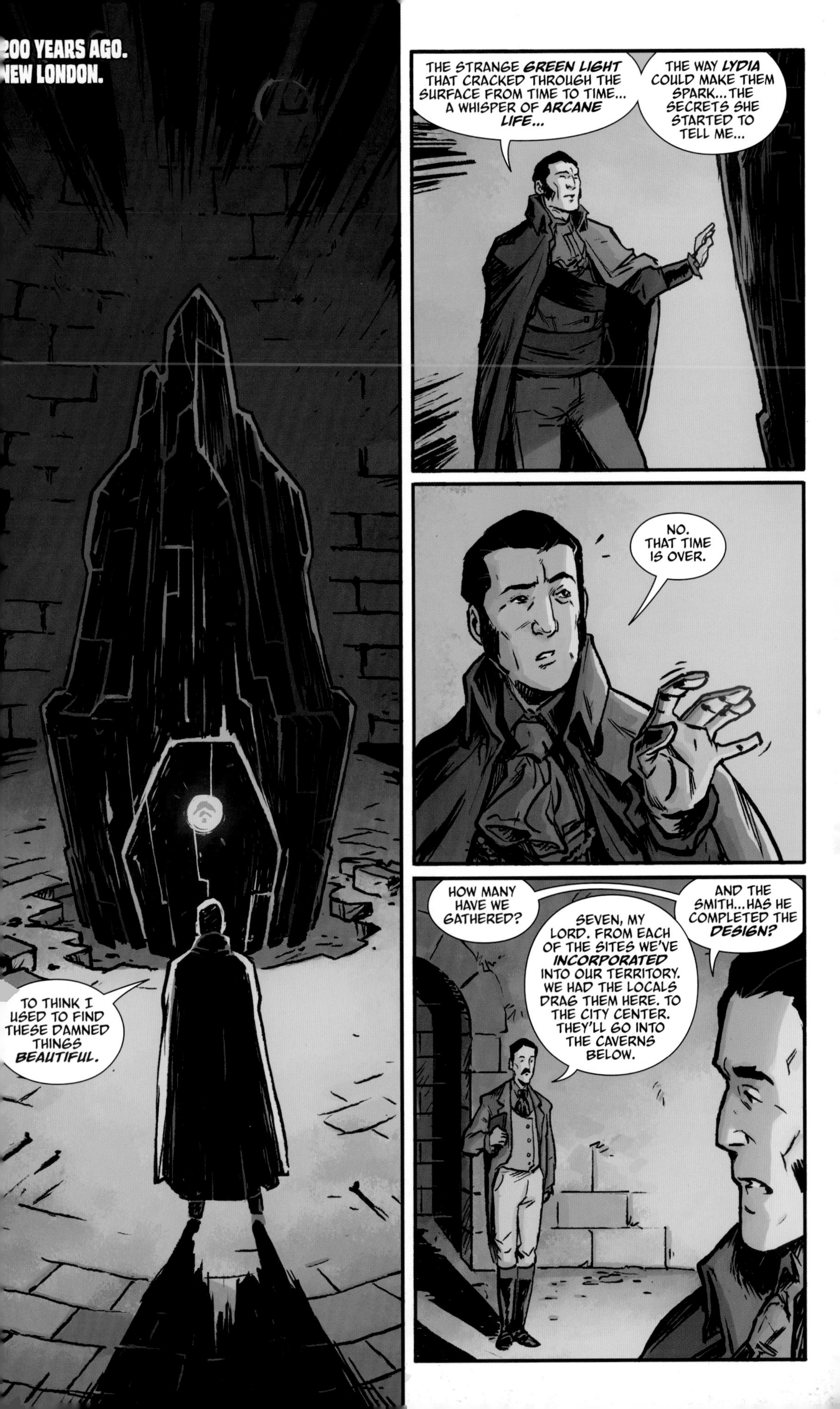

200 YEARS AGO. NEW LONDON.
TO THINK I USED TO FIND THESE DAMNED THINGS *BEAUTIFUL.*
THE STRANGE *GREEN LIGHT* THAT CRACKED THROUGH THE SURFACE FROM TIME TO TIME... A WHISPER OF *ARCANE LIFE...*
THE WAY *LYDIA* COULD MAKE THEM SPARK...THE SECRETS SHE STARTED TO TELL ME...
NO. THAT TIME IS OVER.
HOW MANY HAVE WE GATHERED?
AND THE SMITH...HAS HE COMPLETED THE *DESIGN?*
SEVEN, MY LORD. FROM EACH OF THE SITES WE'VE *INCORPORATED* INTO OUR TERRITORY. WE HAD THE LOCALS DRAG THEM HERE. TO THE CITY CENTER. THEY'LL GO INTO THE CAVERNS BELOW.

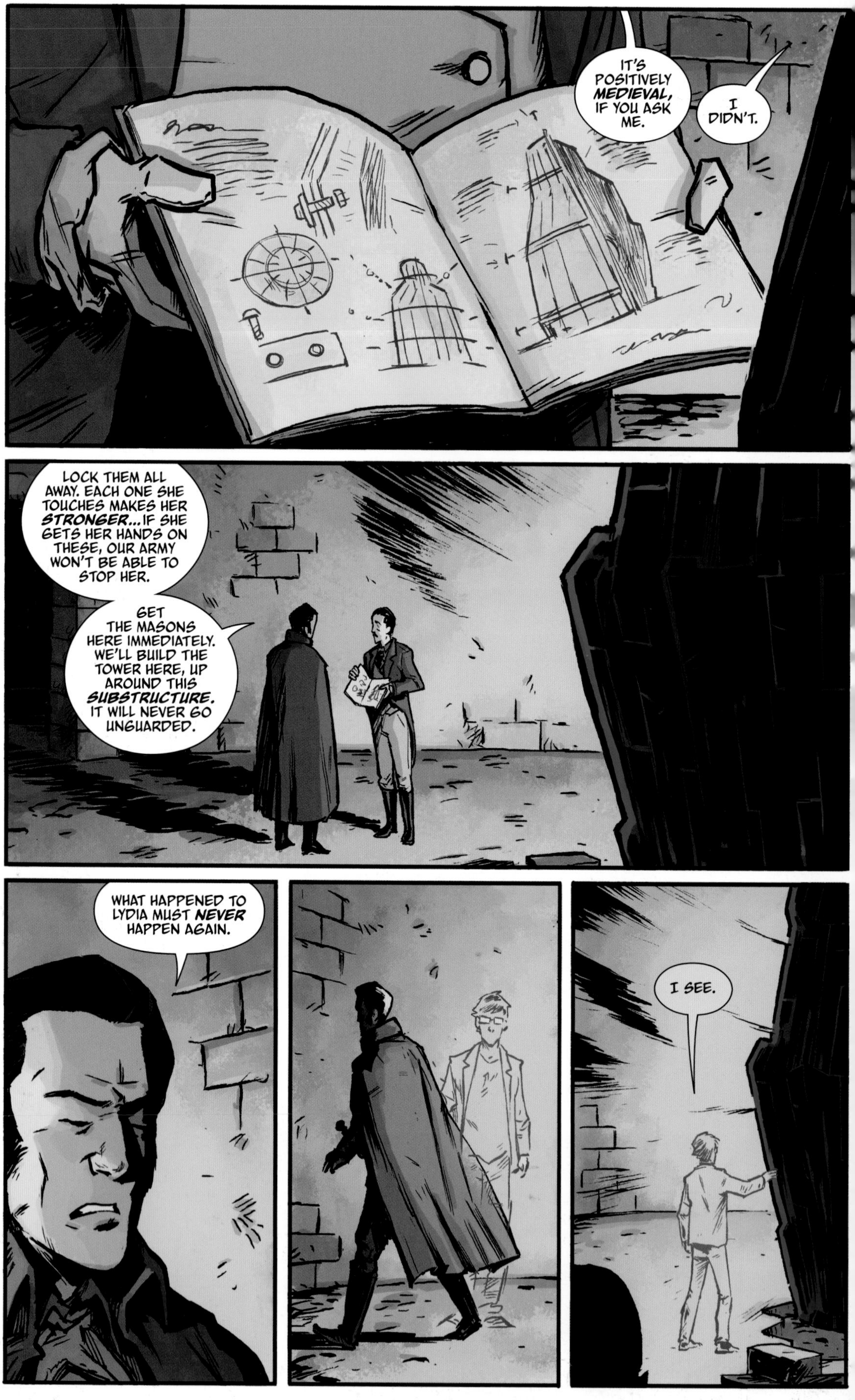
IT'S POSITIVELY MEDIEVAL, IF YOU ASK ME.
I DIDN'T.
LOCK THEM ALL AWAY. EACH ONE SHE TOUCHES MAKES HER STRONGER... IF SHE GETS HER HANDS ON THESE, OUR ARMY WON'T BE ABLE TO STOP HER.
GET THE MASONS HERE IMMEDIATELY. WE'LL BUILD THE TOWER HERE, UP AROUND THIS SUBSTRUCTURE. IT WILL NEVER GO UNGUARDED.
WHAT HAPPENED TO LYDIA MUST NEVER HAPPEN AGAIN.
I SEE.

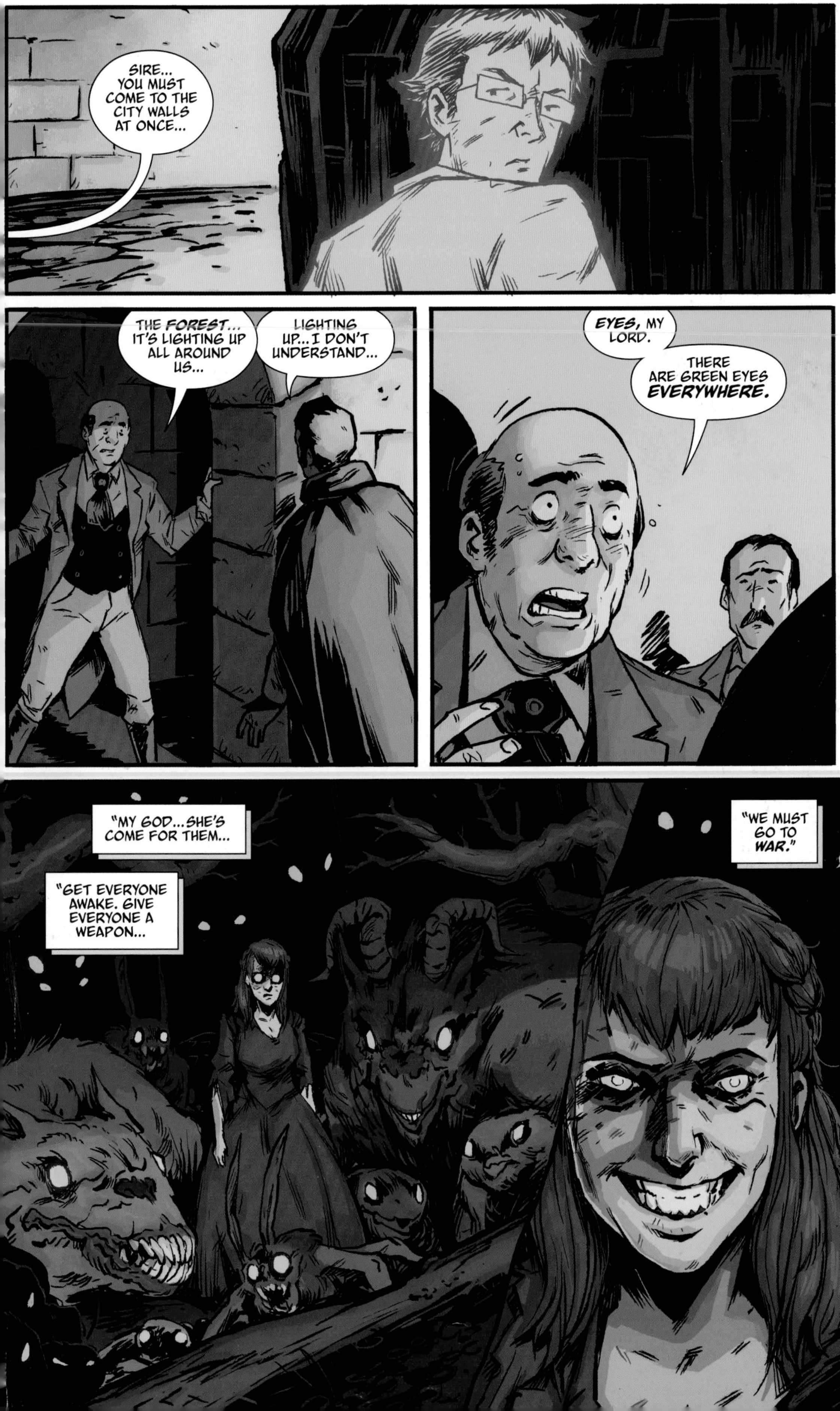
SIRE... YOU MUST COME TO THE CITY WALLS AT ONCE...
THE FOREST... IT'S LIGHTING UP ALL AROUND US...
LIGHTING UP... I DON'T UNDERSTAND...
EYES, MY LORD.
THERE ARE GREEN EYES EVERYWHERE.
"MY GOD... SHE'S COME FOR THEM...
"GET EVERYONE AWAKE. GIVE EVERYONE A WEAPON...
"WE MUST GO TO WAR."

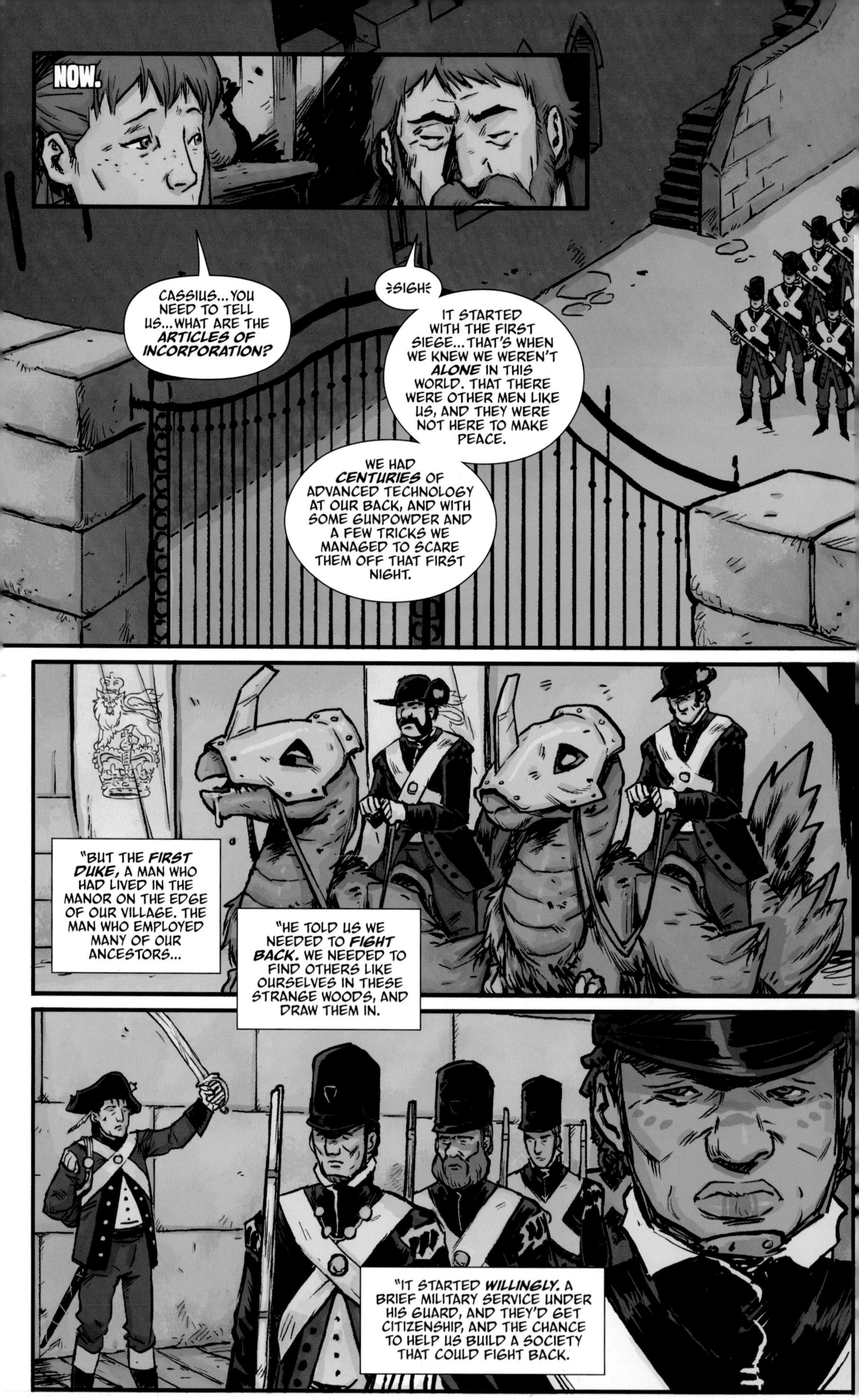
NOW.
CASSIUS...YOU NEED TO TELL US...WHAT ARE THE ARTICLES OF INCORPORATION?
SIGH
IT STARTED WITH THE FIRST SIEGE...THAT'S WHEN WE KNEW WE WEREN'T ALONE IN THIS WORLD. THAT THERE WERE OTHER MEN LIKE US, AND THEY WERE NOT HERE TO MAKE PEACE.
WE HAD CENTURIES OF ADVANCED TECHNOLOGY AT OUR BACK, AND WITH SOME GUNPOWDER AND A FEW TRICKS WE MANAGED TO SCARE THEM OFF THAT FIRST NIGHT.
"BUT THE FIRST DUKE, A MAN WHO HAD LIVED IN THE MANOR ON THE EDGE OF OUR VILLAGE. THE MAN WHO EMPLOYED MANY OF OUR ANCESTORS...
"HE TOLD US WE NEEDED TO FIGHT BACK. WE NEEDED TO FIND OTHERS LIKE OURSELVES IN THESE STRANGE WOODS, AND DRAW THEM IN.
"IT STARTED WILLINGLY. A BRIEF MILITARY SERVICE UNDER HIS GUARD, AND THEY'D GET CITIZENSHIP, AND THE CHANCE TO HELP US BUILD A SOCIETY THAT COULD FIGHT BACK.

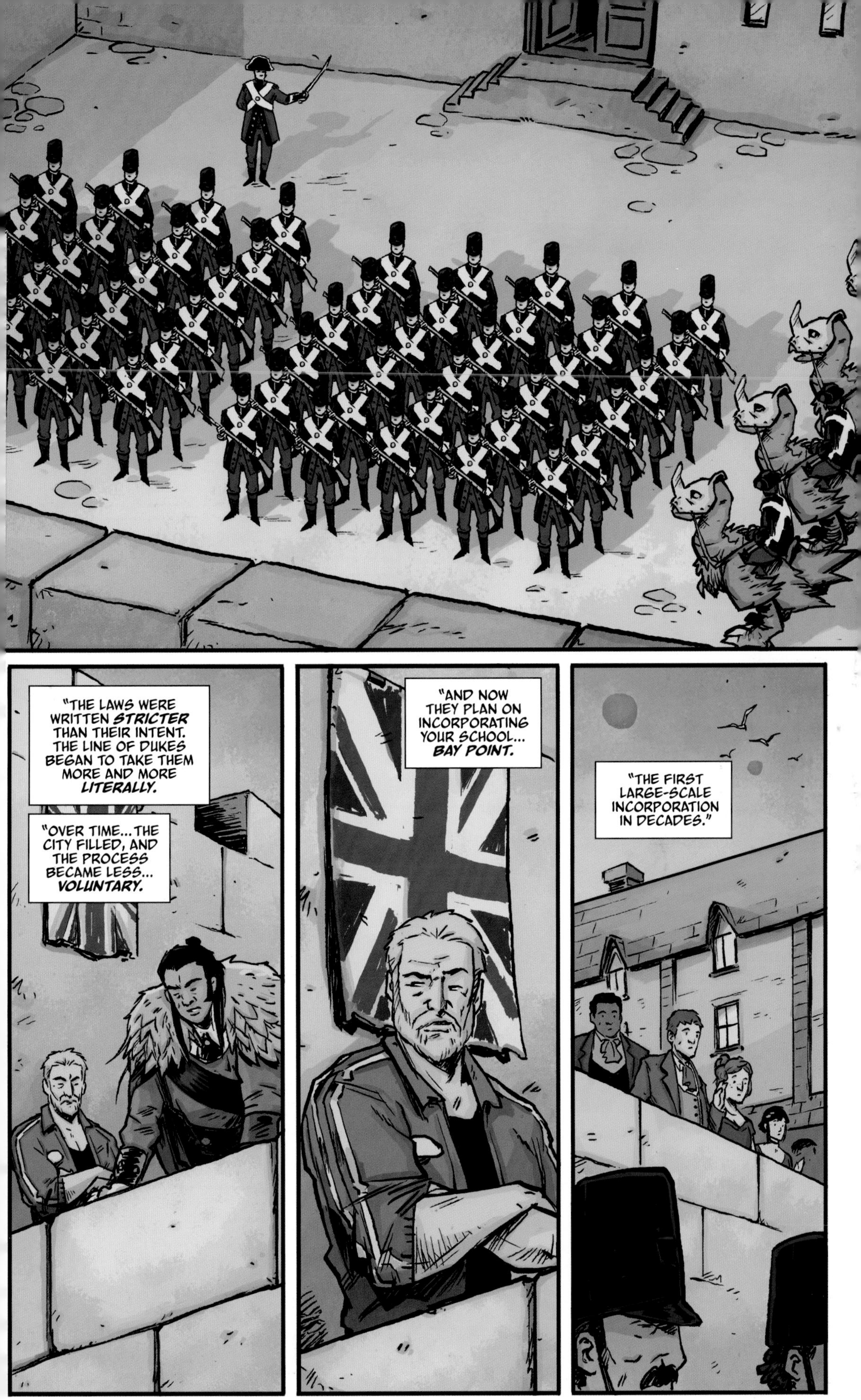
"THE LAWS WERE WRITTEN *STRICTER* THAN THEIR INTENT. THE LINE OF DUKES BEGAN TO TAKE THEM MORE AND MORE *LITERALLY.*
"OVER TIME... THE CITY FILLED, AND THE PROCESS BECAME LESS... *VOLUNTARY.*
"AND NOW THEY PLAN ON INCORPORATING YOUR SCHOOL... *BAY POINT.*
"THE FIRST LARGE-SCALE INCORPORATION IN DECADES."

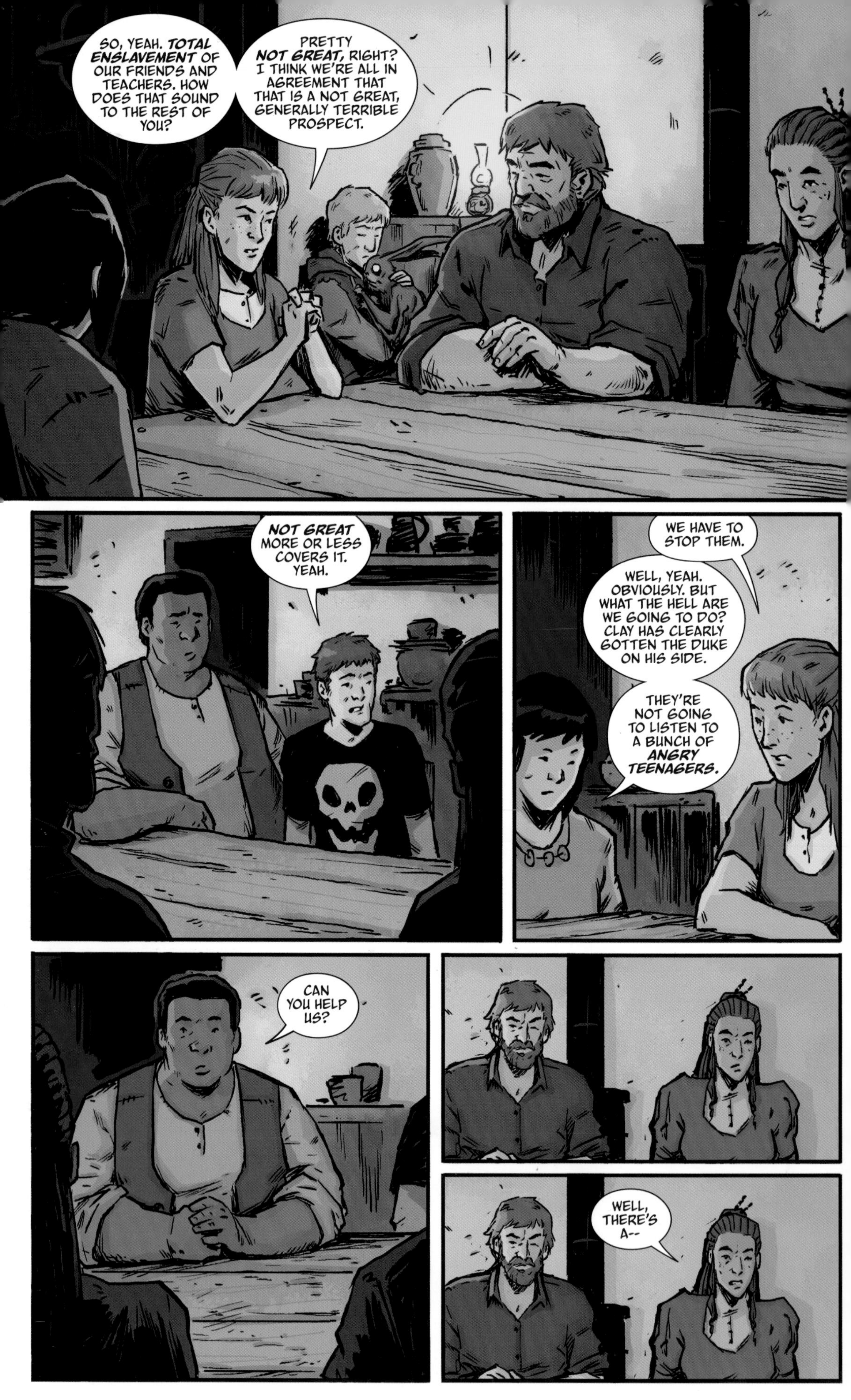
SO, YEAH. TOTAL ENSLAVEMENT OF OUR FRIENDS AND TEACHERS. HOW DOES THAT SOUND TO THE REST OF YOU?
PRETTY NOT GREAT, RIGHT? I THINK WE'RE ALL IN AGREEMENT THAT THAT IS A NOT GREAT, GENERALLY TERRIBLE PROSPECT.
NOT GREAT MORE OR LESS COVERS IT. YEAH.
WE HAVE TO STOP THEM.
WELL, YEAH. OBVIOUSLY. BUT WHAT THE HELL ARE WE GOING TO DO? CLAY HAS CLEARLY GOTTEN THE DUKE ON HIS SIDE.
THEY'RE NOT GOING TO LISTEN TO A BUNCH OF ANGRY TEENAGERS.
CAN YOU HELP US?
WELL, THERE'S A--

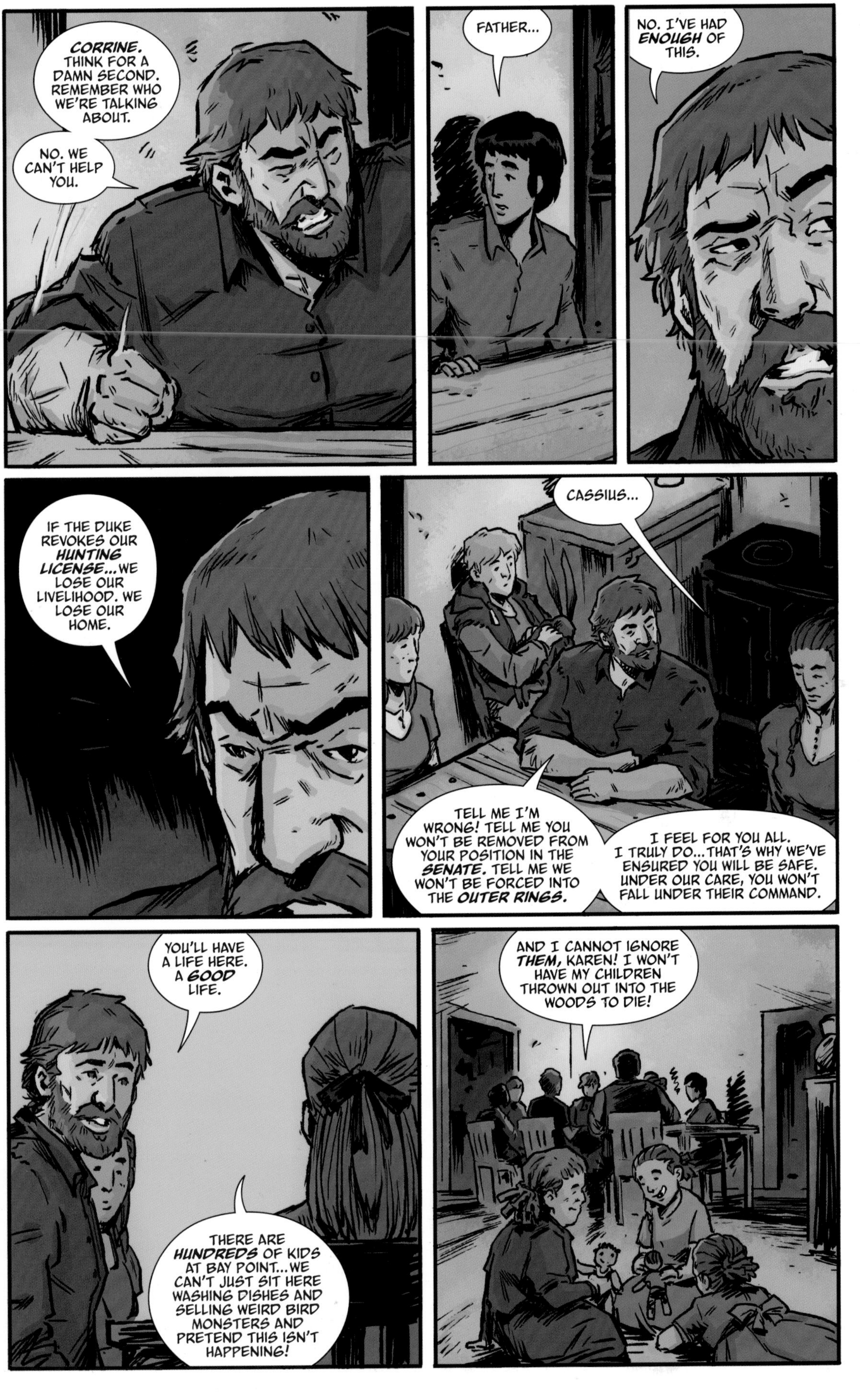
CORRINE. THINK FOR A DAMN SECOND. REMEMBER WHO WE'RE TALKING ABOUT.
NO. WE CAN'T HELP YOU.
FATHER...
NO. I'VE HAD ENOUGH OF THIS.
IF THE DUKE REVOKES OUR HUNTING LICENSE...WE LOSE OUR LIVELIHOOD. WE LOSE OUR HOME.
CASSIUS...
TELL ME I'M WRONG! TELL ME YOU WON'T BE REMOVED FROM YOUR POSITION IN THE SENATE. TELL ME WE WON'T BE FORCED INTO THE OUTER RINGS.
I FEEL FOR YOU ALL. I TRULY DO...THAT'S WHY WE'VE ENSURED YOU WILL BE SAFE. UNDER OUR CARE, YOU WON'T FALL UNDER THEIR COMMAND.
YOU'LL HAVE A LIFE HERE. A GOOD LIFE.
THERE ARE HUNDREDS OF KIDS AT BAY POINT...WE CAN'T JUST SIT HERE WASHING DISHES AND SELLING WEIRD BIRD MONSTERS AND PRETEND THIS ISN'T HAPPENING!
AND I CANNOT IGNORE THEM, KAREN! I WON'T HAVE MY CHILDREN THROWN OUT INTO THE WOODS TO DIE!

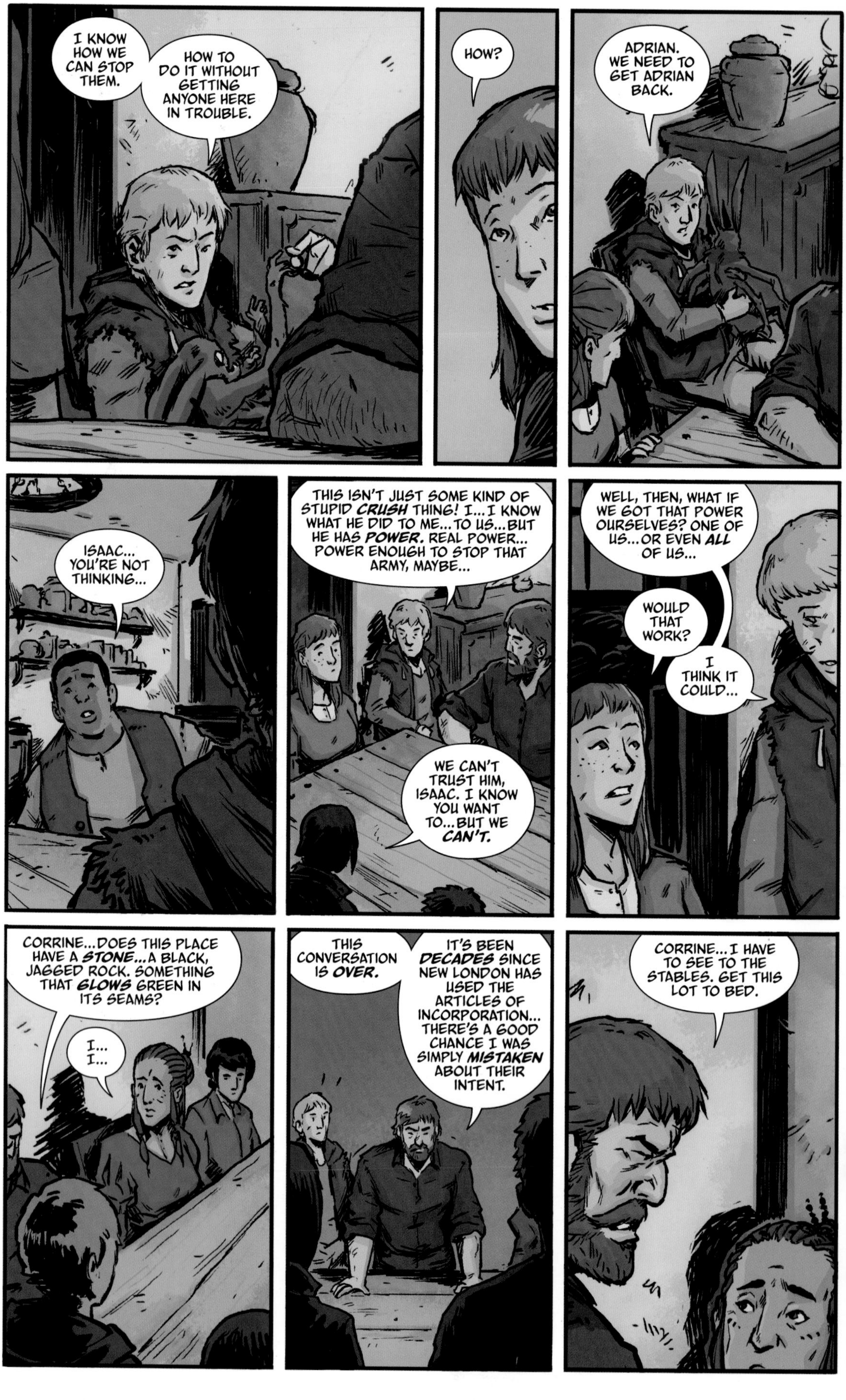

I KNOW HOW WE CAN STOP THEM.
HOW TO DO IT WITHOUT GETTING ANYONE HERE IN TROUBLE.
HOW?
ADRIAN. WE NEED TO GET ADRIAN BACK.
ISAAC... YOU'RE NOT THINKING...
THIS ISN'T JUST SOME KIND OF STUPID CRUSH THING! I...I KNOW WHAT HE DID TO ME...TO US...BUT HE HAS POWER. REAL POWER... POWER ENOUGH TO STOP THAT ARMY, MAYBE...
WE CAN'T TRUST HIM, ISAAC. I KNOW YOU WANT TO...BUT WE CAN'T.
WELL, THEN, WHAT IF WE GOT THAT POWER OURSELVES? ONE OF US...OR EVEN ALL OF US...
WOULD THAT WORK?
I THINK IT COULD...
CORRINE...DOES THIS PLACE HAVE A STONE...A BLACK, JAGGED ROCK. SOMETHING THAT GLOWS GREEN IN ITS SEAMS?
I... I...
THIS CONVERSATION IS OVER.
IT'S BEEN DECADES SINCE NEW LONDON HAS USED THE ARTICLES OF INCORPORATION... THERE'S A GOOD CHANCE I WAS SIMPLY MISTAKEN ABOUT THEIR INTENT.
CORRINE... I HAVE TO SEE TO THE STABLES. GET THIS LOT TO BED.

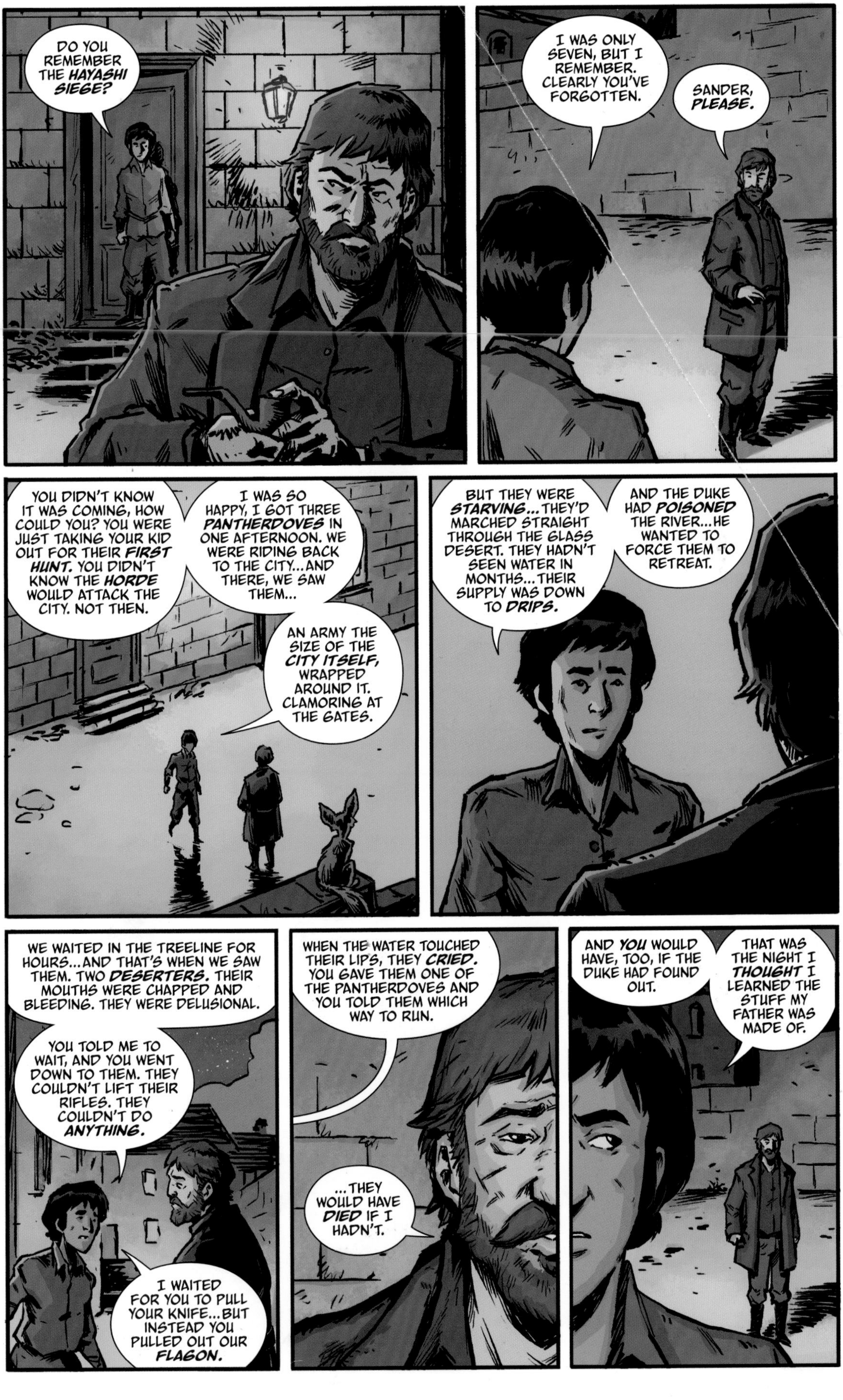

DO YOU REMEMBER THE HAYASHI SIEGE?
I WAS ONLY SEVEN, BUT I REMEMBER. CLEARLY YOU'VE FORGOTTEN.
SANDER, PLEASE.
YOU DIDN'T KNOW IT WAS COMING, HOW COULD YOU? YOU WERE JUST TAKING YOUR KID OUT FOR THEIR FIRST HUNT. YOU DIDN'T KNOW THE HORDE WOULD ATTACK THE CITY. NOT THEN.
I WAS SO HAPPY, I GOT THREE PANTHERDOVES IN ONE AFTERNOON. WE WERE RIDING BACK TO THE CITY...AND THERE, WE SAW THEM...
AN ARMY THE SIZE OF THE CITY ITSELF, WRAPPED AROUND IT. CLAMORING AT THE GATES.
BUT THEY WERE STARVING...THEY'D MARCHED STRAIGHT THROUGH THE GLASS DESERT. THEY HADN'T SEEN WATER IN MONTHS...THEIR SUPPLY WAS DOWN TO DRIPS.
AND THE DUKE HAD POISONED THE RIVER...HE WANTED TO FORCE THEM TO RETREAT.
WE WAITED IN THE TREELINE FOR HOURS...AND THAT'S WHEN WE SAW THEM. TWO DESERTERS. THEIR MOUTHS WERE CHAPPED AND BLEEDING. THEY WERE DELUSIONAL.
YOU TOLD ME TO WAIT, AND YOU WENT DOWN TO THEM. THEY COULDN'T LIFT THEIR RIFLES. THEY COULDN'T DO ANYTHING.
I WAITED FOR YOU TO PULL YOUR KNIFE...BUT INSTEAD YOU PULLED OUT OUR FLAGON.
WHEN THE WATER TOUCHED THEIR LIPS, THEY CRIED. YOU GAVE THEM ONE OF THE PANTHERDOVES AND YOU TOLD THEM WHICH WAY TO RUN.
...THEY WOULD HAVE DIED IF I HADN'T.
AND YOU WOULD HAVE, TOO, IF THE DUKE HAD FOUND OUT.
THAT WAS THE NIGHT I THOUGHT I LEARNED THE STUFF MY FATHER WAS MADE OF.

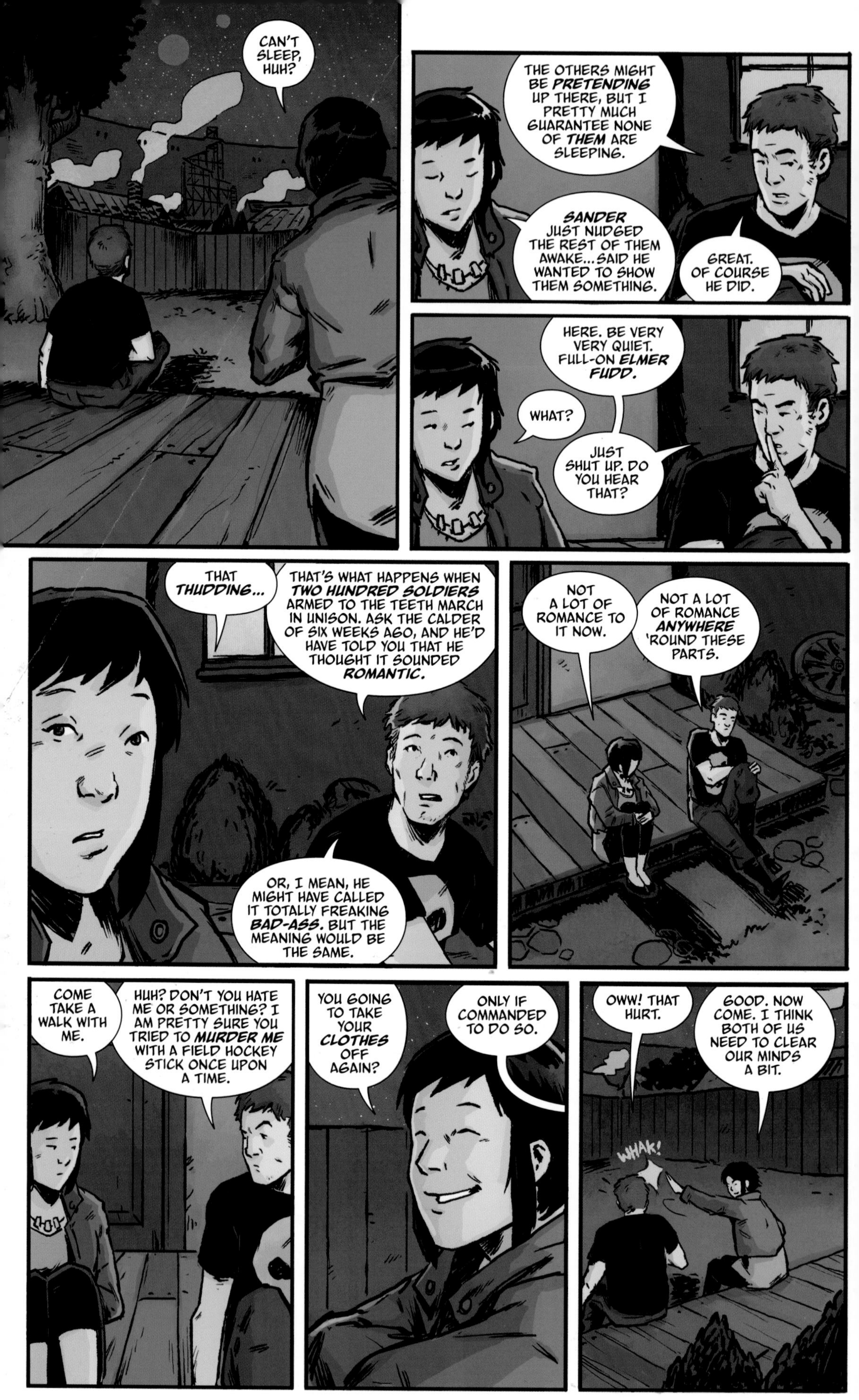
CAN'T SLEEP, HUH?
THE OTHERS MIGHT BE PRETENDING UP THERE, BUT I PRETTY MUCH GUARANTEE NONE OF THEM ARE SLEEPING.
SANDER JUST NUDGED THE REST OF THEM AWAKE... SAID HE WANTED TO SHOW THEM SOMETHING.
GREAT. OF COURSE HE DID.
HERE. BE VERY VERY QUIET. FULL-ON ELMER FUDD.
WHAT?
JUST SHUT UP. DO YOU HEAR THAT?
THAT THUDDING...
THAT'S WHAT HAPPENS WHEN TWO HUNDRED SOLDIERS ARMED TO THE TEETH MARCH IN UNISON. ASK THE CALDER OF SIX WEEKS AGO, AND HE'D HAVE TOLD YOU THAT HE THOUGHT IT SOUNDED ROMANTIC.
OR, I MEAN, HE MIGHT HAVE CALLED IT TOTALLY FREAKING BAD-ASS. BUT THE MEANING WOULD BE THE SAME.
NOT A LOT OF ROMANCE TO IT NOW.
NOT A LOT OF ROMANCE ANYWHERE 'ROUND THESE PARTS.
COME TAKE A WALK WITH ME.
HUH? DON'T YOU HATE ME OR SOMETHING? I AM PRETTY SURE YOU TRIED TO MURDER ME WITH A FIELD HOCKEY STICK ONCE UPON A TIME.
YOU GOING TO TAKE YOUR CLOTHES OFF AGAIN?
ONLY IF COMMANDED TO DO SO.
WHAK!
OWW! THAT HURT.
GOOD. NOW COME. I THINK BOTH OF US NEED TO CLEAR OUR MINDS A BIT.

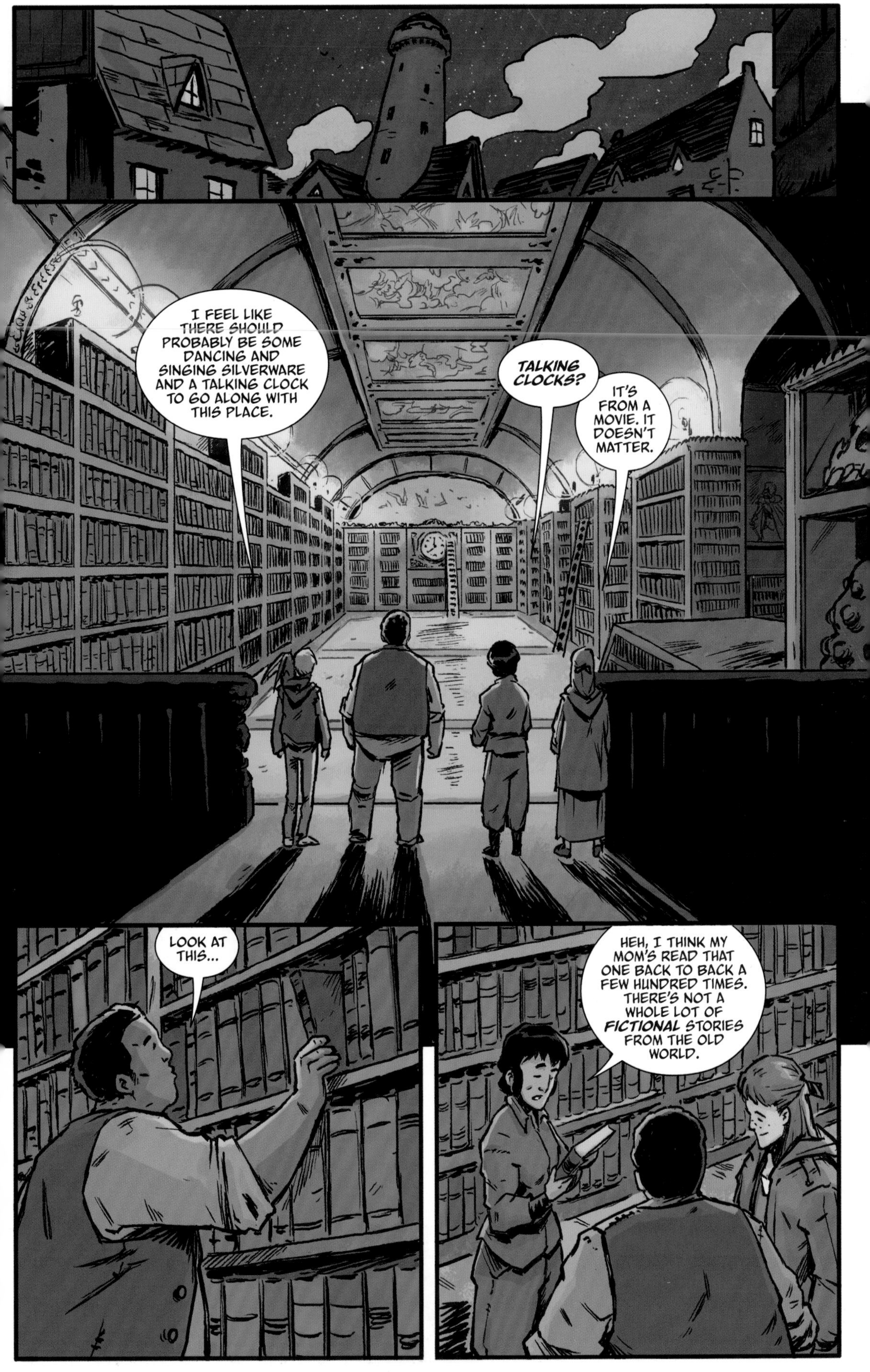
I FEEL LIKE THERE SHOULD PROBABLY BE SOME DANCING AND SINGING SILVERWARE AND A TALKING CLOCK TO GO ALONG WITH THIS PLACE.
TALKING CLOCKS?
IT'S FROM A MOVIE. IT DOESN'T MATTER.
LOOK AT THIS...
HEH, I THINK MY MOM'S READ THAT ONE BACK TO BACK A FEW HUNDRED TIMES. THERE'S NOT A WHOLE LOT OF FICTIONAL STORIES FROM THE OLD WORLD.

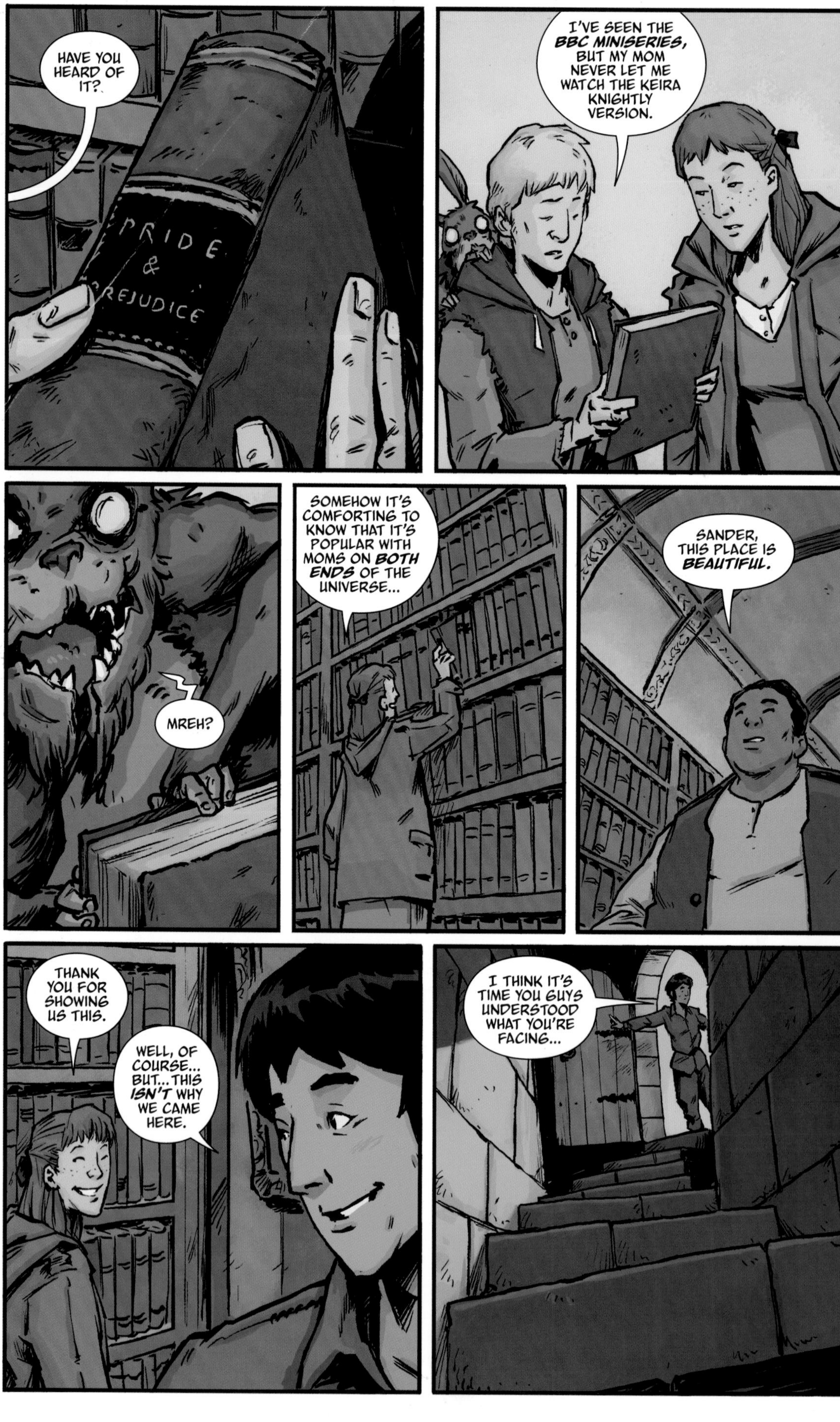
HAVE YOU HEARD OF IT?
I'VE SEEN THE BBC MINISERIES, BUT MY MOM NEVER LET ME WATCH THE KEIRA KNIGHTLY VERSION.
PRIDE & PREJUDICE
MREH?
SOMEHOW IT'S COMFORTING TO KNOW THAT IT'S POPULAR WITH MOMS ON BOTH ENDS OF THE UNIVERSE...
SANDER, THIS PLACE IS BEAUTIFUL.
THANK YOU FOR SHOWING US THIS.
WELL, OF COURSE... BUT... THIS ISN'T WHY WE CAME HERE.
I THINK IT'S TIME YOU GUYS UNDERSTOOD WHAT YOU'RE FACING...

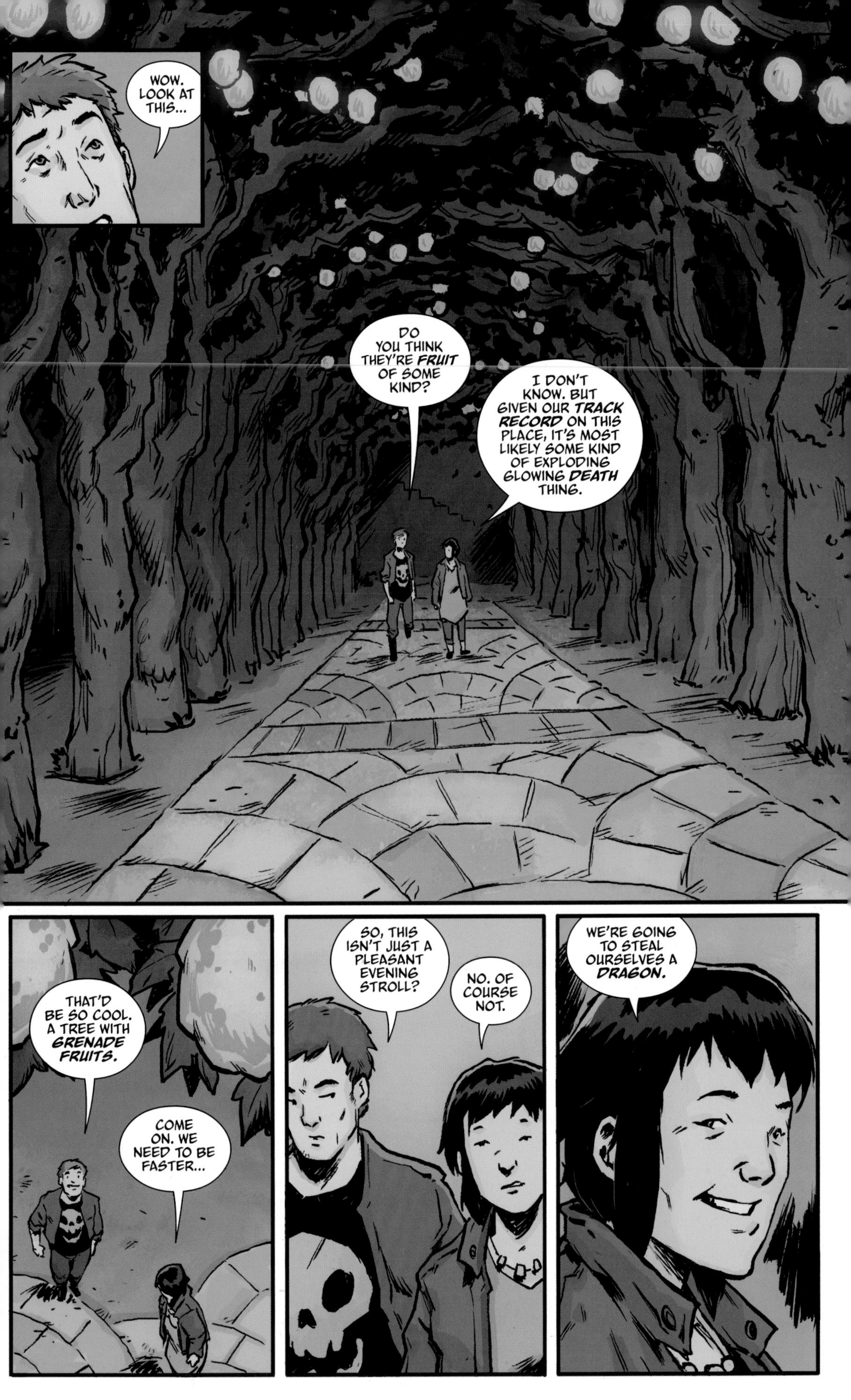

WOW. LOOK AT THIS...
DO YOU THINK THEY'RE FRUIT OF SOME KIND?
I DON'T KNOW. BUT GIVEN OUR TRACK RECORD ON THIS PLACE, IT'S MOST LIKELY SOME KIND OF EXPLODING GLOWING DEATH THING.
THAT'D BE SO COOL. A TREE WITH GRENADE FRUITS.
COME ON. WE NEED TO BE FASTER...
SO, THIS ISN'T JUST A PLEASANT EVENING STROLL?
NO. OF COURSE NOT.
WE'RE GOING TO STEAL OURSELVES A DRAGON.

IT'S A *TOMB*...

YOU ASKED ABOUT THE STONES... THIS IS WHAT WE DID WITH *OURS*, AND WHAT WE HAD TO DO WITH THE *OTHERS* WE'VE FOUND.

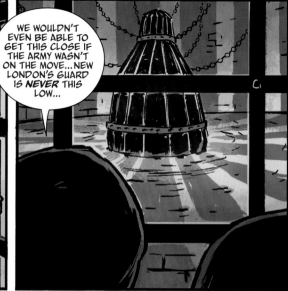

WE WOULDN'T EVEN BE ABLE TO GET THIS CLOSE IF THE ARMY WASN'T ON THE MOVE... NEW LONDON'S GUARD IS *NEVER* THIS LOW...

AND NOBODY IS ALLOWED TO GET THIS CLOSE. IT'S TOO DANGEROUS.

WHY?

SHA!

THE GREEN LIGHT...AND THE *BLACK CITY*.

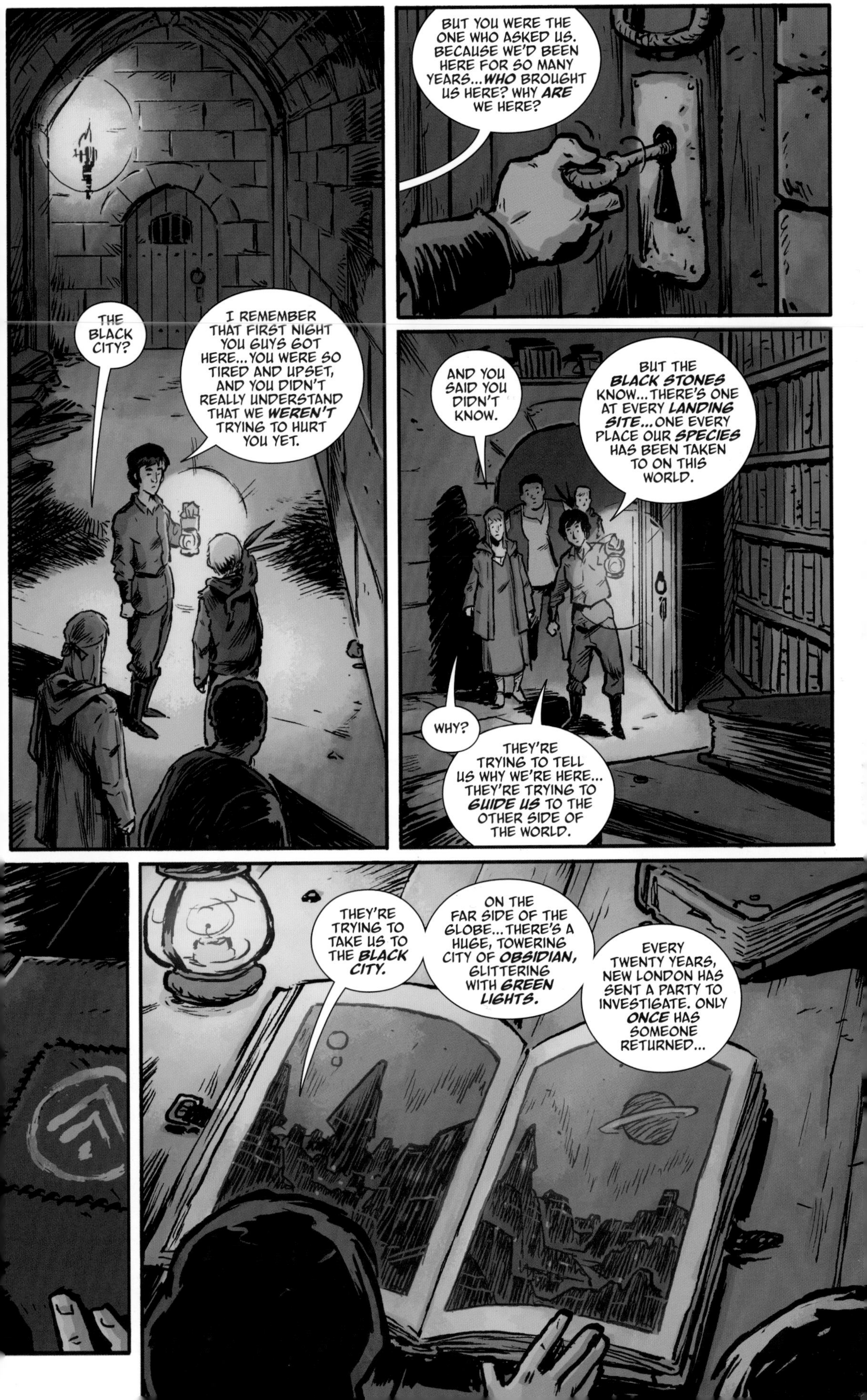
I REMEMBER THAT FIRST NIGHT YOU GUYS GOT HERE... YOU WERE SO TIRED AND UPSET, AND YOU DIDN'T REALLY UNDERSTAND THAT WE WEREN'T TRYING TO HURT YOU YET.
BUT YOU WERE THE ONE WHO ASKED US. BECAUSE WE'D BEEN HERE FOR SO MANY YEARS... WHO BROUGHT US HERE? WHY ARE WE HERE?
THE BLACK CITY?
AND YOU SAID YOU DIDN'T KNOW.
BUT THE BLACK STONES KNOW... THERE'S ONE AT EVERY LANDING SITE... ONE EVERY PLACE OUR SPECIES HAS BEEN TAKEN TO ON THIS WORLD.
WHY?
THEY'RE TRYING TO TELL US WHY WE'RE HERE... THEY'RE TRYING TO GUIDE US TO THE OTHER SIDE OF THE WORLD.
THEY'RE TRYING TO TAKE US TO THE BLACK CITY.
ON THE FAR SIDE OF THE GLOBE... THERE'S A HUGE, TOWERING CITY OF OBSIDIAN, GLITTERING WITH GREEN LIGHTS.
EVERY TWENTY YEARS, NEW LONDON HAS SENT A PARTY TO INVESTIGATE. ONLY ONCE HAS SOMEONE RETURNED...

HIS EYES GLOWED BRIGHT GREEN...SO DID HIS *BLOOD*, THROUGH HIS SKIN... BUT HE COULDN'T SPEAK...ALL THAT WAS LEFT IN HIM WAS *SCREAMS*.

HE ENDED UP *RIPPING OPEN* HIS WRISTS, TRYING TO BLEED THE ESSENCE OF THE BLACK CITY OUT OF HIMSELF...

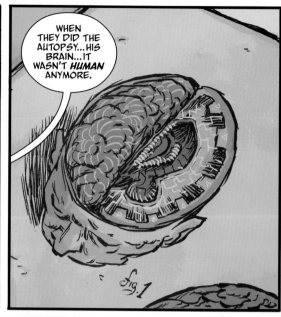

WHEN THEY DID THE AUTOPSY...HIS BRAIN...IT WASN'T *HUMAN* ANYMORE.

fig.1

IS THAT...IS THAT WHAT HAPPENS WITH THE STONES? WHEN YOU START *TALKING* TO THEM?

AS FAR AS WE UNDERSTAND IT, YES.

THEY WANT US TO BE SOMETHING WE'RE *NOT*. SOMETHING WE CAN *NEVER* BE...AND INEVITABLY IT DESTROYS US.

THAT'S WHY YOU CAN'T LET YOURSELF *PLAY* WITH THAT POWER. THAT'S WHY MY FATHER TRIED TO END YOUR *FRIEND'S* LIFE.

IT WASN'T MALICE. IT WAS *MERCY*.

BECAUSE HE'S ON THE PATH TO *DEATH'S DOOR* EITHER WAY.

ISAAC!

I'M SORRY, KAREN. I JUST NEEDED TO SHOW YOU WHY IT WAS HOPELESS. I WANT TO HELP YOU GUYS...

I WANT TO HELP *YOU*, ESPECIALLY. I JUST DON'T KNOW HOW.

SANDER...

YOU REALLY THINK WE DIDN'T HAVE A *PLAN* THE SECOND WE WALKED AWAY FROM THAT DINNER TABLE?

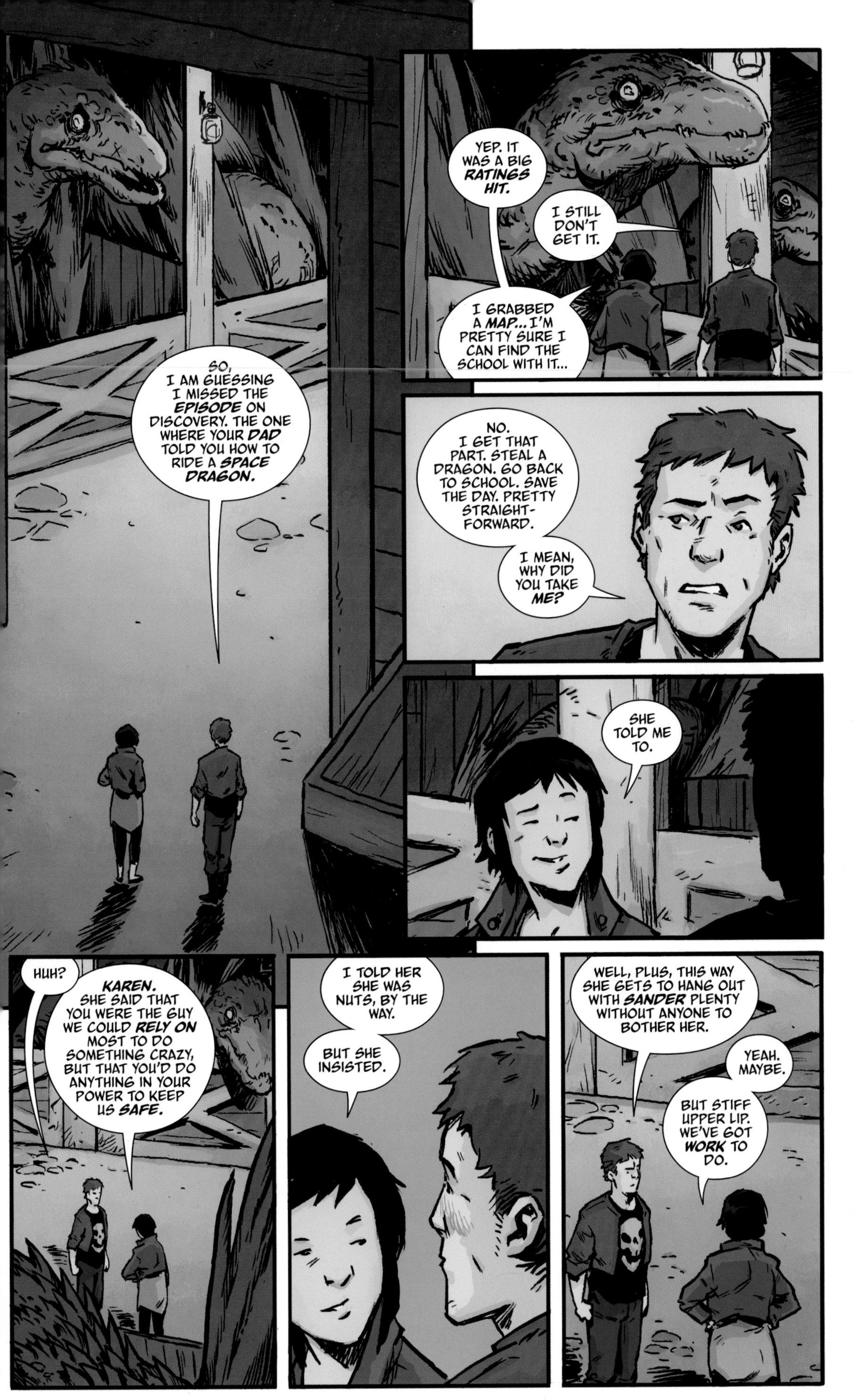
YEP. IT WAS A BIG RATINGS HIT.
I STILL DON'T GET IT.
I GRABBED A MAP... I'M PRETTY SURE I CAN FIND THE SCHOOL WITH IT...
SO, I AM GUESSING I MISSED THE EPISODE ON DISCOVERY. THE ONE WHERE YOUR DAD TOLD YOU HOW TO RIDE A SPACE DRAGON.
NO. I GET THAT PART. STEAL A DRAGON. GO BACK TO SCHOOL. SAVE THE DAY. PRETTY STRAIGHT-FORWARD.
I MEAN, WHY DID YOU TAKE ME?
SHE TOLD ME TO.
HUH?
KAREN. SHE SAID THAT YOU WERE THE GUY WE COULD RELY ON MOST TO DO SOMETHING CRAZY, BUT THAT YOU'D DO ANYTHING IN YOUR POWER TO KEEP US SAFE.
I TOLD HER SHE WAS NUTS, BY THE WAY.
BUT SHE INSISTED.
WELL, PLUS, THIS WAY SHE GETS TO HANG OUT WITH SANDER PLENTY WITHOUT ANYONE TO BOTHER HER.
YEAH. MAYBE.
BUT STIFF UPPER LIP. WE'VE GOT WORK TO DO.

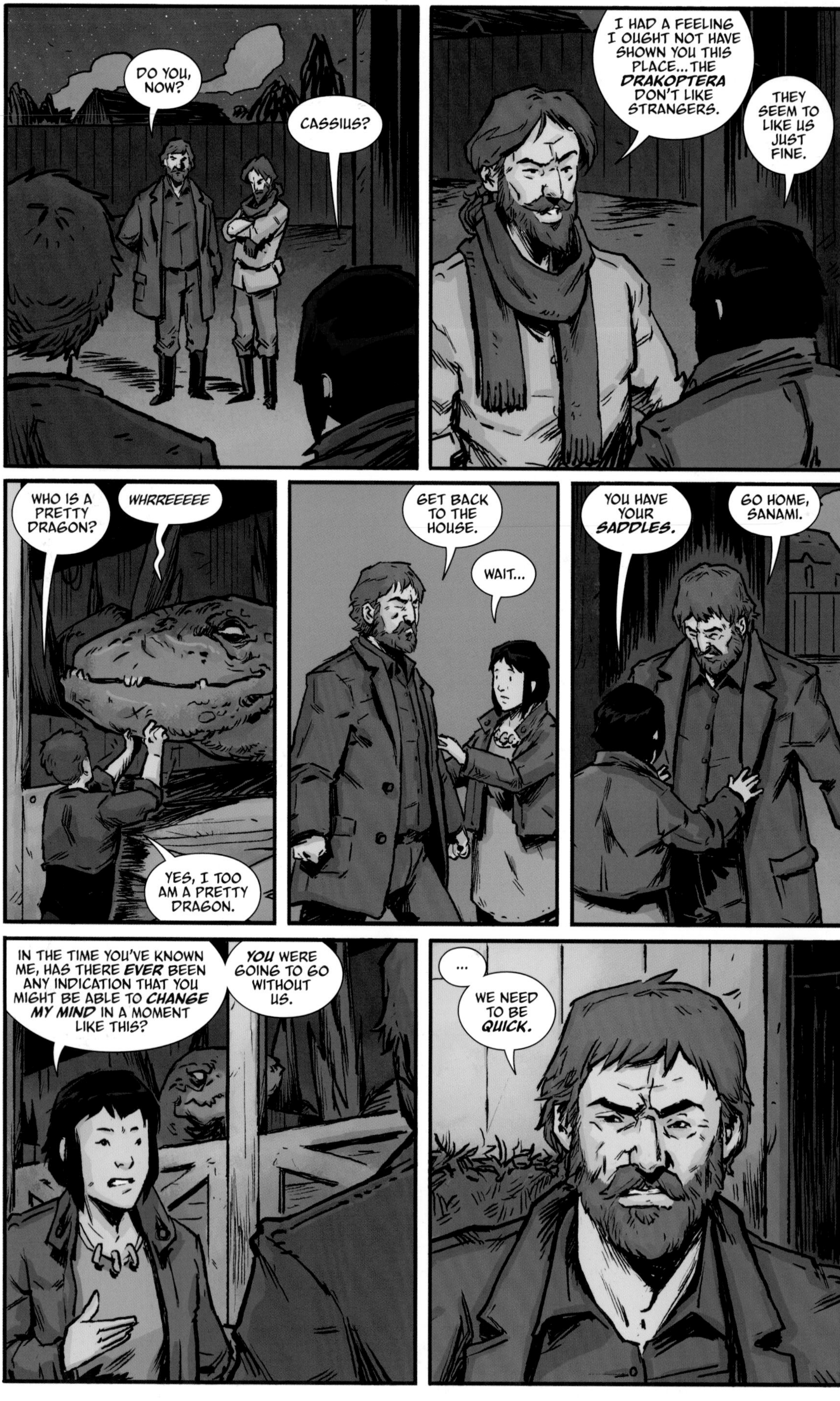
DO YOU, NOW?
CASSIUS?
I HAD A FEELING I OUGHT NOT HAVE SHOWN YOU THIS PLACE... THE DRAKOPTERA DON'T LIKE STRANGERS.
THEY SEEM TO LIKE US JUST FINE.
WHO IS A PRETTY DRAGON?
WHRREEEEE
YES, I TOO AM A PRETTY DRAGON.
GET BACK TO THE HOUSE.
WAIT...
YOU HAVE YOUR SADDLES.
GO HOME, SANAMI.
IN THE TIME YOU'VE KNOWN ME, HAS THERE EVER BEEN ANY INDICATION THAT YOU MIGHT BE ABLE TO CHANGE MY MIND IN A MOMENT LIKE THIS?
YOU WERE GOING TO GO WITHOUT US.
...
WE NEED TO BE QUICK.

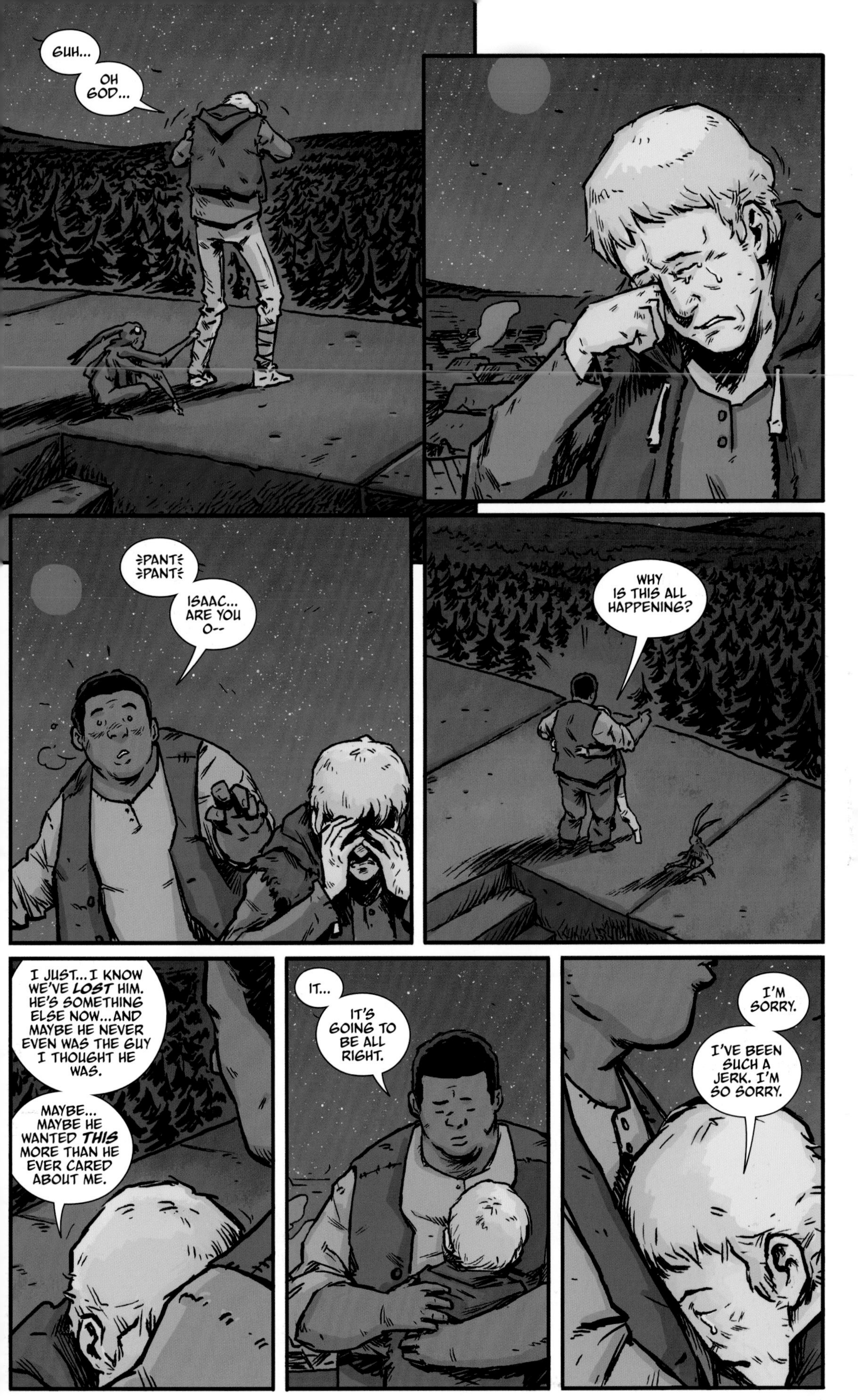
GUH...
OH GOD...
⪢PANT⪡ ⪢PANT⪡
ISAAC... ARE YOU O--
WHY IS THIS ALL HAPPENING?
I JUST... I KNOW WE'VE *LOST* HIM. HE'S SOMETHING ELSE NOW... AND MAYBE HE NEVER EVEN WAS THE GUY I THOUGHT HE WAS.
MAYBE... MAYBE HE WANTED ***THIS*** MORE THAN HE EVER CARED ABOUT ME.
IT...
IT'S GOING TO BE ALL RIGHT.
I'M SORRY.
I'VE BEEN SUCH A JERK. I'M SO SORRY.

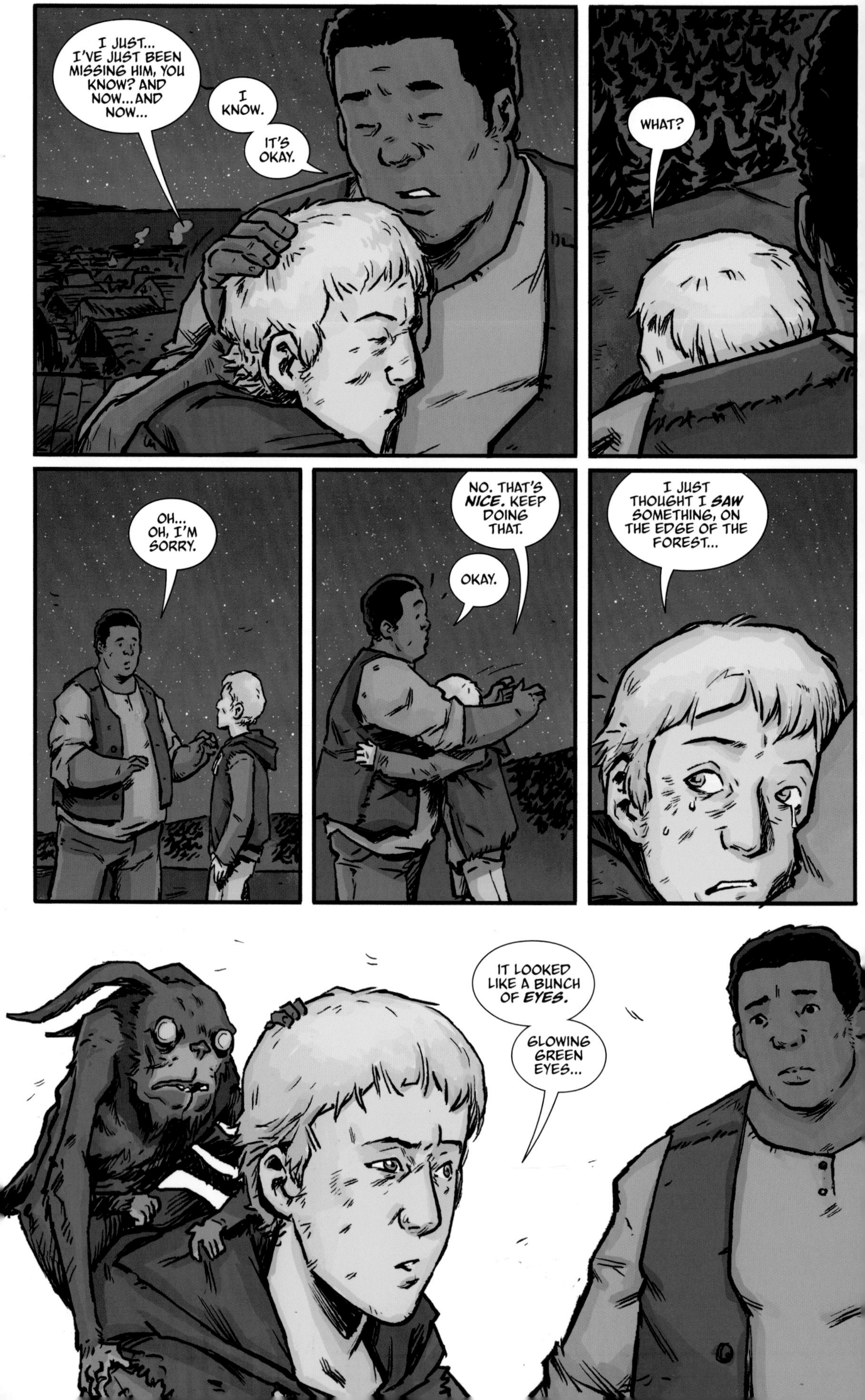
I JUST... I'VE JUST BEEN MISSING HIM, YOU KNOW? AND NOW...AND NOW...
I KNOW.
IT'S OKAY.
WHAT?
OH... OH, I'M SORRY.
NO. THAT'S NICE. KEEP DOING THAT.
OKAY.
I JUST THOUGHT I SAW SOMETHING, ON THE EDGE OF THE FOREST...
IT LOOKED LIKE A BUNCH OF EYES.
GLOWING GREEN EYES...

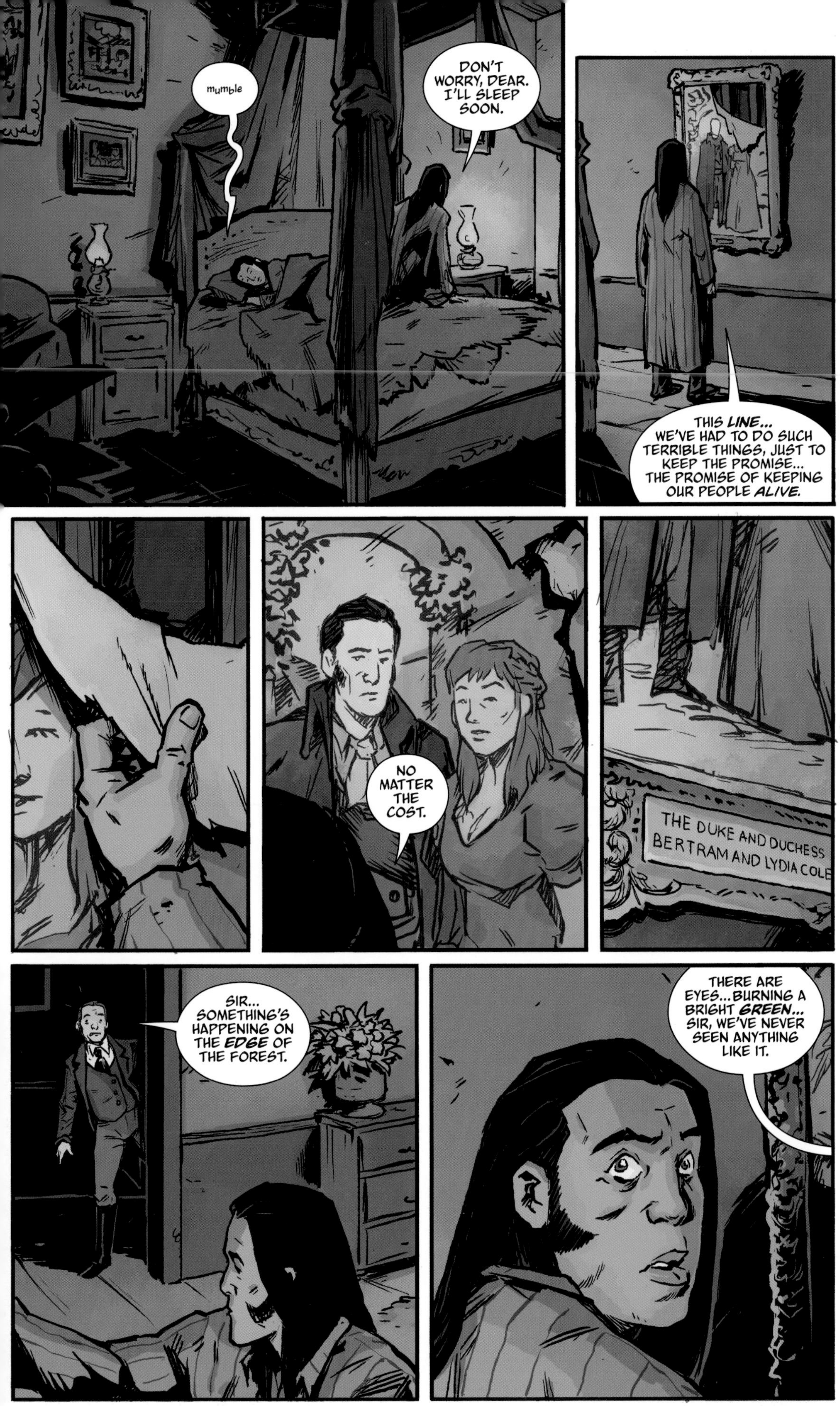
mumble
DON'T WORRY, DEAR. I'LL SLEEP SOON.
THIS LINE... WE'VE HAD TO DO SUCH TERRIBLE THINGS, JUST TO KEEP THE PROMISE... THE PROMISE OF KEEPING OUR PEOPLE ALIVE.
NO MATTER THE COST.
THE DUKE AND DUCHESS
BERTRAM AND LYDIA COLE
SIR... SOMETHING'S HAPPENING ON THE EDGE OF THE FOREST.
THERE ARE EYES... BURNING A BRIGHT GREEN... SIR, WE'VE NEVER SEEN ANYTHING LIKE IT.

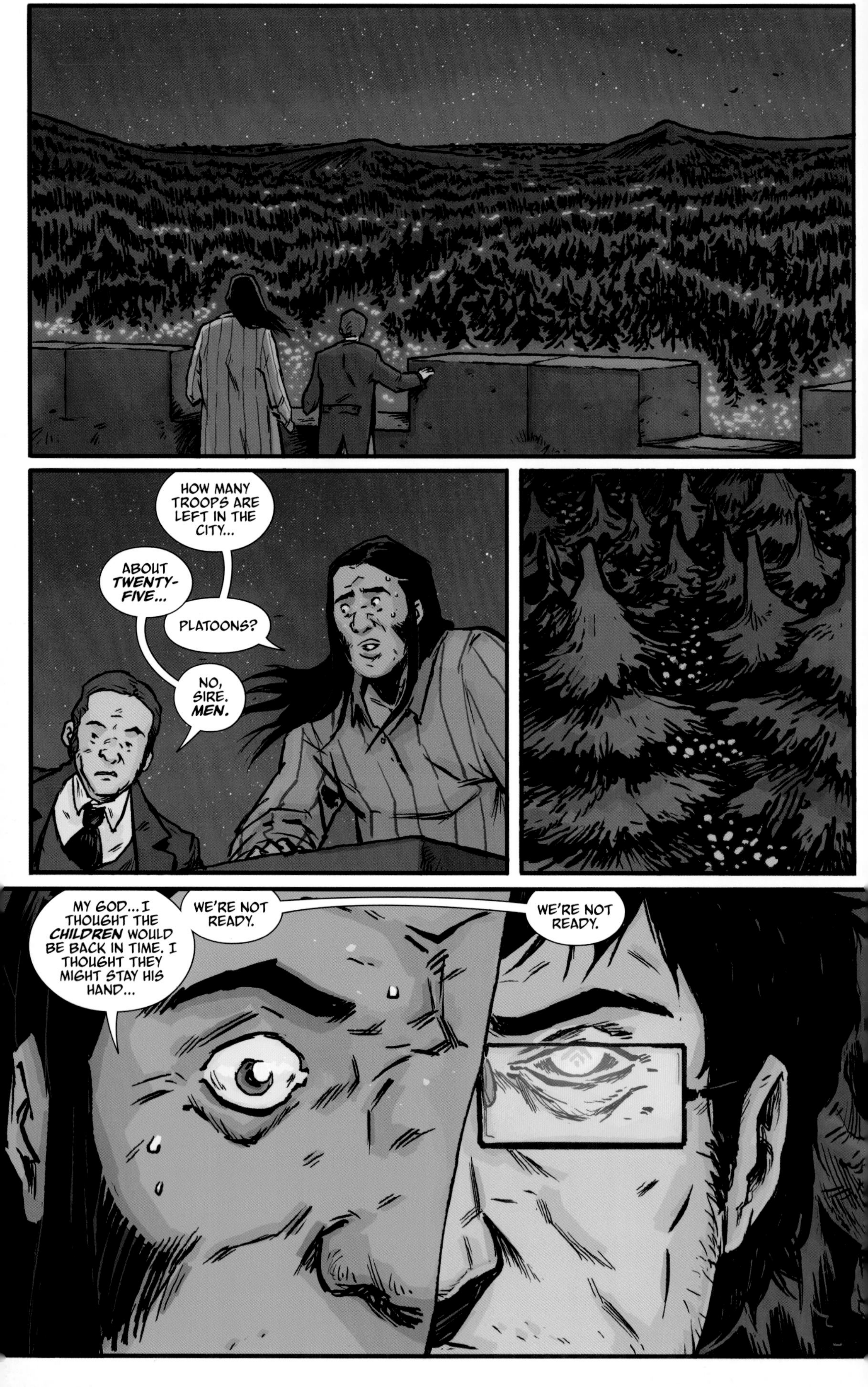
HOW MANY TROOPS ARE LEFT IN THE CITY...
ABOUT TWENTY-FIVE...
PLATOONS?
NO, SIRE. MEN.
MY GOD... I THOUGHT THE CHILDREN WOULD BE BACK IN TIME. I THOUGHT THEY MIGHT STAY HIS HAND...
WE'RE NOT READY.
WE'RE NOT READY.

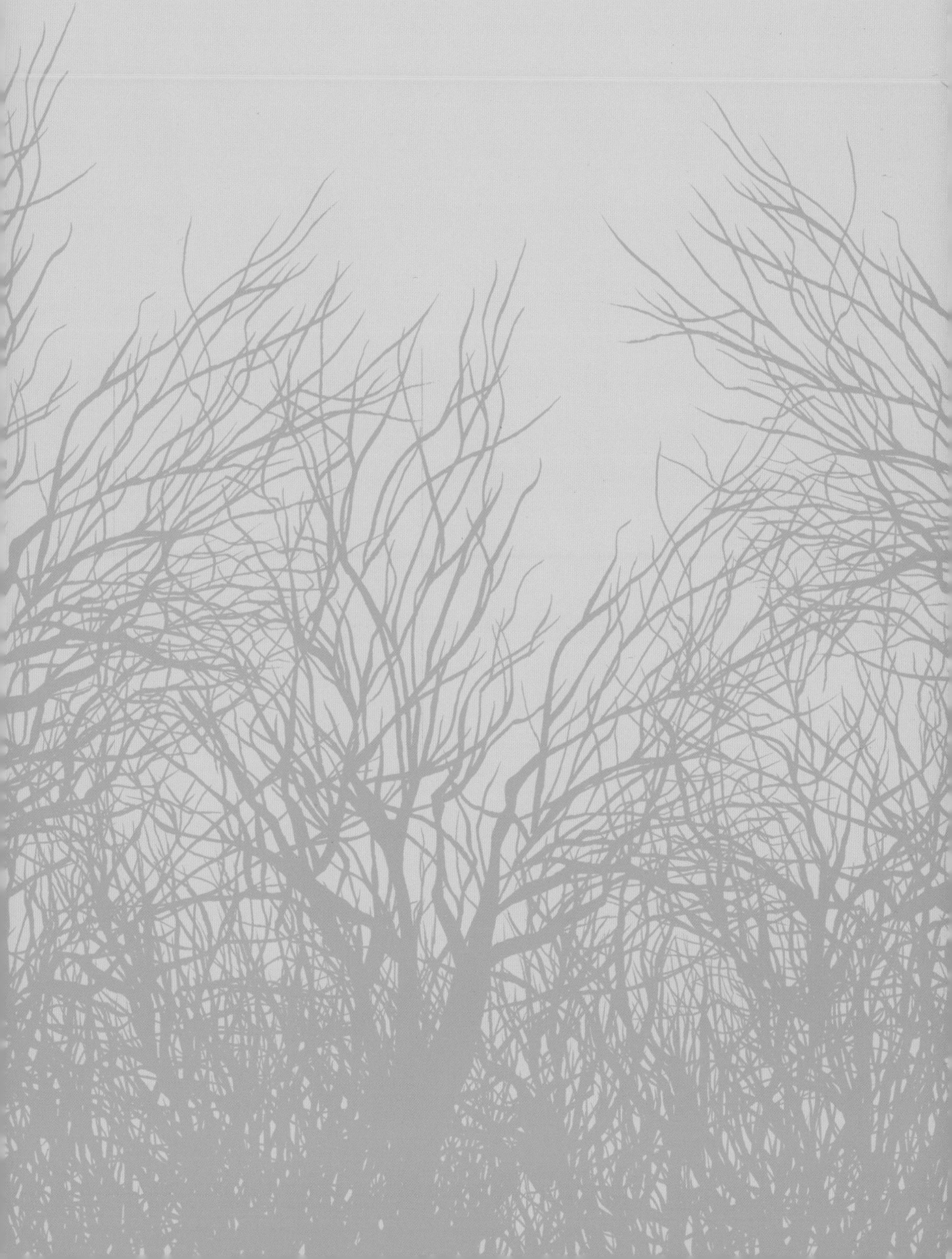

CHAPTER
ELEVEN

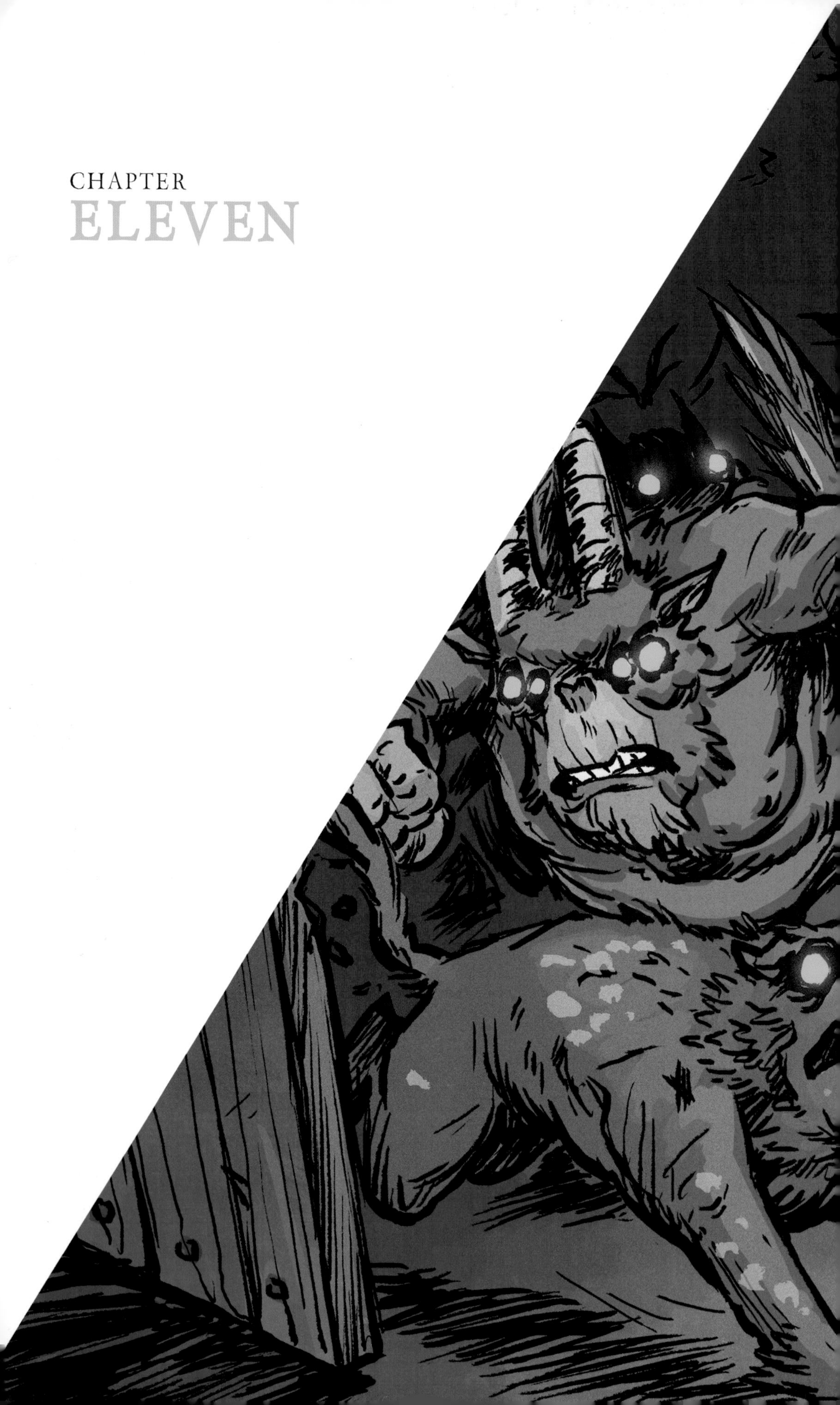

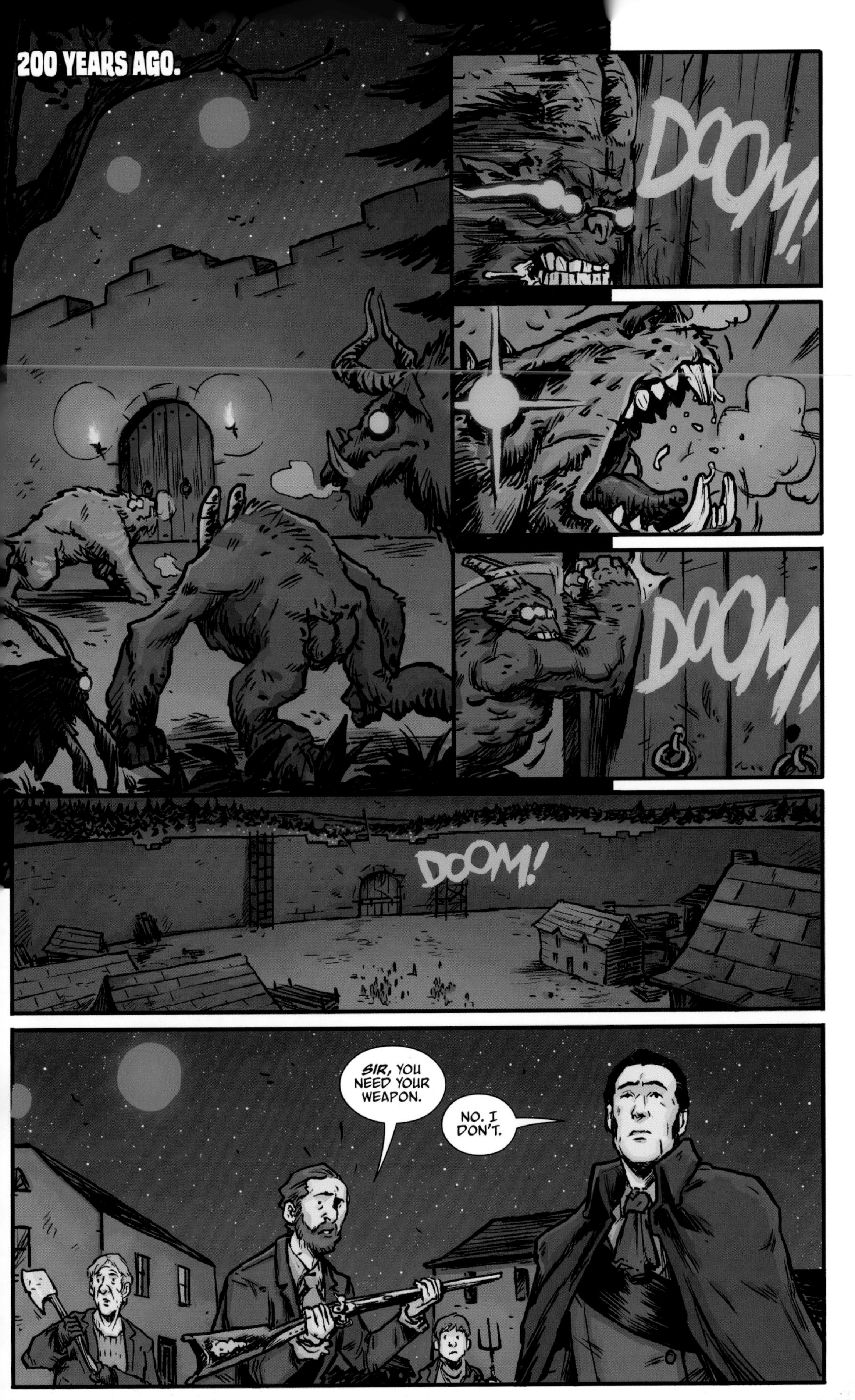
200 YEARS AGO.
DOOM!
DOOM!
DOOM!
SIR, YOU NEED YOUR WEAPON.
NO. I DON'T.

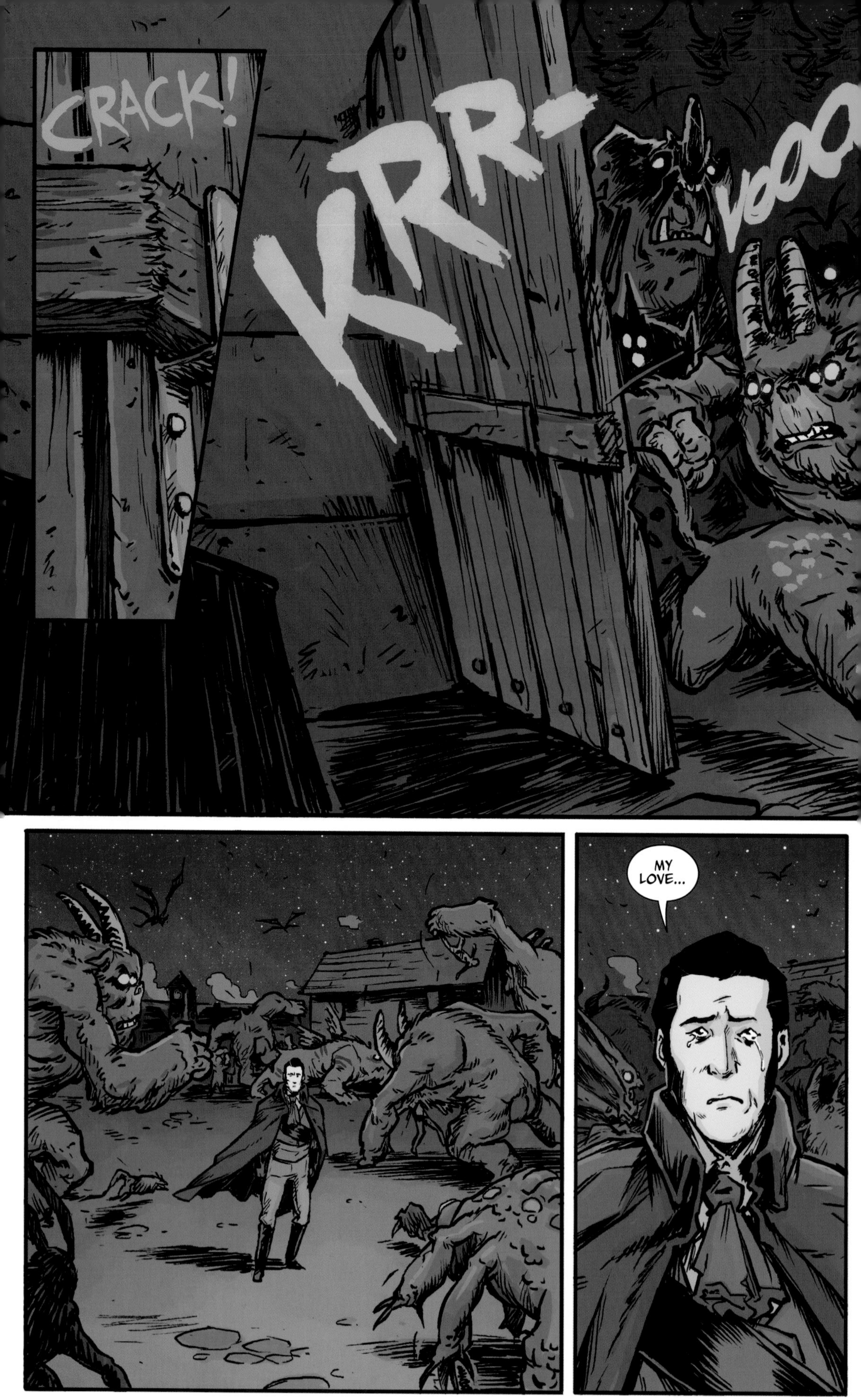
CRACK!
KRR-
VOOO
MY LOVE...

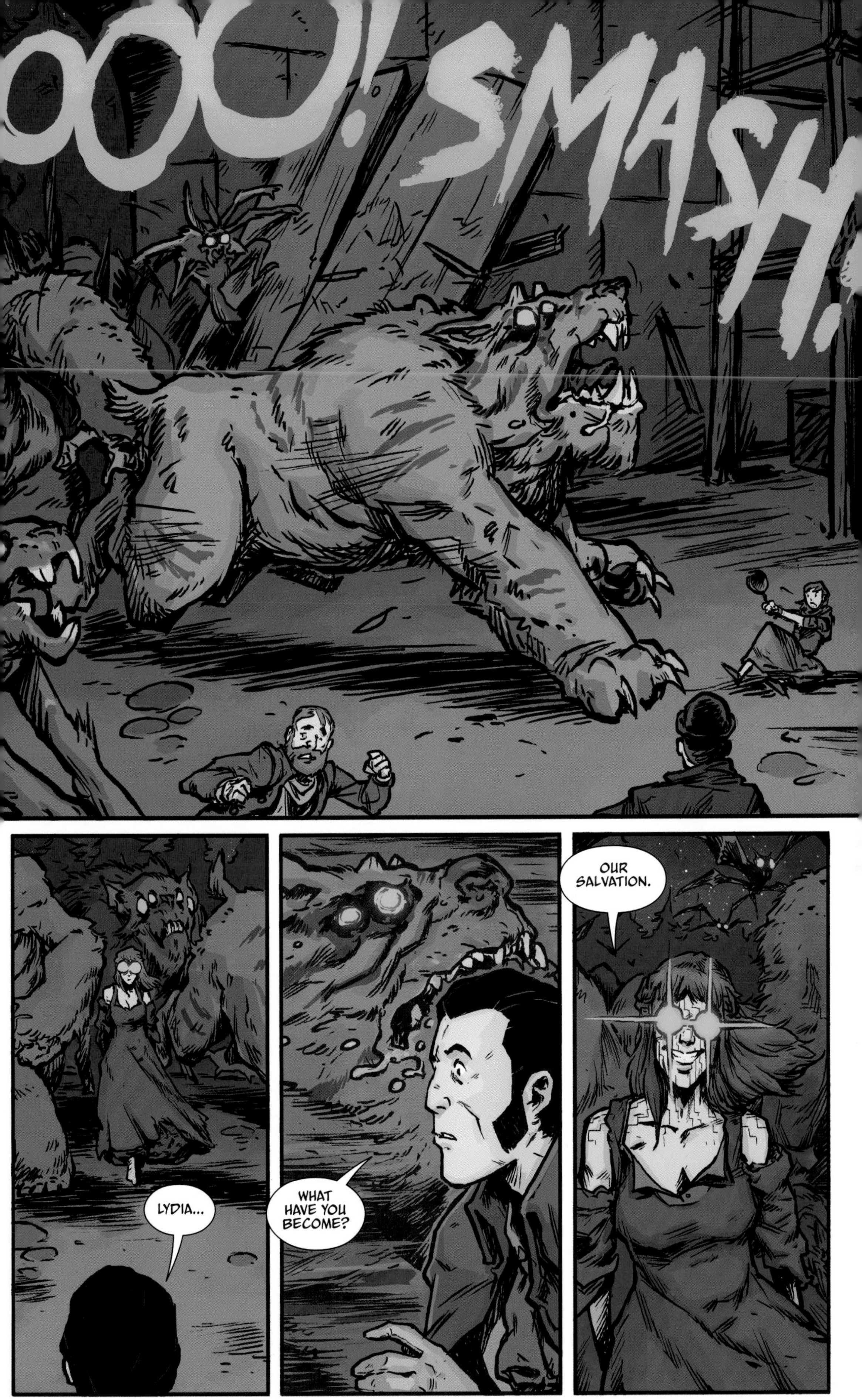
OOO! SMASH!!
LYDIA...
WHAT HAVE YOU BECOME?
OUR SALVATION.

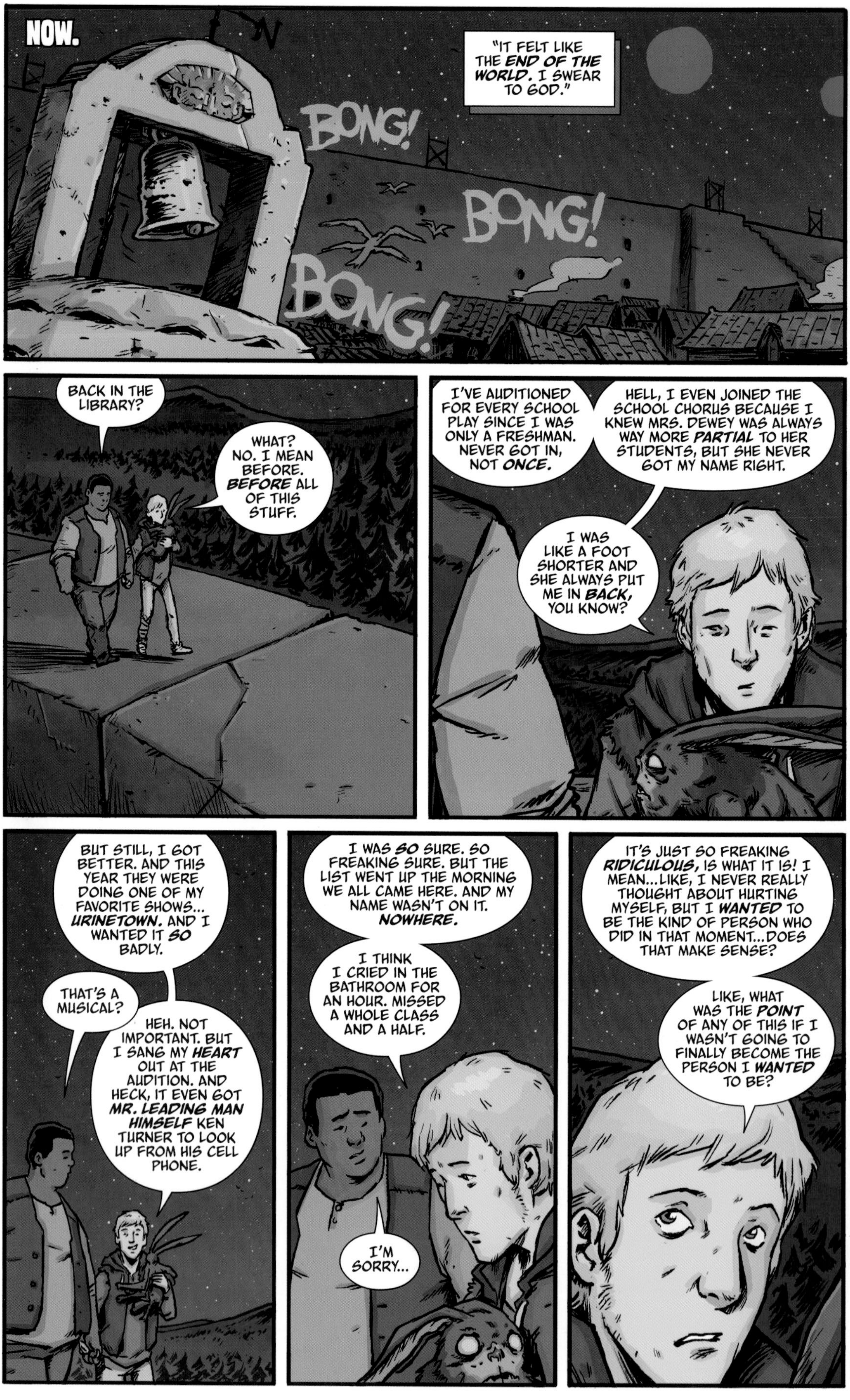
NOW.
"IT FELT LIKE THE END OF THE WORLD. I SWEAR TO GOD."
BONG!
BONG!
BONG!
BACK IN THE LIBRARY?
WHAT? NO. I MEAN BEFORE. BEFORE ALL OF THIS STUFF.
I'VE AUDITIONED FOR EVERY SCHOOL PLAY SINCE I WAS ONLY A FRESHMAN. NEVER GOT IN, NOT ONCE.
HELL, I EVEN JOINED THE SCHOOL CHORUS BECAUSE I KNEW MRS. DEWEY WAS ALWAYS WAY MORE PARTIAL TO HER STUDENTS, BUT SHE NEVER GOT MY NAME RIGHT.
I WAS LIKE A FOOT SHORTER AND SHE ALWAYS PUT ME IN BACK, YOU KNOW?
BUT STILL, I GOT BETTER. AND THIS YEAR THEY WERE DOING ONE OF MY FAVORITE SHOWS... URINETOWN. AND I WANTED IT SO BADLY.
THAT'S A MUSICAL?
HEH. NOT IMPORTANT. BUT I SANG MY HEART OUT AT THE AUDITION. AND HECK, IT EVEN GOT MR. LEADING MAN HIMSELF KEN TURNER TO LOOK UP FROM HIS CELL PHONE.
I WAS SO SURE. SO FREAKING SURE. BUT THE LIST WENT UP THE MORNING WE ALL CAME HERE. AND MY NAME WASN'T ON IT. NOWHERE.
I THINK I CRIED IN THE BATHROOM FOR AN HOUR. MISSED A WHOLE CLASS AND A HALF.
I'M SORRY...
IT'S JUST SO FREAKING RIDICULOUS, IS WHAT IT IS! I MEAN...LIKE, I NEVER REALLY THOUGHT ABOUT HURTING MYSELF, BUT I WANTED TO BE THE KIND OF PERSON WHO DID IN THAT MOMENT...DOES THAT MAKE SENSE?
LIKE, WHAT WAS THE POINT OF ANY OF THIS IF I WASN'T GOING TO FINALLY BECOME THE PERSON I WANTED TO BE?

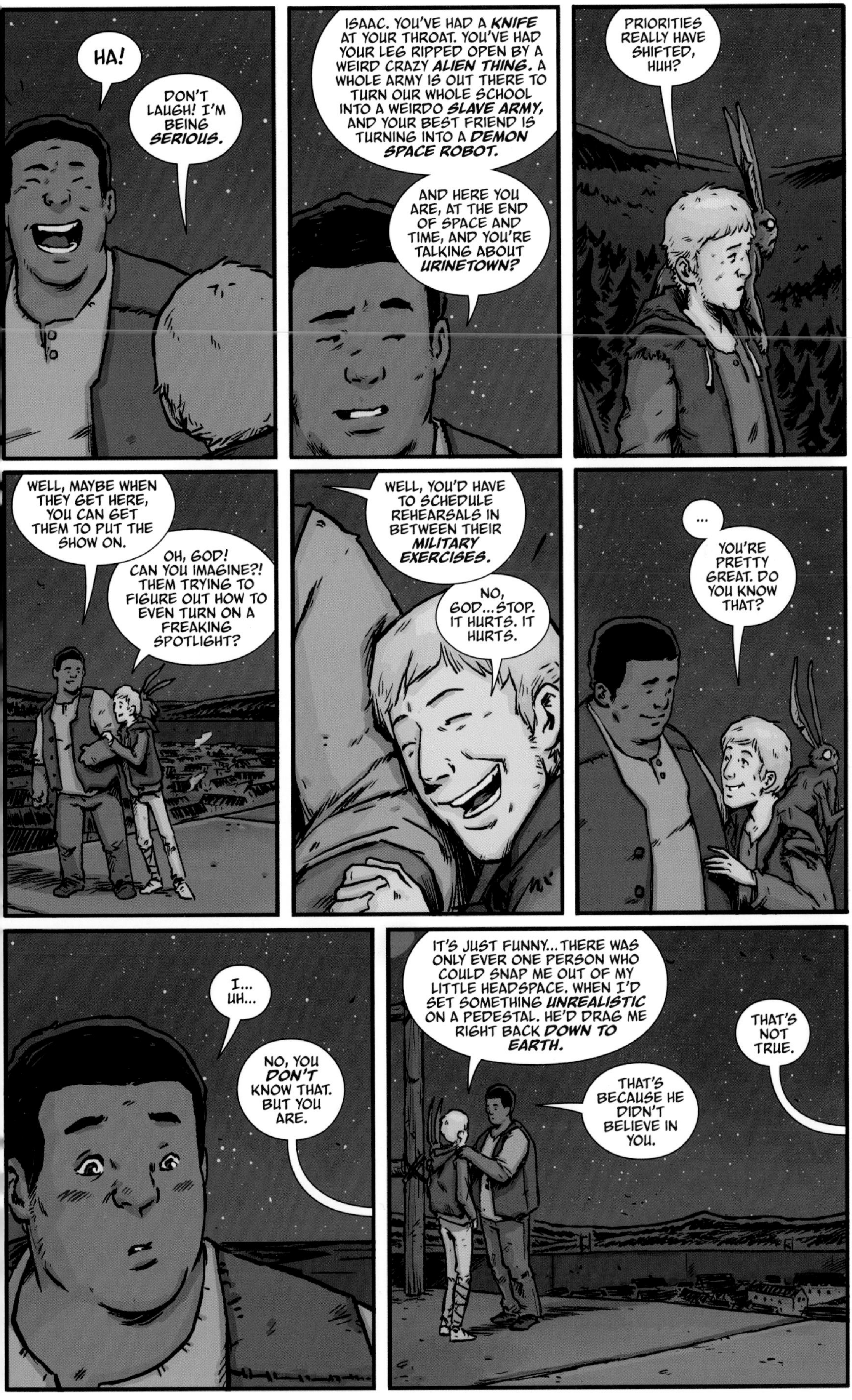
HA!
DON'T LAUGH! I'M BEING *SERIOUS.*
ISAAC. YOU'VE HAD A *KNIFE* AT YOUR THROAT. YOU'VE HAD YOUR LEG RIPPED OPEN BY A WEIRD CRAZY *ALIEN THING.* A WHOLE ARMY IS OUT THERE TO TURN OUR WHOLE SCHOOL INTO A WEIRDO *SLAVE ARMY,* AND YOUR BEST FRIEND IS TURNING INTO A *DEMON SPACE ROBOT.*
AND HERE YOU ARE, AT THE END OF SPACE AND TIME, AND YOU'RE TALKING ABOUT *URINETOWN?*
PRIORITIES REALLY HAVE SHIFTED, HUH?
WELL, MAYBE WHEN THEY GET HERE, YOU CAN GET THEM TO PUT THE SHOW ON.
OH, GOD! CAN YOU IMAGINE?! THEM TRYING TO FIGURE OUT HOW TO EVEN TURN ON A FREAKING SPOTLIGHT?
WELL, YOU'D HAVE TO SCHEDULE REHEARSALS IN BETWEEN THEIR *MILITARY EXERCISES.*
NO, GOD...STOP. IT HURTS. IT HURTS.
...
YOU'RE PRETTY GREAT. DO YOU KNOW THAT?
I... UH...
NO, YOU *DON'T* KNOW THAT. BUT YOU ARE.
IT'S JUST FUNNY...THERE WAS ONLY EVER ONE PERSON WHO COULD SNAP ME OUT OF MY LITTLE HEADSPACE. WHEN I'D SET SOMETHING *UNREALISTIC* ON A PEDESTAL. HE'D DRAG ME RIGHT BACK *DOWN TO EARTH.*
THAT'S NOT TRUE.
THAT'S BECAUSE HE DIDN'T BELIEVE IN YOU.

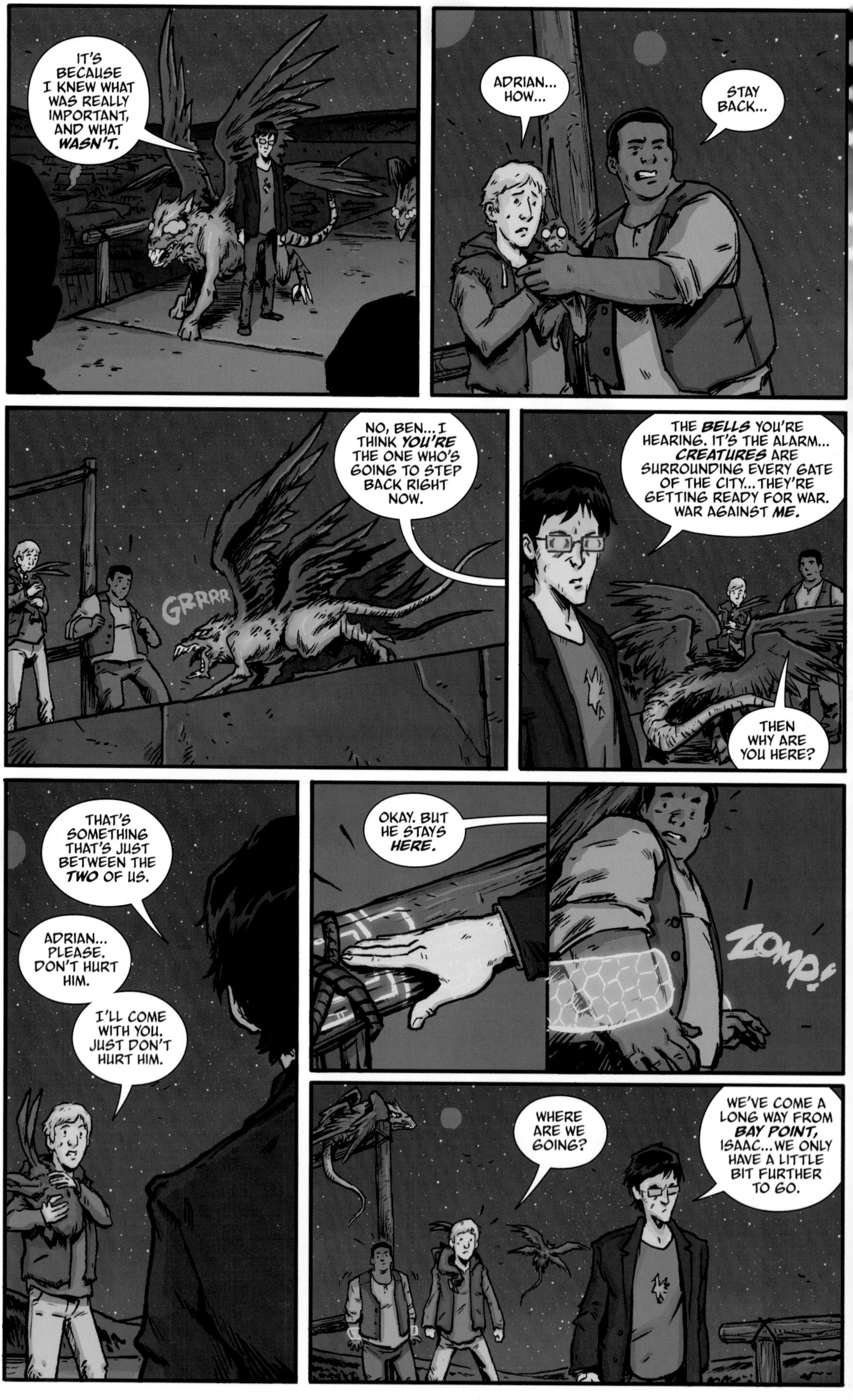
IT'S BECAUSE I KNEW WHAT WAS REALLY IMPORTANT, AND WHAT WASN'T.
ADRIAN... HOW...
STAY BACK...
NO, BEN... I THINK YOU'RE THE ONE WHO'S GOING TO STEP BACK RIGHT NOW.
GRRRR
THE BELLS YOU'RE HEARING. IT'S THE ALARM... CREATURES ARE SURROUNDING EVERY GATE OF THE CITY... THEY'RE GETTING READY FOR WAR. WAR AGAINST ME.
THEN WHY ARE YOU HERE?
THAT'S SOMETHING THAT'S JUST BETWEEN THE TWO OF US.
ADRIAN... PLEASE. DON'T HURT HIM.
I'LL COME WITH YOU. JUST DON'T HURT HIM.
OKAY. BUT HE STAYS HERE.
ZOMP!
WHERE ARE WE GOING?
WE'VE COME A LONG WAY FROM BAY POINT, ISAAC... WE ONLY HAVE A LITTLE BIT FURTHER TO GO.

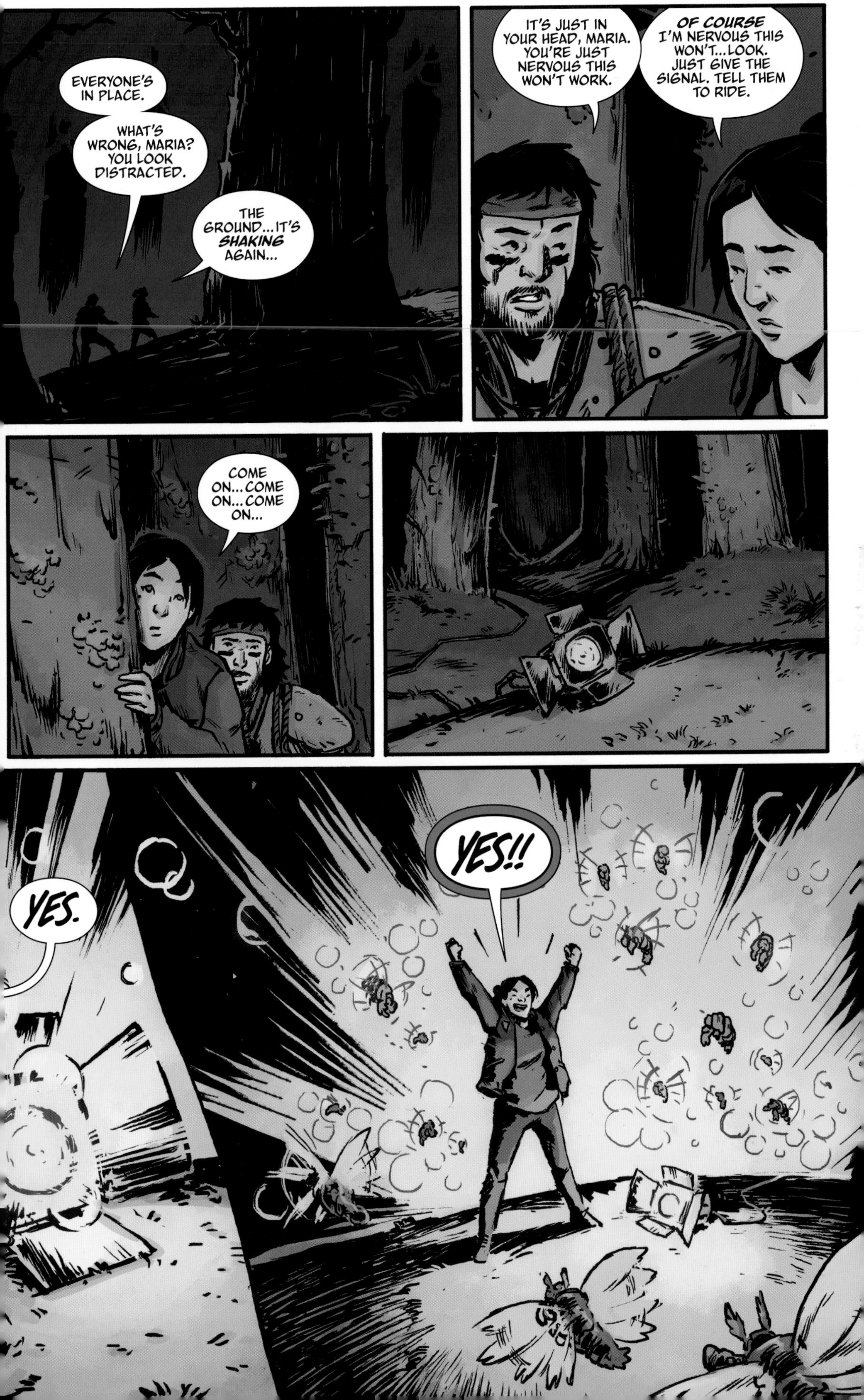
EVERYONE'S IN PLACE.
WHAT'S WRONG, MARIA? YOU LOOK DISTRACTED.
THE GROUND...IT'S SHAKING AGAIN...
IT'S JUST IN YOUR HEAD, MARIA. YOU'RE JUST NERVOUS THIS WON'T WORK.
OF COURSE I'M NERVOUS THIS WON'T...LOOK. JUST GIVE THE SIGNAL. TELL THEM TO RIDE.
COME ON...COME ON...COME ON...
YES.
YES!!

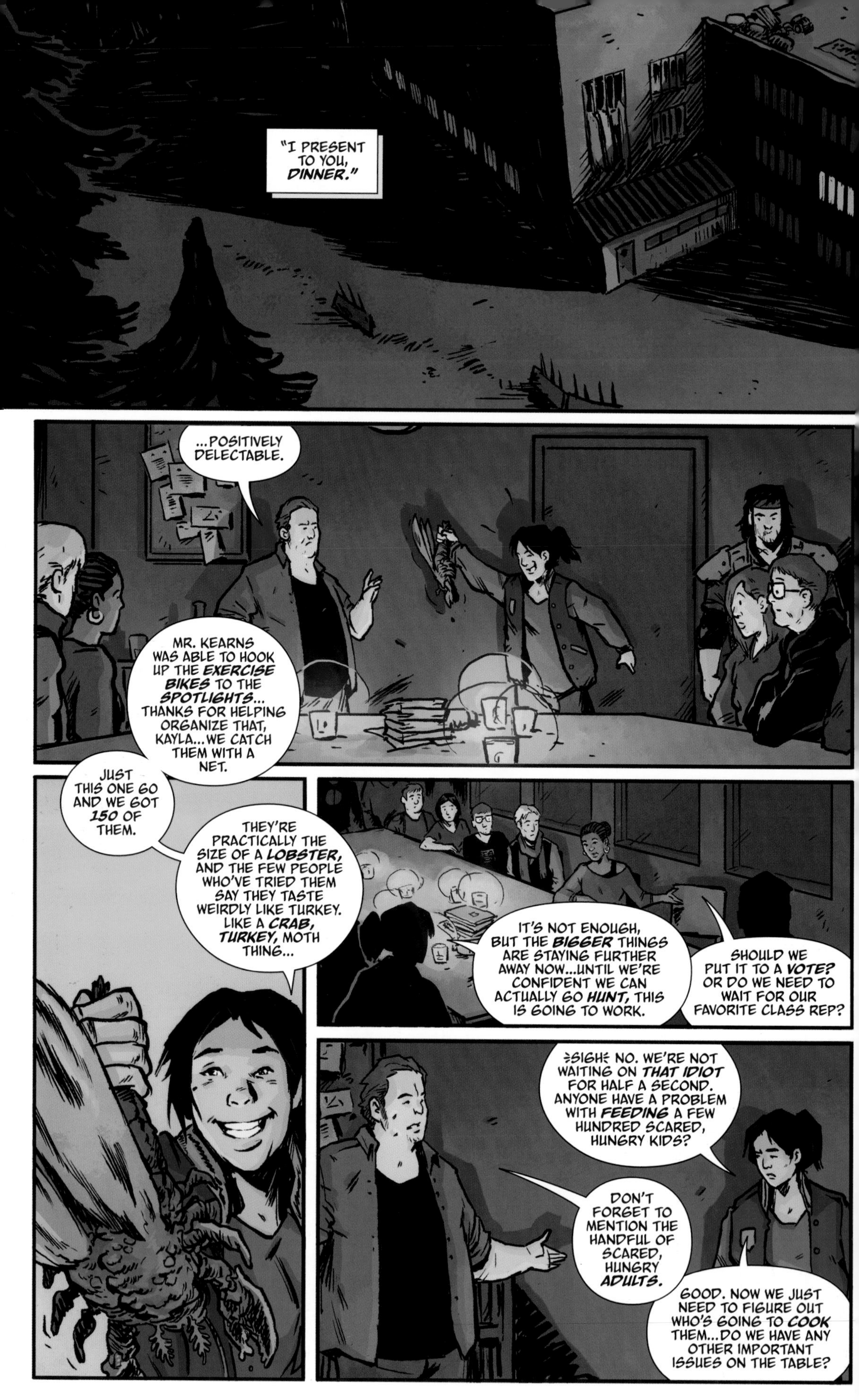
"I PRESENT TO YOU, DINNER."
...POSITIVELY DELECTABLE.
MR. KEARNS WAS ABLE TO HOOK UP THE EXERCISE BIKES TO THE SPOTLIGHTS... THANKS FOR HELPING ORGANIZE THAT, KAYLA...WE CATCH THEM WITH A NET.
JUST THIS ONE GO AND WE GOT 150 OF THEM.
THEY'RE PRACTICALLY THE SIZE OF A LOBSTER, AND THE FEW PEOPLE WHO'VE TRIED THEM SAY THEY TASTE WEIRDLY LIKE TURKEY. LIKE A CRAB, TURKEY, MOTH THING...
IT'S NOT ENOUGH, BUT THE BIGGER THINGS ARE STAYING FURTHER AWAY NOW...UNTIL WE'RE CONFIDENT WE CAN ACTUALLY GO HUNT, THIS IS GOING TO WORK.
SHOULD WE PUT IT TO A VOTE? OR DO WE NEED TO WAIT FOR OUR FAVORITE CLASS REP?
=SIGH= NO. WE'RE NOT WAITING ON THAT IDIOT FOR HALF A SECOND. ANYONE HAVE A PROBLEM WITH FEEDING A FEW HUNDRED SCARED, HUNGRY KIDS?
DON'T FORGET TO MENTION THE HANDFUL OF SCARED, HUNGRY ADULTS.
GOOD. NOW WE JUST NEED TO FIGURE OUT WHO'S GOING TO COOK THEM...DO WE HAVE ANY OTHER IMPORTANT ISSUES ON THE TABLE?

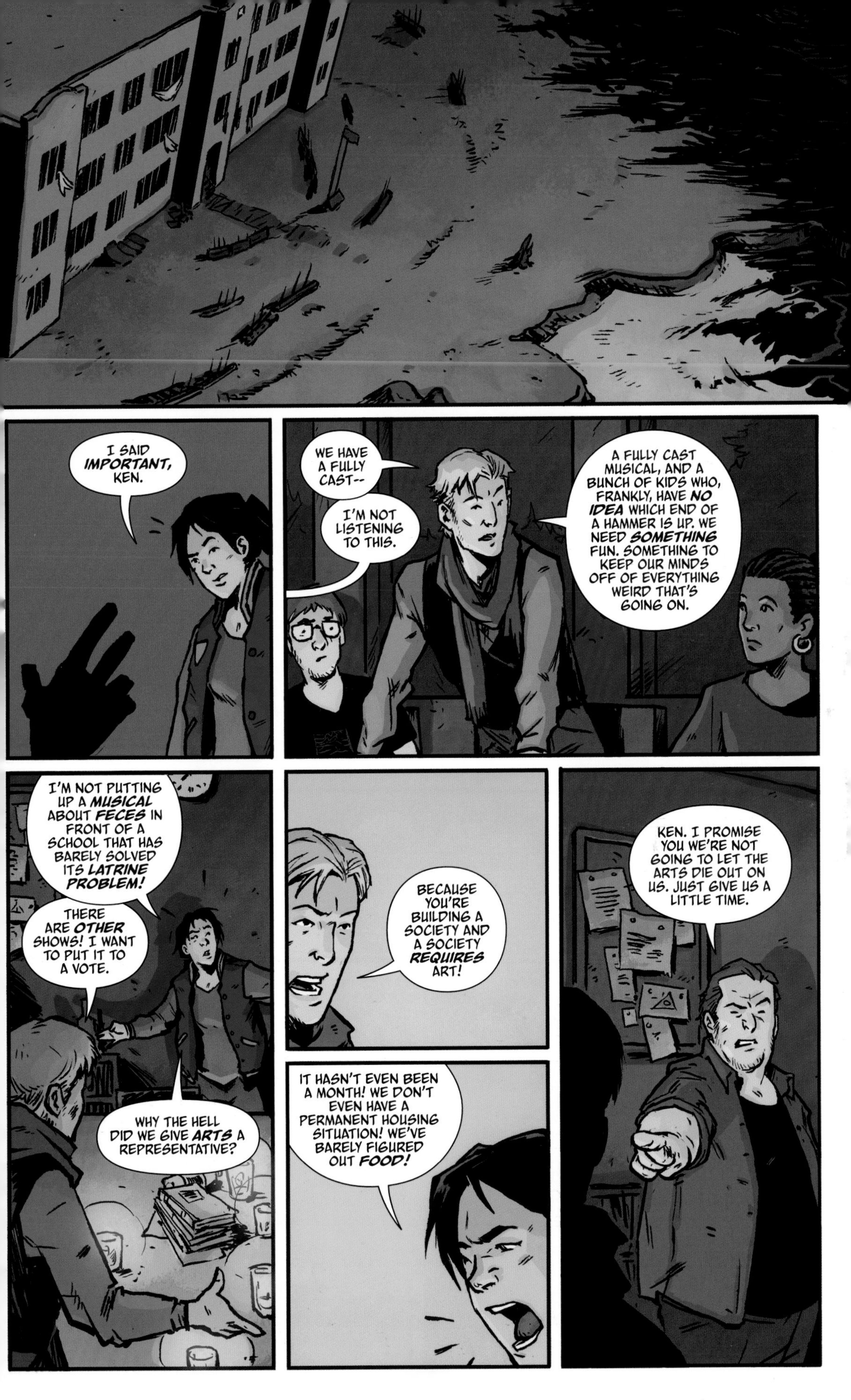
I SAID *IMPORTANT*, KEN.
WE HAVE A FULLY CAST--
I'M NOT LISTENING TO THIS.
A FULLY CAST MUSICAL, AND A BUNCH OF KIDS WHO, FRANKLY, HAVE *NO IDEA* WHICH END OF A HAMMER IS UP. WE NEED *SOMETHING* FUN. SOMETHING TO KEEP OUR MINDS OFF OF EVERYTHING WEIRD THAT'S GOING ON.
I'M NOT PUTTING UP A *MUSICAL* ABOUT *FECES* IN FRONT OF A SCHOOL THAT HAS BARELY SOLVED ITS *LATRINE PROBLEM!*
THERE ARE *OTHER* SHOWS! I WANT TO PUT IT TO A VOTE.
WHY THE HELL DID WE GIVE *ARTS* A REPRESENTATIVE?
BECAUSE YOU'RE BUILDING A SOCIETY AND A SOCIETY *REQUIRES* ART!
IT HASN'T EVEN BEEN A MONTH! WE DON'T EVEN HAVE A PERMANENT HOUSING SITUATION! WE'VE BARELY FIGURED OUT *FOOD!*
KEN. I PROMISE YOU WE'RE NOT GOING TO LET THE ARTS DIE OUT ON US. JUST GIVE US A LITTLE TIME.

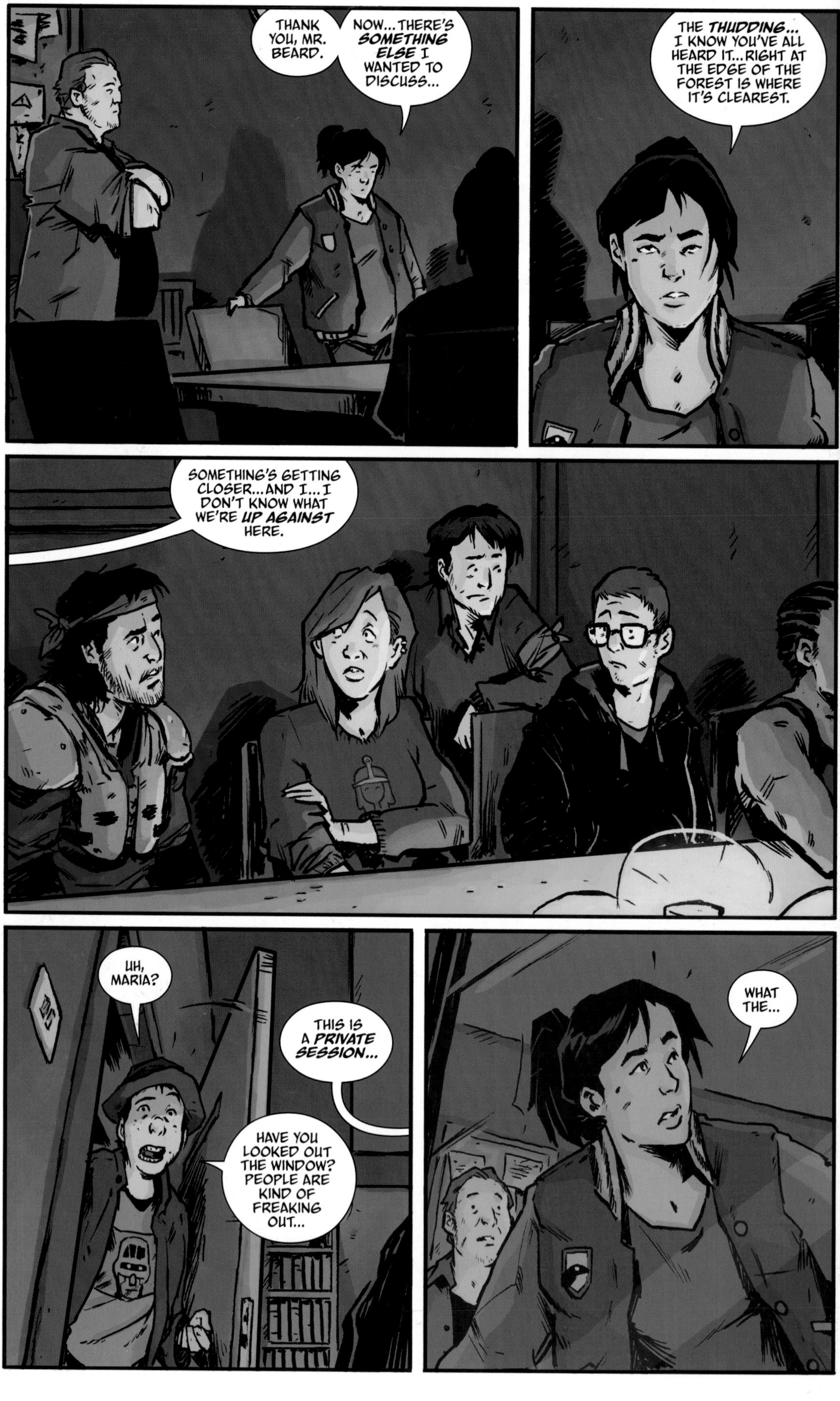
THANK YOU, MR. BEARD.
NOW... THERE'S SOMETHING ELSE I WANTED TO DISCUSS...
THE THUDDING... I KNOW YOU'VE ALL HEARD IT... RIGHT AT THE EDGE OF THE FOREST IS WHERE IT'S CLEAREST.
SOMETHING'S GETTING CLOSER... AND I... I DON'T KNOW WHAT WE'RE UP AGAINST HERE.
UH, MARIA?
THIS IS A PRIVATE SESSION...
HAVE YOU LOOKED OUT THE WINDOW? PEOPLE ARE KIND OF FREAKING OUT...
WHAT THE...

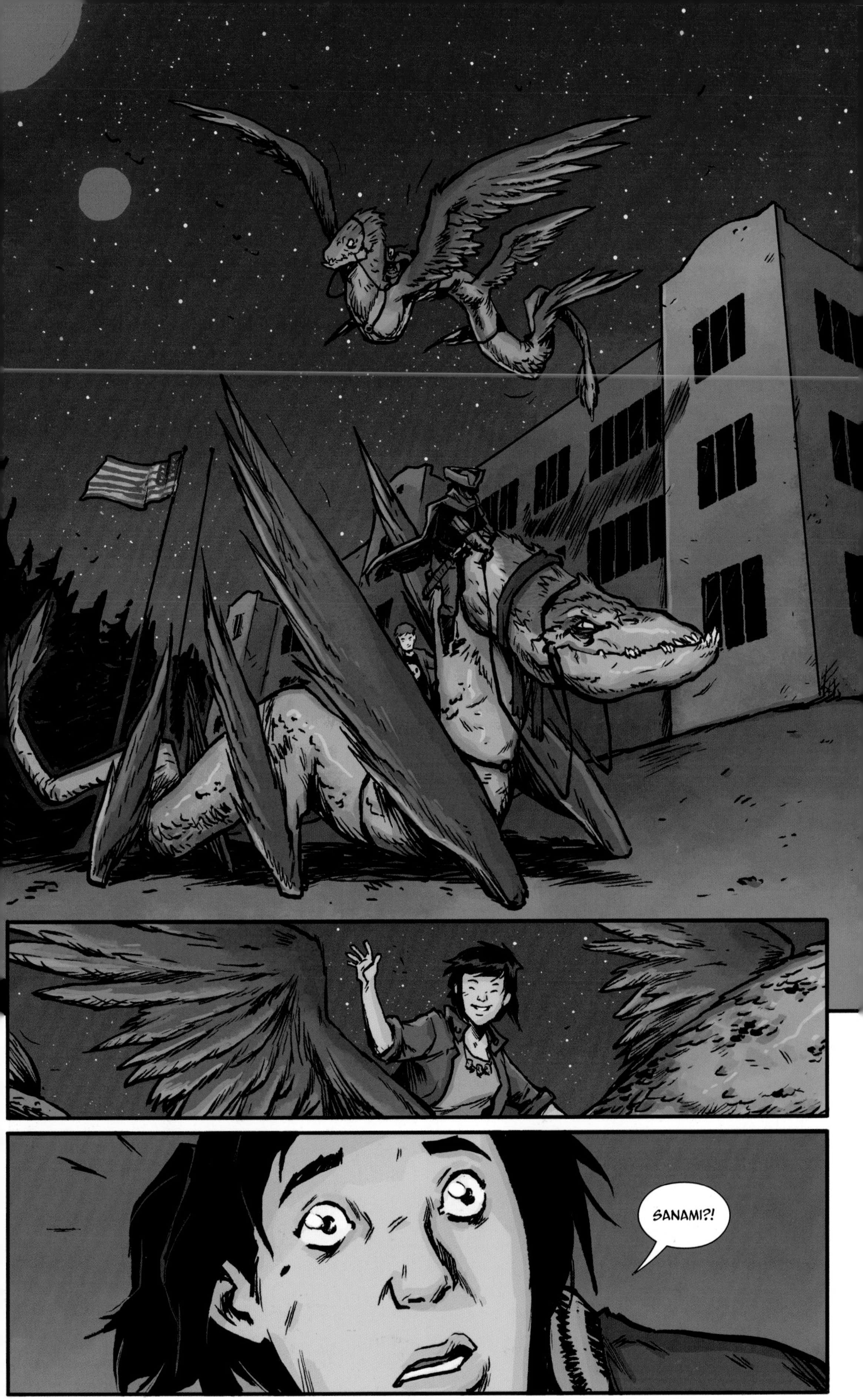
SANAMI?!

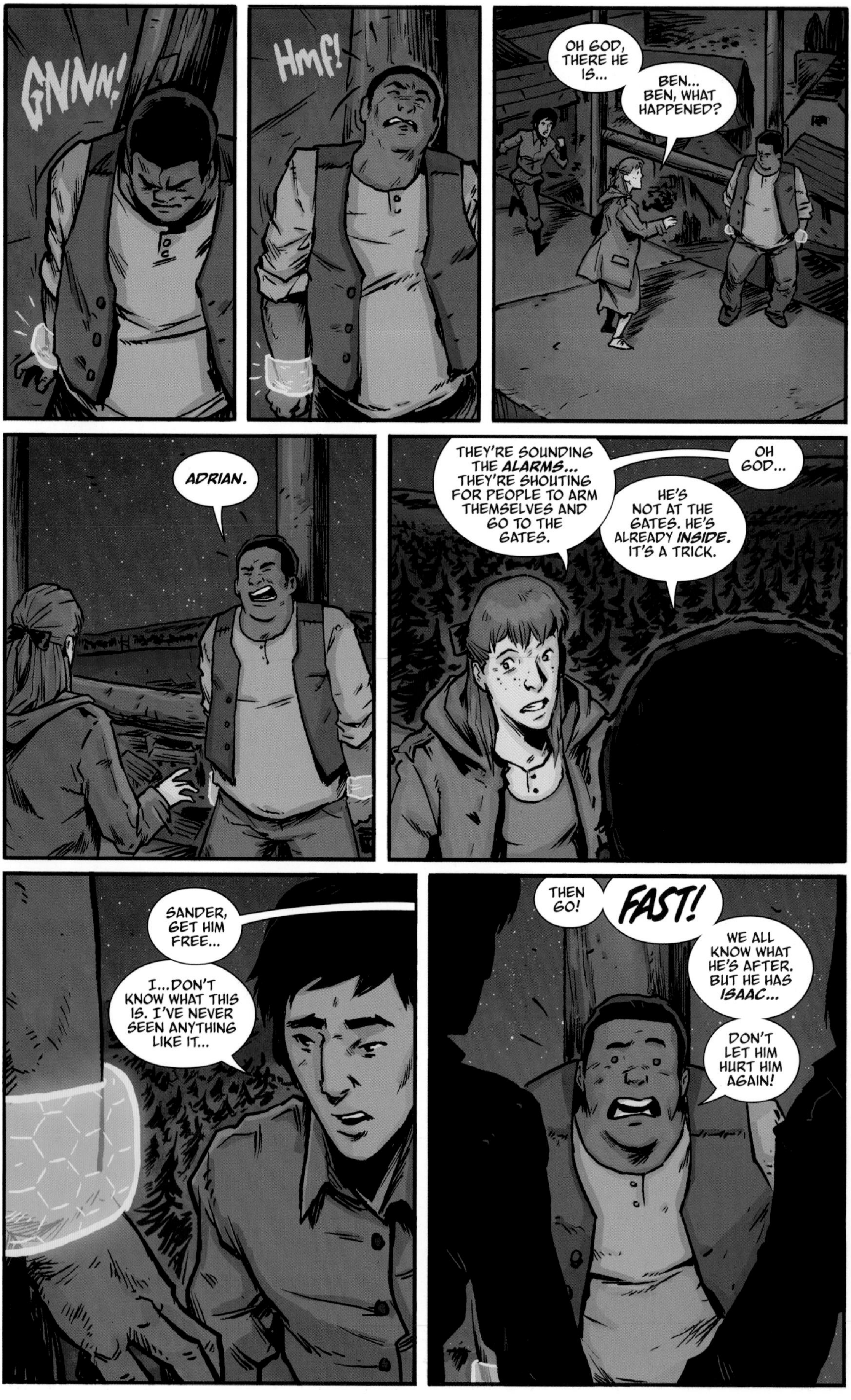
GNNN!
Hmf!
OH GOD, THERE HE IS...
BEN... BEN, WHAT HAPPENED?
ADRIAN.
THEY'RE SOUNDING THE *ALARMS...* THEY'RE SHOUTING FOR PEOPLE TO ARM THEMSELVES AND GO TO THE GATES.
OH GOD...
HE'S NOT AT THE GATES. HE'S ALREADY *INSIDE.* IT'S A TRICK.
SANDER, GET HIM FREE...
I...DON'T KNOW WHAT THIS IS. I'VE NEVER SEEN ANYTHING LIKE IT...
THEN GO!
FAST!
WE ALL KNOW WHAT HE'S AFTER. BUT HE HAS *ISAAC...*
DON'T LET HIM HURT HIM AGAIN!

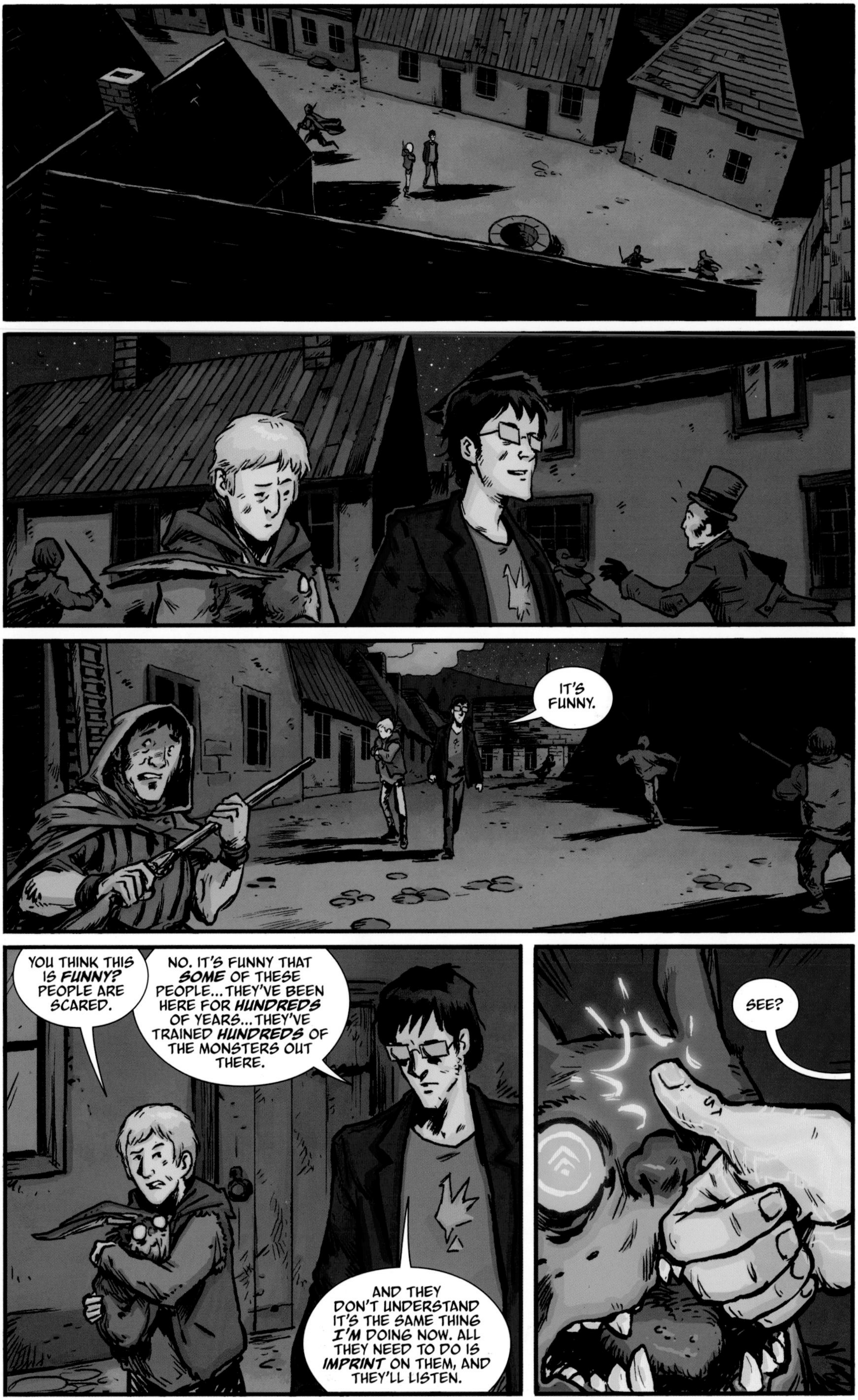
IT'S FUNNY.
YOU THINK THIS IS FUNNY? PEOPLE ARE SCARED.
NO. IT'S FUNNY THAT SOME OF THESE PEOPLE... THEY'VE BEEN HERE FOR HUNDREDS OF YEARS... THEY'VE TRAINED HUNDREDS OF THE MONSTERS OUT THERE.
AND THEY DON'T UNDERSTAND IT'S THE SAME THING I'M DOING NOW. ALL THEY NEED TO DO IS IMPRINT ON THEM, AND THEY'LL LISTEN.
SEE?

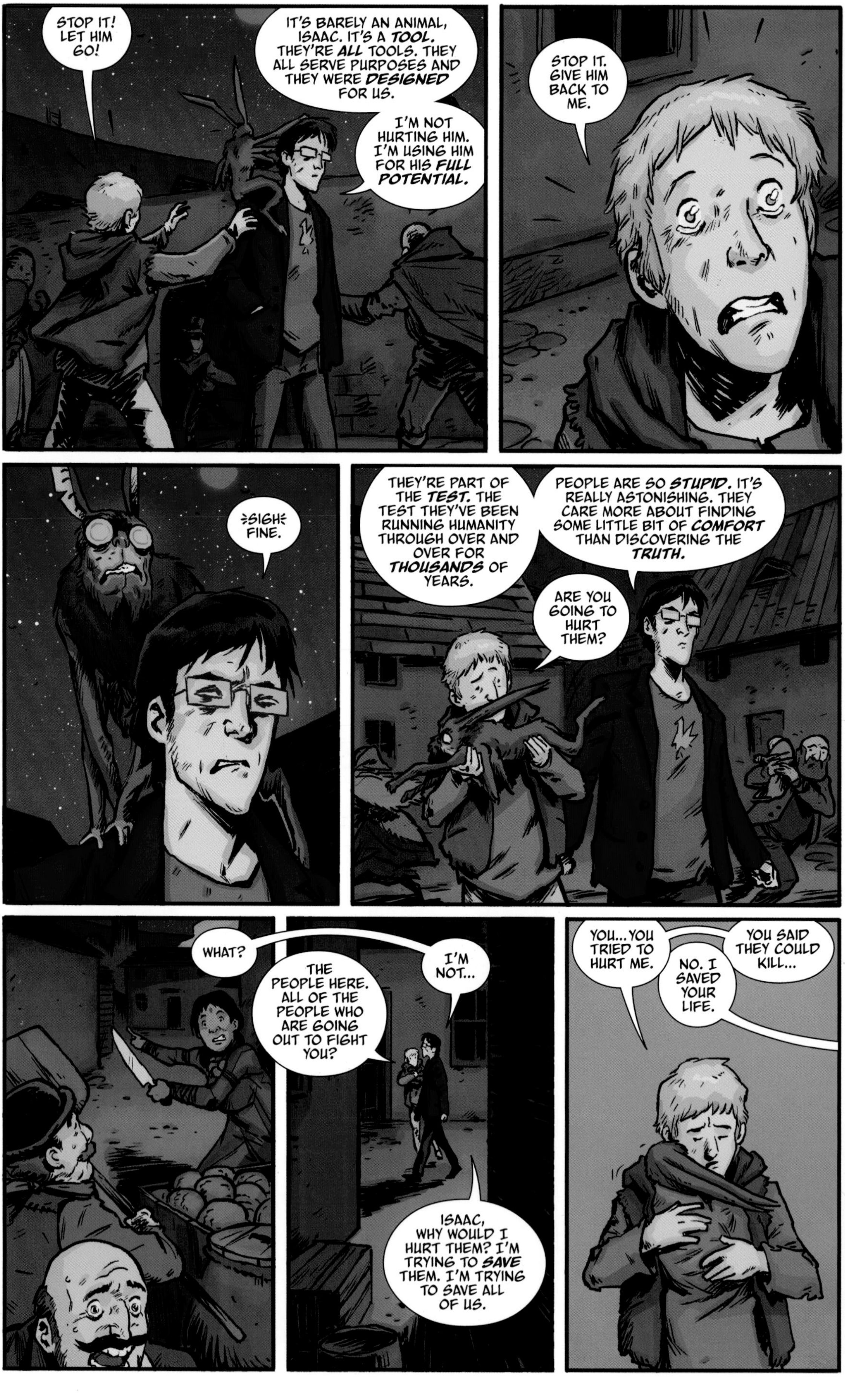
STOP IT! LET HIM GO!
IT'S BARELY AN ANIMAL, ISAAC. IT'S A TOOL. THEY'RE ALL TOOLS. THEY ALL SERVE PURPOSES AND THEY WERE DESIGNED FOR US.
I'M NOT HURTING HIM. I'M USING HIM FOR HIS FULL POTENTIAL.
STOP IT. GIVE HIM BACK TO ME.
SIGH FINE.
THEY'RE PART OF THE TEST. THE TEST THEY'VE BEEN RUNNING HUMANITY THROUGH OVER AND OVER FOR THOUSANDS OF YEARS.
PEOPLE ARE SO STUPID. IT'S REALLY ASTONISHING. THEY CARE MORE ABOUT FINDING SOME LITTLE BIT OF COMFORT THAN DISCOVERING THE TRUTH.
ARE YOU GOING TO HURT THEM?
WHAT?
THE PEOPLE HERE. ALL OF THE PEOPLE WHO ARE GOING OUT TO FIGHT YOU?
I'M NOT...
ISAAC, WHY WOULD I HURT THEM? I'M TRYING TO SAVE THEM. I'M TRYING TO SAVE ALL OF US.
YOU... YOU TRIED TO HURT ME.
YOU SAID THEY COULD KILL...
NO. I SAVED YOUR LIFE.

I CALLED THEIR BLUFF TO SAVE BOTH YOU AND ME. WHY ON EARTH WOULD I WANT YOU TO *DIE?* WHAT KIND OF PERSON DO YOU THINK I AM?

A KIND OF *CRAPPY* ONE, TO BE HONEST.

THAT'S... THAT'S FAIR.

...

WHY WERE YOU EVER MY FRIEND?

WHAT?

THAT'S...THAT'S WHY I WANTED TO TALK TO YOU. I JUST...I DON'T *UNDERSTAND.* I NEVER REALLY DID.

ADRIAN...

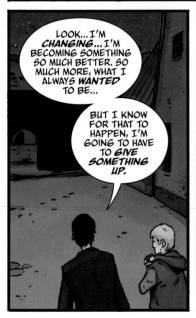

LOOK...I'M *CHANGING...* I'M BECOMING SOMETHING SO MUCH BETTER. SO MUCH MORE, WHAT I ALWAYS *WANTED* TO BE...

BUT I KNOW FOR THAT TO HAPPEN, I'M GOING TO HAVE TO *GIVE SOMETHING UP.*

WHEN SHE...WHEN SHE TOUCHED THE *FIFTH STONE,* SHE KILLED HER SISTER BECAUSE IT WAS THE EASY THING TO DO. AND SHE DIDN'T CARE ANYMORE.

I JUST WANT TO UNDERSTAND WHAT YOU EVER SAW IN ME, BEFORE I DO THIS TO MYSELF.

BEFORE I STOP BEING ANYTHING CLOSE TO *HUMAN.*

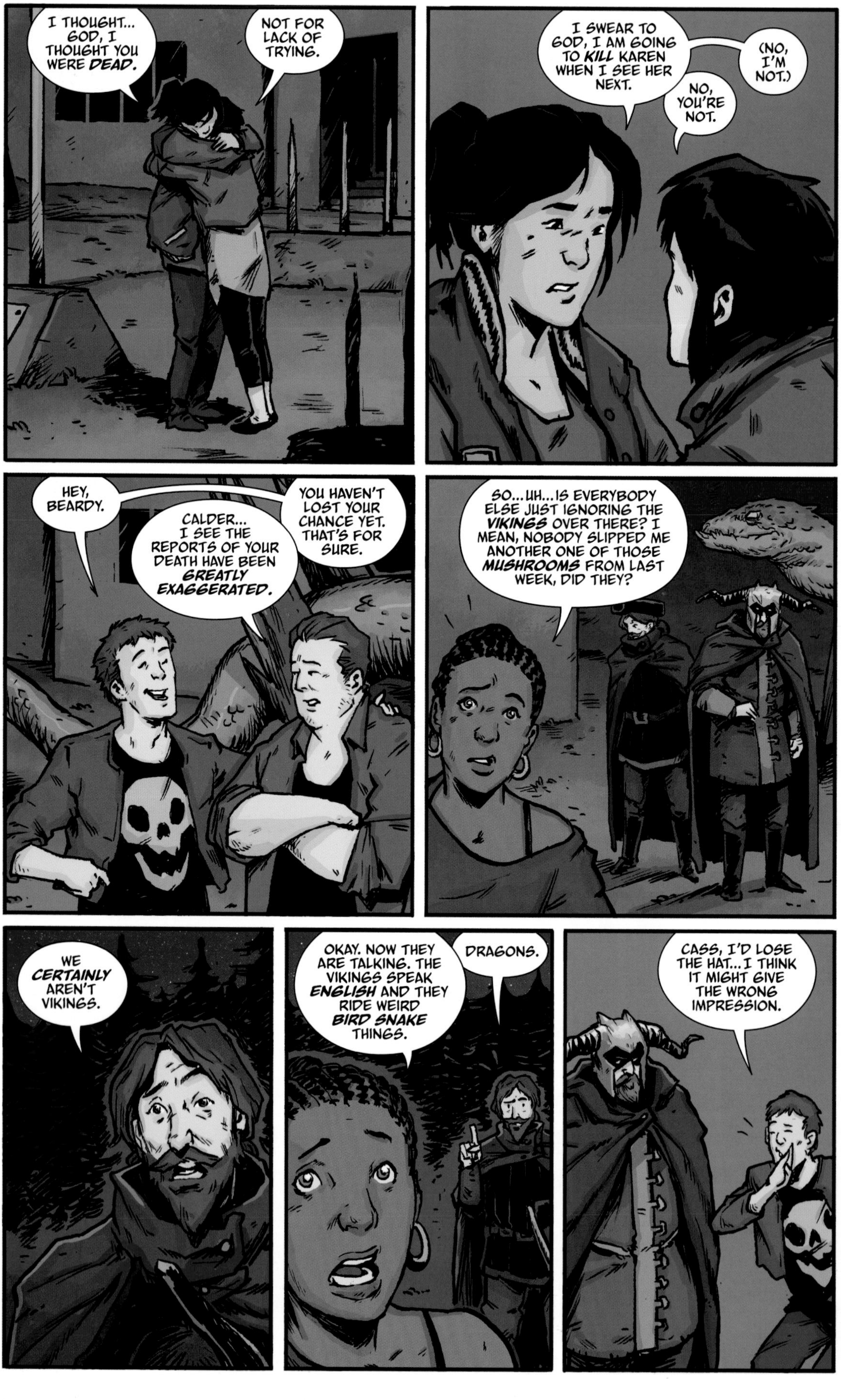
I THOUGHT... GOD, I THOUGHT YOU WERE DEAD.
NOT FOR LACK OF TRYING.
I SWEAR TO GOD, I AM GOING TO KILL KAREN WHEN I SEE HER NEXT.
(NO, I'M NOT.)
NO, YOU'RE NOT.
HEY, BEARDY.
YOU HAVEN'T LOST YOUR CHANCE YET. THAT'S FOR SURE.
CALDER... I SEE THE REPORTS OF YOUR DEATH HAVE BEEN GREATLY EXAGGERATED.
SO...UH...IS EVERYBODY ELSE JUST IGNORING THE VIKINGS OVER THERE? I MEAN, NOBODY SLIPPED ME ANOTHER ONE OF THOSE MUSHROOMS FROM LAST WEEK, DID THEY?
WE CERTAINLY AREN'T VIKINGS.
OKAY. NOW THEY ARE TALKING. THE VIKINGS SPEAK ENGLISH AND THEY RIDE WEIRD BIRD SNAKE THINGS.
DRAGONS.
CASS, I'D LOSE THE HAT...I THINK IT MIGHT GIVE THE WRONG IMPRESSION.

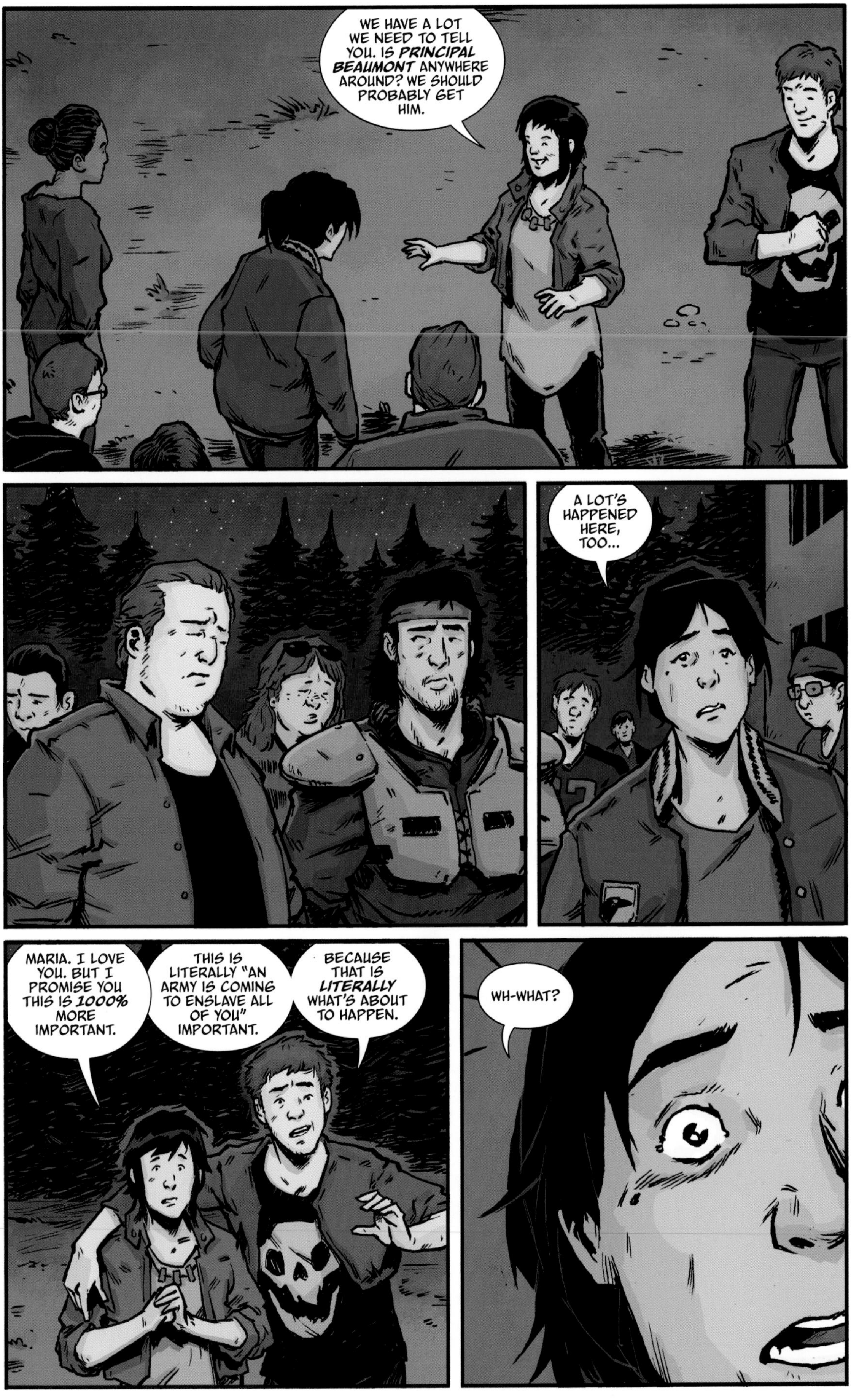
WE HAVE A LOT WE NEED TO TELL YOU. IS *PRINCIPAL BEAUMONT* ANYWHERE AROUND? WE SHOULD PROBABLY GET HIM.
A LOT'S HAPPENED HERE, TOO...
MARIA. I LOVE YOU. BUT I PROMISE YOU THIS IS *1000%* MORE IMPORTANT.
THIS IS LITERALLY "AN ARMY IS COMING TO ENSLAVE ALL OF YOU" IMPORTANT.
BECAUSE THAT IS *LITERALLY* WHAT'S ABOUT TO HAPPEN.
WH-WHAT?

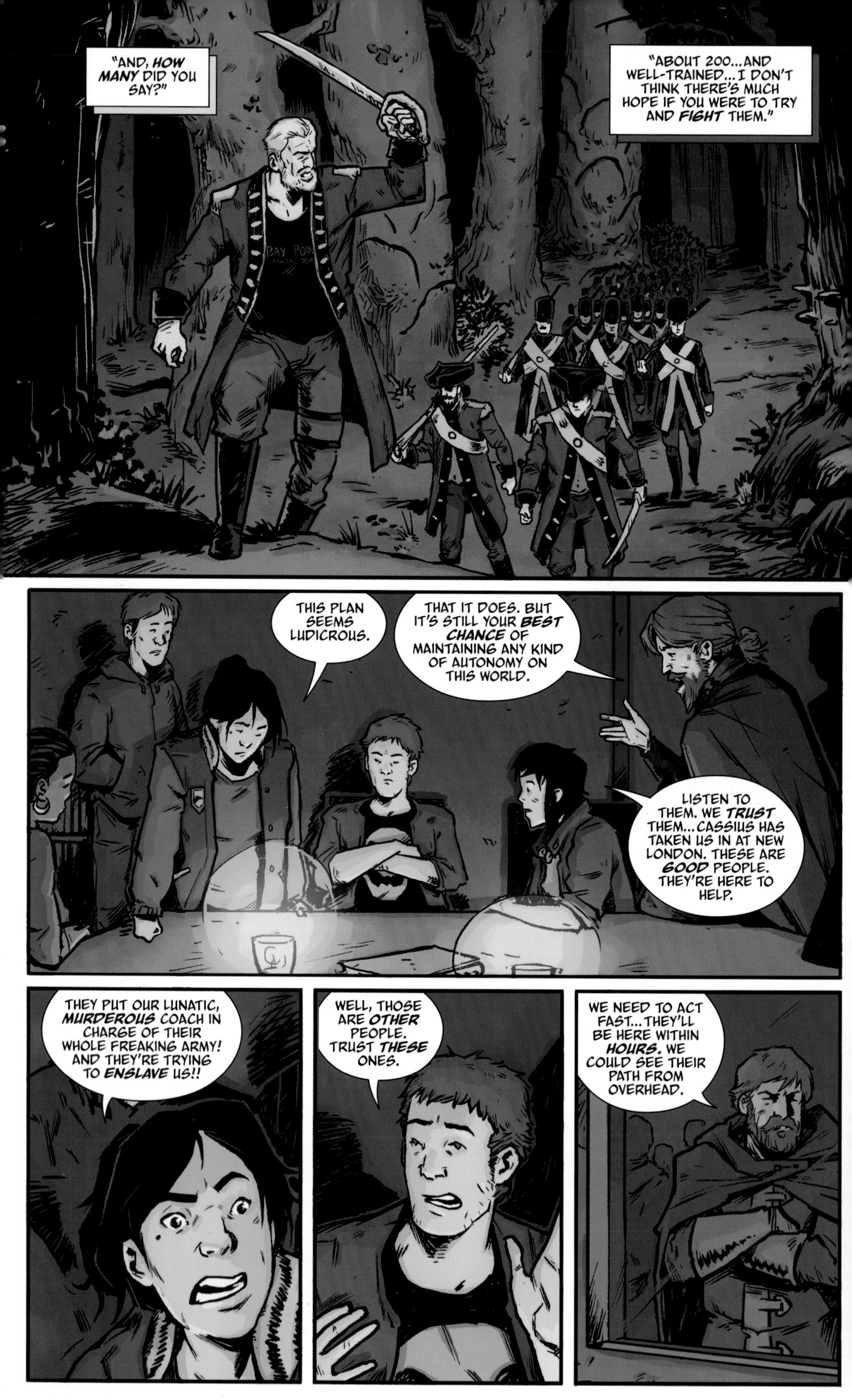
"AND, HOW MANY DID YOU SAY?"
"ABOUT 200...AND WELL-TRAINED...I DON'T THINK THERE'S MUCH HOPE IF YOU WERE TO TRY AND FIGHT THEM."
THIS PLAN SEEMS LUDICROUS.
THAT IT DOES. BUT IT'S STILL YOUR BEST CHANCE OF MAINTAINING ANY KIND OF AUTONOMY ON THIS WORLD.
LISTEN TO THEM. WE TRUST THEM...CASSIUS HAS TAKEN US IN AT NEW LONDON. THESE ARE GOOD PEOPLE. THEY'RE HERE TO HELP.
THEY PUT OUR LUNATIC, MURDEROUS COACH IN CHARGE OF THEIR WHOLE FREAKING ARMY! AND THEY'RE TRYING TO ENSLAVE US!!
WELL, THOSE ARE OTHER PEOPLE. TRUST THESE ONES.
WE NEED TO ACT FAST...THEY'LL BE HERE WITHIN HOURS. WE COULD SEE THEIR PATH FROM OVERHEAD.

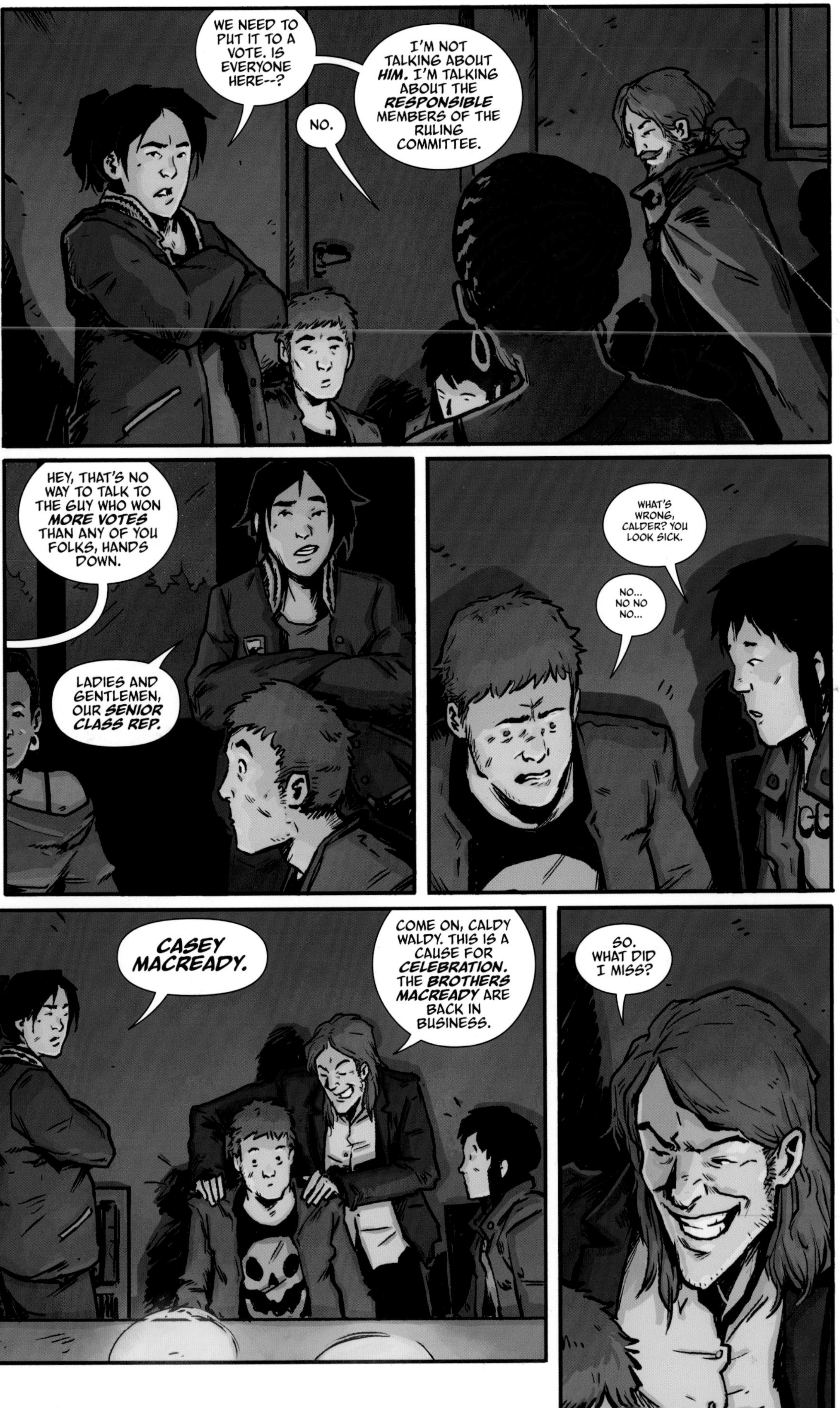
WE NEED TO PUT IT TO A VOTE. IS EVERYONE HERE--?
I'M NOT TALKING ABOUT HIM. I'M TALKING ABOUT THE RESPONSIBLE MEMBERS OF THE RULING COMMITTEE.
NO.
HEY, THAT'S NO WAY TO TALK TO THE GUY WHO WON MORE VOTES THAN ANY OF YOU FOLKS, HANDS DOWN.
LADIES AND GENTLEMEN, OUR SENIOR CLASS REP.
WHAT'S WRONG, CALDER? YOU LOOK SICK.
NO... NO NO NO...
CASEY MACREADY.
COME ON, CALDY WALDY. THIS IS A CAUSE FOR CELEBRATION. THE BROTHERS MACREADY ARE BACK IN BUSINESS.
SO. WHAT DID I MISS?

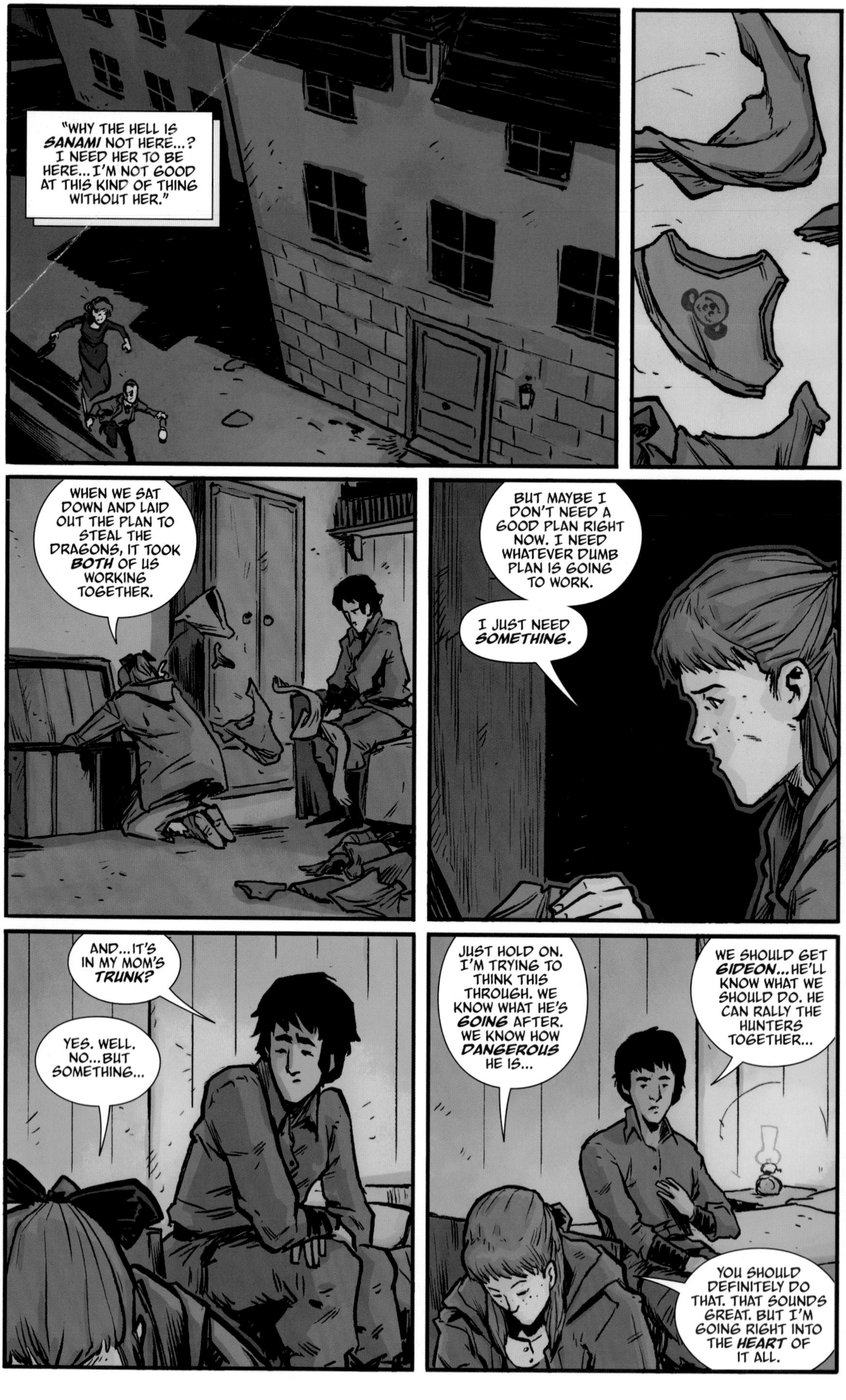
"WHY THE HELL IS SANAMI NOT HERE...? I NEED HER TO BE HERE...I'M NOT GOOD AT THIS KIND OF THING WITHOUT HER."
WHEN WE SAT DOWN AND LAID OUT THE PLAN TO STEAL THE DRAGONS, IT TOOK BOTH OF US WORKING TOGETHER.
BUT MAYBE I DON'T NEED A GOOD PLAN RIGHT NOW. I NEED WHATEVER DUMB PLAN IS GOING TO WORK.
I JUST NEED SOMETHING.
AND...IT'S IN MY MOM'S TRUNK?
YES. WELL. NO...BUT SOMETHING...
JUST HOLD ON. I'M TRYING TO THINK THIS THROUGH. WE KNOW WHAT HE'S GOING AFTER. WE KNOW HOW DANGEROUS HE IS...
WE SHOULD GET GIDEON...HE'LL KNOW WHAT WE SHOULD DO. HE CAN RALLY THE HUNTERS TOGETHER...
YOU SHOULD DEFINITELY DO THAT. THAT SOUNDS GREAT. BUT I'M GOING RIGHT INTO THE HEART OF IT ALL.

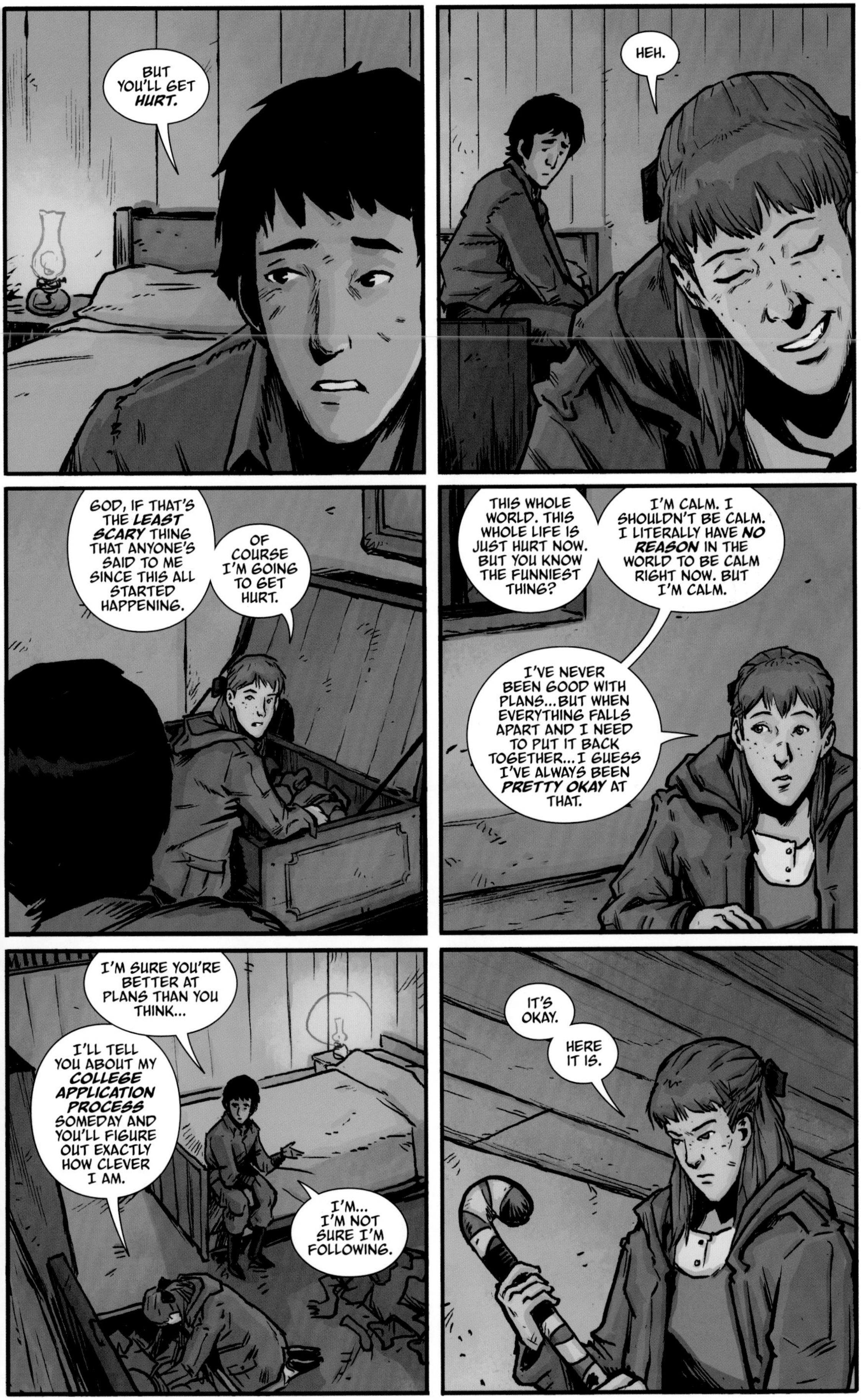
BUT YOU'LL GET **HURT.**
HEH.
GOD, IF THAT'S THE **LEAST SCARY** THING THAT ANYONE'S SAID TO ME SINCE THIS ALL STARTED HAPPENING.
OF COURSE I'M GOING TO GET HURT.
THIS WHOLE WORLD. THIS WHOLE LIFE IS JUST HURT NOW. BUT YOU KNOW THE FUNNIEST THING?
I'M CALM. I SHOULDN'T BE CALM. I LITERALLY HAVE **NO REASON** IN THE WORLD TO BE CALM RIGHT NOW. BUT I'M CALM.
I'VE NEVER BEEN GOOD WITH PLANS...BUT WHEN EVERYTHING FALLS APART AND I NEED TO PUT IT BACK TOGETHER...I GUESS I'VE ALWAYS BEEN **PRETTY OKAY** AT THAT.
I'M SURE YOU'RE BETTER AT PLANS THAN YOU THINK...
I'LL TELL YOU ABOUT MY **COLLEGE APPLICATION PROCESS** SOMEDAY AND YOU'LL FIGURE OUT EXACTLY HOW CLEVER I AM.
I'M... I'M NOT SURE I'M FOLLOWING.
IT'S OKAY.
HERE IT IS.

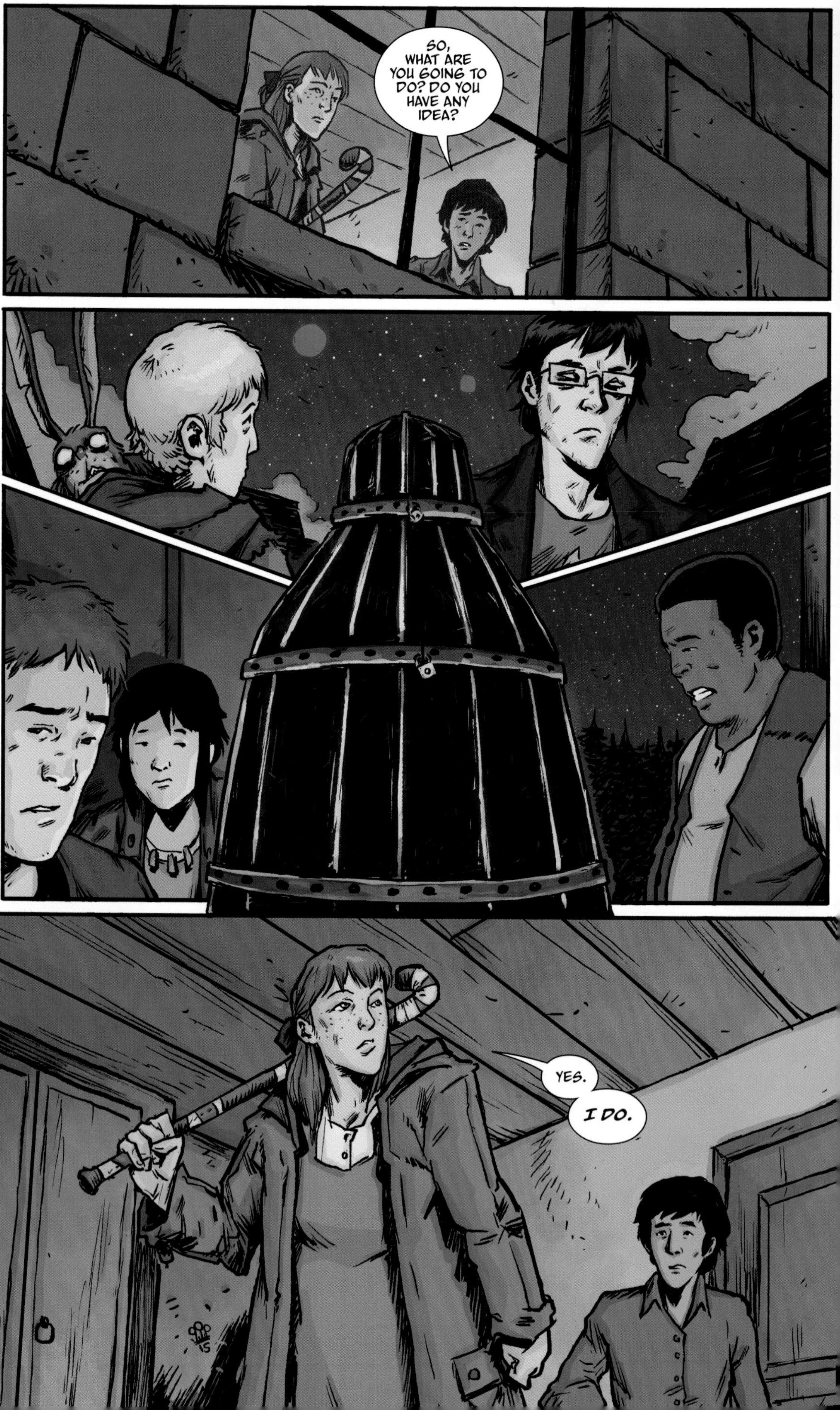
SO, WHAT ARE YOU GOING TO DO? DO YOU HAVE ANY IDEA?
YES.
I DO.

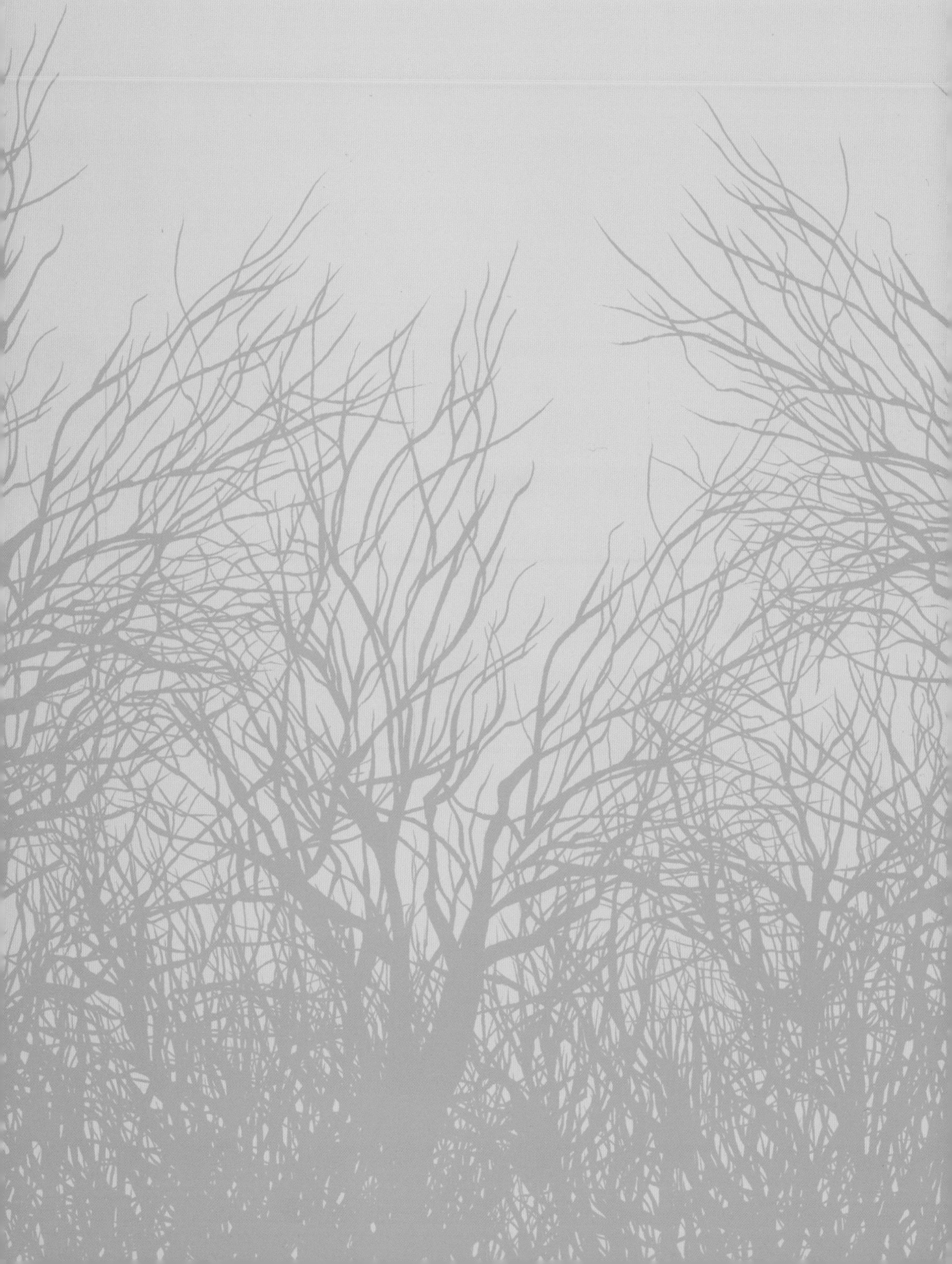

CHAPTER
TWELVE

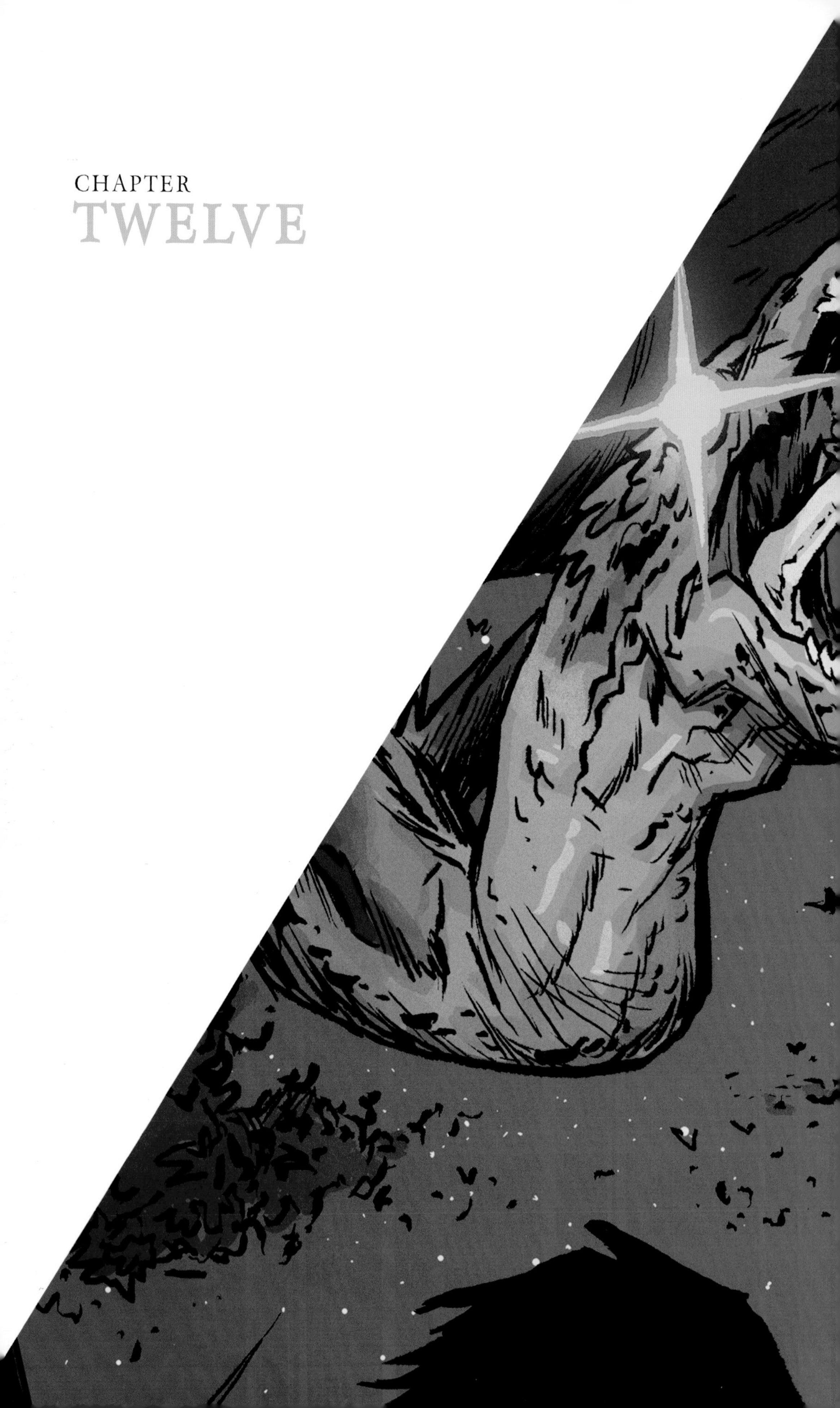

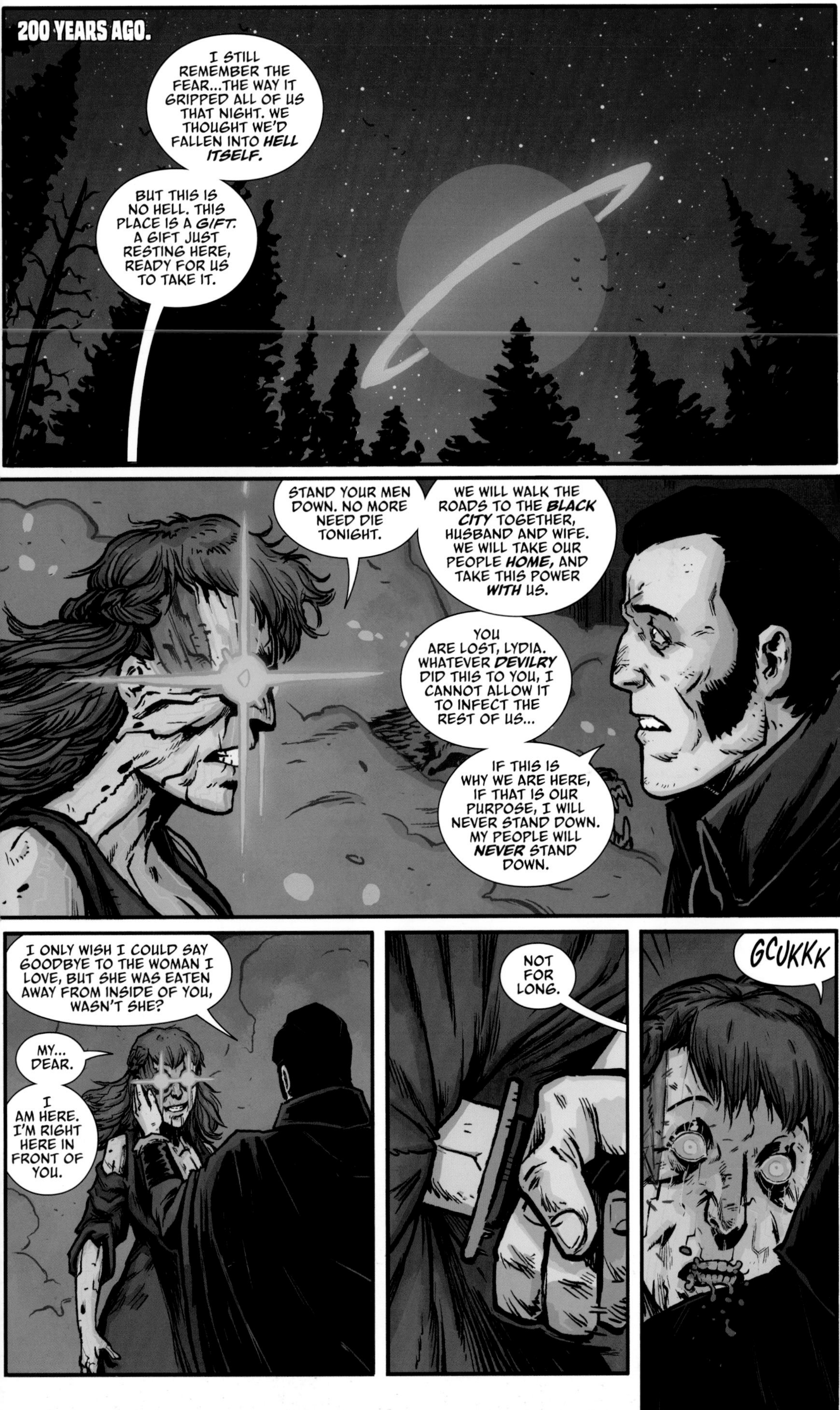
200 YEARS AGO.
I STILL REMEMBER THE FEAR...THE WAY IT GRIPPED ALL OF US THAT NIGHT. WE THOUGHT WE'D FALLEN INTO HELL ITSELF.
BUT THIS IS NO HELL. THIS PLACE IS A GIFT. A GIFT JUST RESTING HERE, READY FOR US TO TAKE IT.
STAND YOUR MEN DOWN. NO MORE NEED DIE TONIGHT.
WE WILL WALK THE ROADS TO THE BLACK CITY TOGETHER, HUSBAND AND WIFE. WE WILL TAKE OUR PEOPLE HOME, AND TAKE THIS POWER WITH US.
YOU ARE LOST, LYDIA. WHATEVER DEVILRY DID THIS TO YOU, I CANNOT ALLOW IT TO INFECT THE REST OF US...
IF THIS IS WHY WE ARE HERE, IF THAT IS OUR PURPOSE, I WILL NEVER STAND DOWN. MY PEOPLE WILL NEVER STAND DOWN.
I ONLY WISH I COULD SAY GOODBYE TO THE WOMAN I LOVE, BUT SHE WAS EATEN AWAY FROM INSIDE OF YOU, WASN'T SHE?
MY... DEAR.
I AM HERE. I'M RIGHT HERE IN FRONT OF YOU.
NOT FOR LONG.
GCUKKK

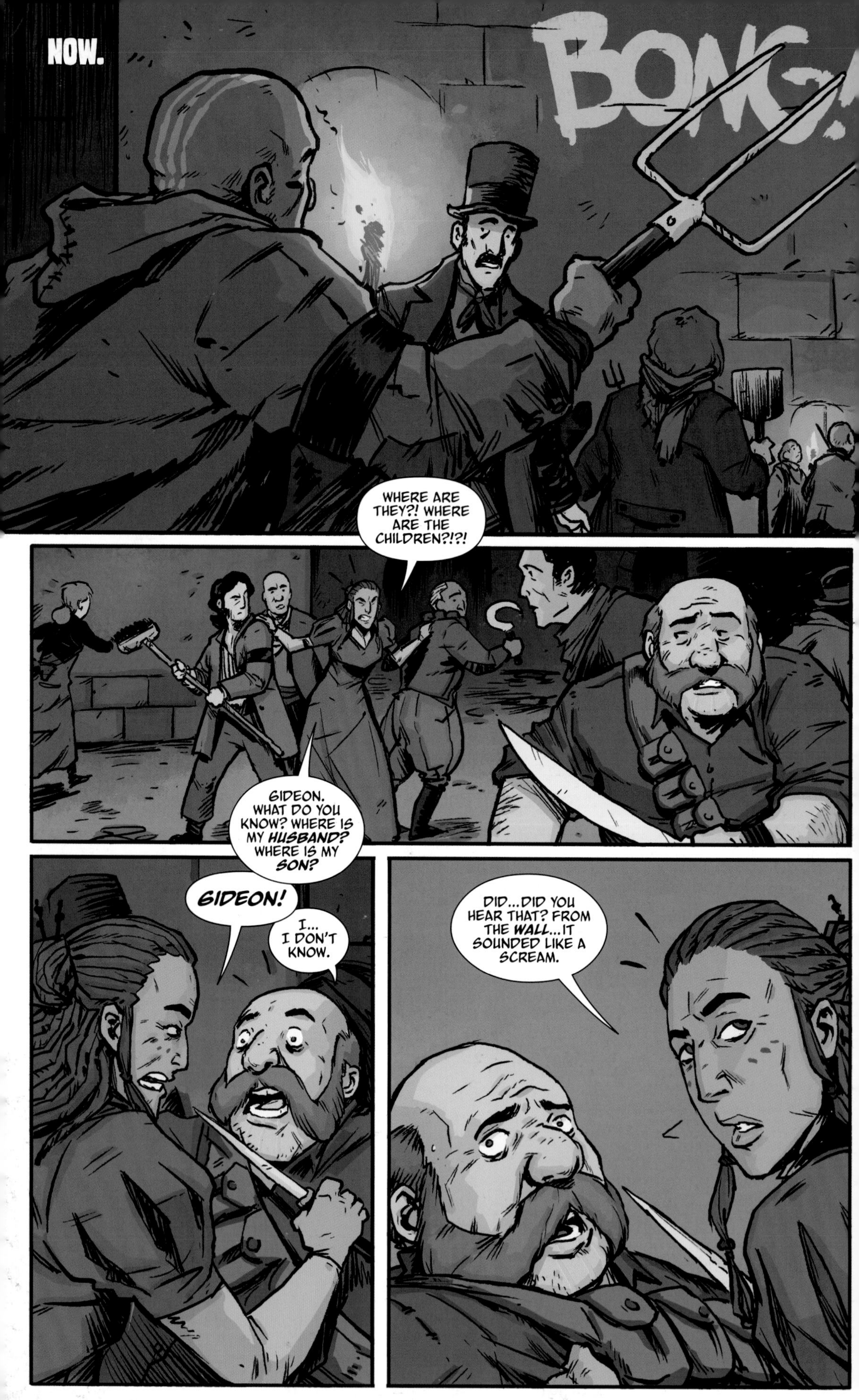
NOW.
BONG!
WHERE ARE THEY?! WHERE ARE THE CHILDREN?!?!
GIDEON. WHAT DO YOU KNOW? WHERE IS MY HUSBAND? WHERE IS MY SON?
GIDEON!
I... I DON'T KNOW.
DID...DID YOU HEAR THAT? FROM THE WALL...IT SOUNDED LIKE A SCREAM.

BONG! BONG!

AAAHHHHA!!!

SNAP!

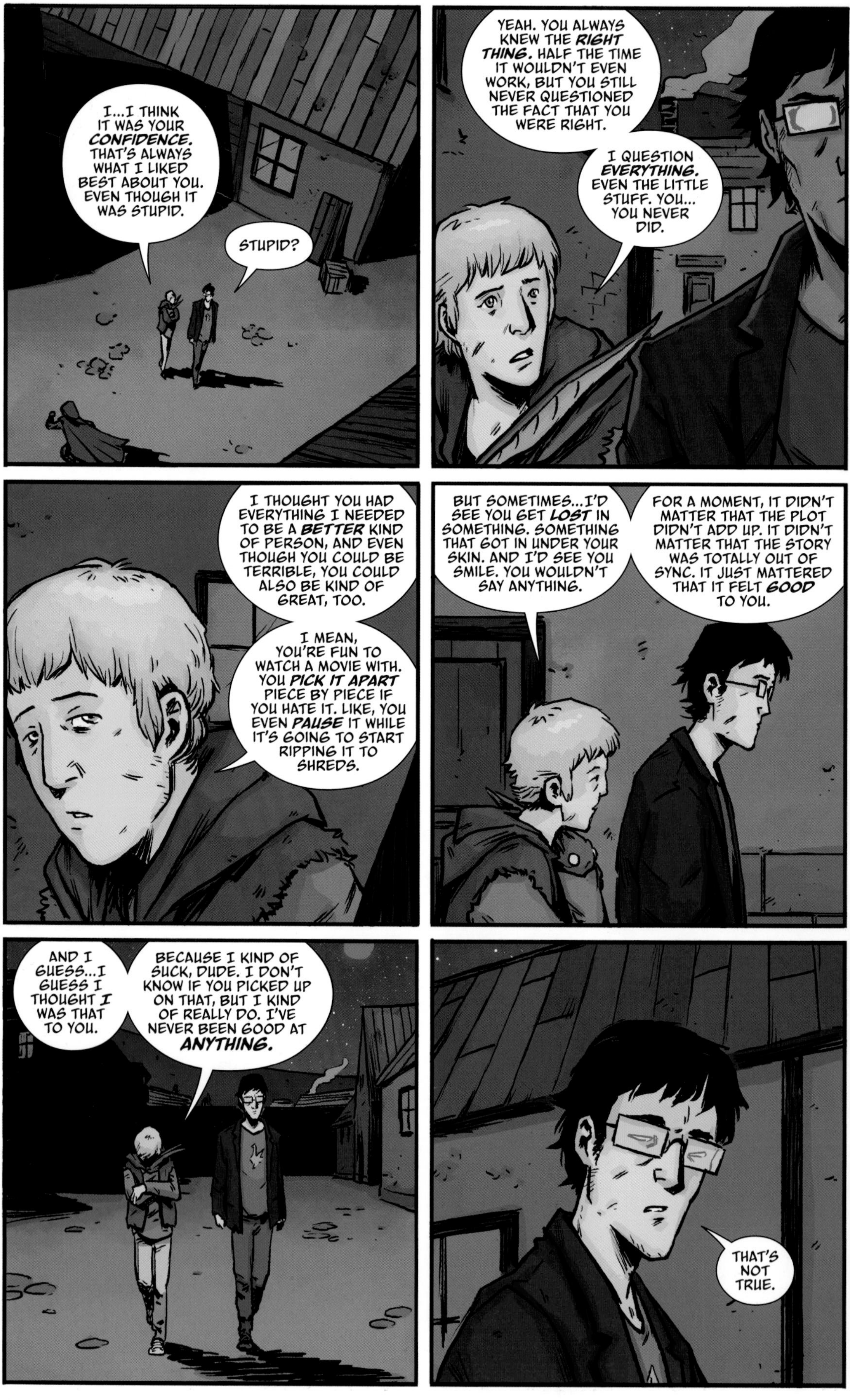
I...I THINK IT WAS YOUR CONFIDENCE. THAT'S ALWAYS WHAT I LIKED BEST ABOUT YOU. EVEN THOUGH IT WAS STUPID.
STUPID?
YEAH. YOU ALWAYS KNEW THE RIGHT THING. HALF THE TIME IT WOULDN'T EVEN WORK, BUT YOU STILL NEVER QUESTIONED THE FACT THAT YOU WERE RIGHT.
I QUESTION EVERYTHING. EVEN THE LITTLE STUFF. YOU... YOU NEVER DID.
I THOUGHT YOU HAD EVERYTHING I NEEDED TO BE A BETTER KIND OF PERSON, AND EVEN THOUGH YOU COULD BE TERRIBLE, YOU COULD ALSO BE KIND OF GREAT, TOO.
I MEAN, YOU'RE FUN TO WATCH A MOVIE WITH. YOU PICK IT APART PIECE BY PIECE IF YOU HATE IT. LIKE, YOU EVEN PAUSE IT WHILE IT'S GOING TO START RIPPING IT TO SHREDS.
BUT SOMETIMES...I'D SEE YOU GET LOST IN SOMETHING. SOMETHING THAT GOT IN UNDER YOUR SKIN. AND I'D SEE YOU SMILE. YOU WOULDN'T SAY ANYTHING.
FOR A MOMENT, IT DIDN'T MATTER THAT THE PLOT DIDN'T ADD UP. IT DIDN'T MATTER THAT THE STORY WAS TOTALLY OUT OF SYNC. IT JUST MATTERED THAT IT FELT GOOD TO YOU.
AND I GUESS...I GUESS I THOUGHT I WAS THAT TO YOU.
BECAUSE I KIND OF SUCK, DUDE. I DON'T KNOW IF YOU PICKED UP ON THAT, BUT I KIND OF REALLY DO. I'VE NEVER BEEN GOOD AT ANYTHING.
THAT'S NOT TRUE.

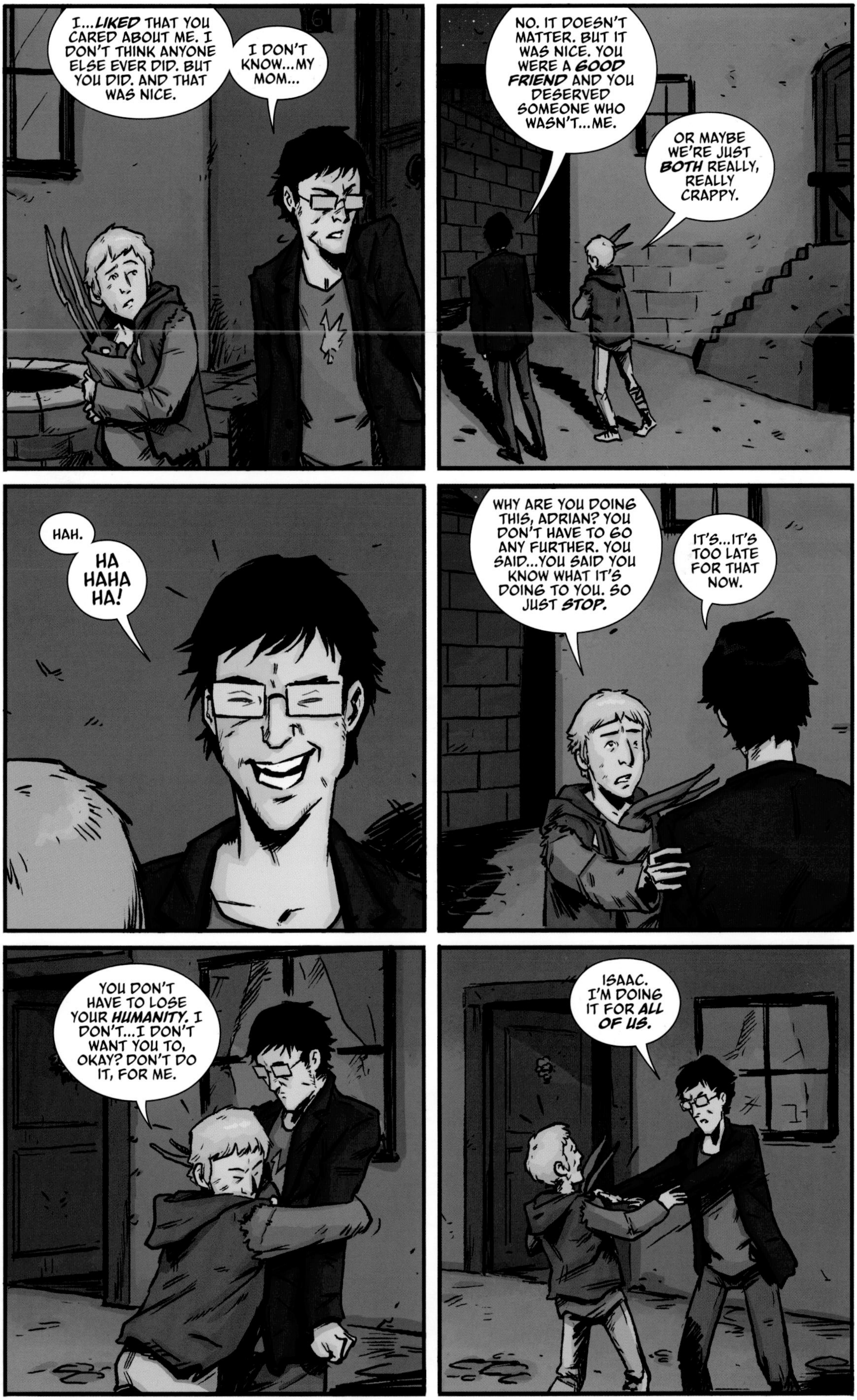
I...LIKED THAT YOU CARED ABOUT ME. I DON'T THINK ANYONE ELSE EVER DID. BUT YOU DID. AND THAT WAS NICE.
I DON'T KNOW...MY MOM...
NO. IT DOESN'T MATTER. BUT IT WAS NICE. YOU WERE A GOOD FRIEND AND YOU DESERVED SOMEONE WHO WASN'T...ME.
OR MAYBE WE'RE JUST BOTH REALLY, REALLY CRAPPY.
HAH.
HA HAHA HA!
WHY ARE YOU DOING THIS, ADRIAN? YOU DON'T HAVE TO GO ANY FURTHER. YOU SAID...YOU SAID YOU KNOW WHAT IT'S DOING TO YOU. SO JUST STOP.
IT'S...IT'S TOO LATE FOR THAT NOW.
YOU DON'T HAVE TO LOSE YOUR HUMANITY. I DON'T...I DON'T WANT YOU TO, OKAY? DON'T DO IT, FOR ME.
ISAAC. I'M DOING IT FOR ALL OF US.

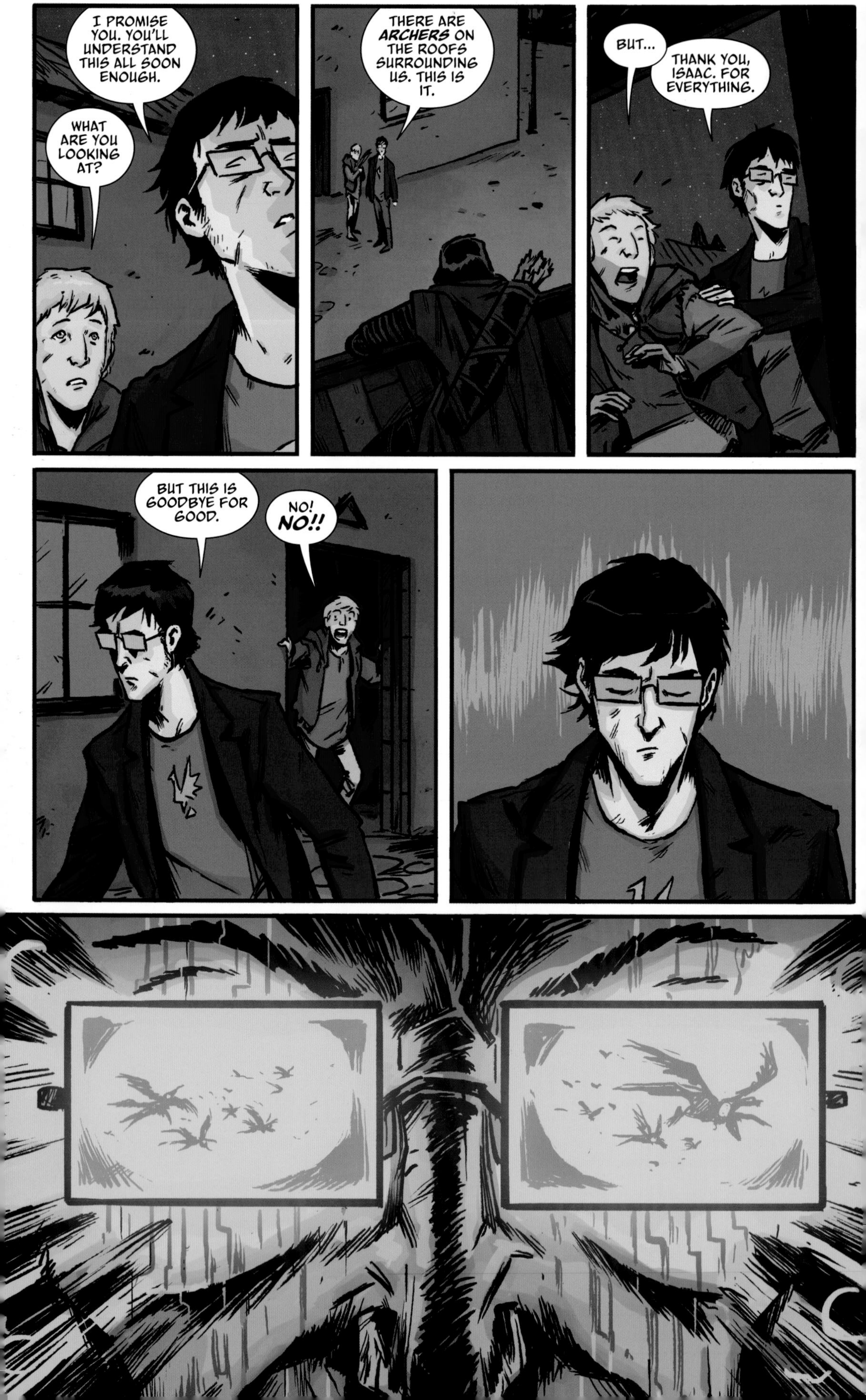
I PROMISE YOU. YOU'LL UNDERSTAND THIS ALL SOON ENOUGH.
WHAT ARE YOU LOOKING AT?
THERE ARE ARCHERS ON THE ROOFS SURROUNDING US. THIS IS IT.
BUT...
THANK YOU, ISAAC. FOR EVERYTHING.
BUT THIS IS GOODBYE FOR GOOD.
NO! NO!!

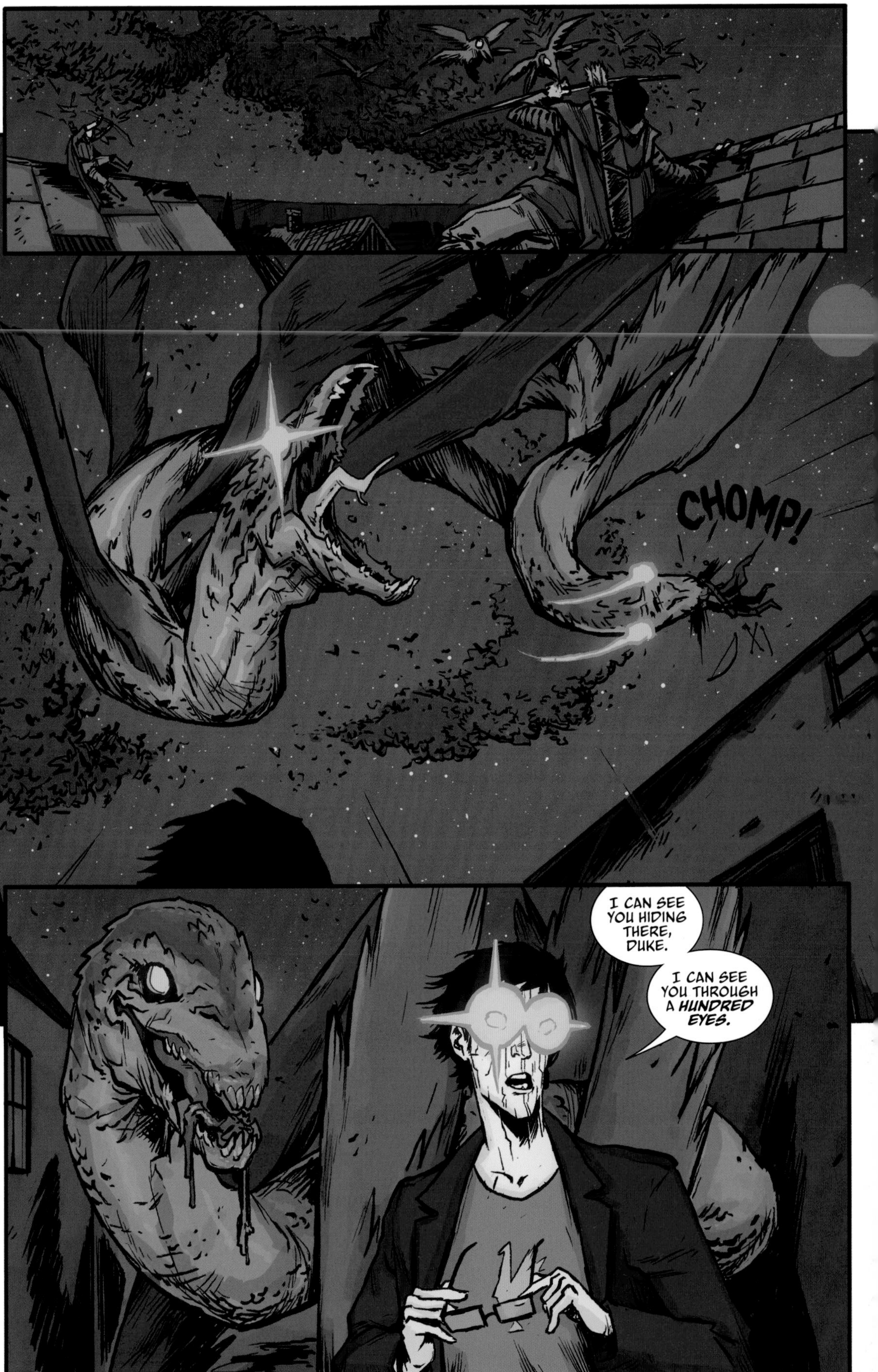
CHOMP!
I CAN SEE YOU HIDING THERE, DUKE.
I CAN SEE YOU THROUGH A HUNDRED EYES.

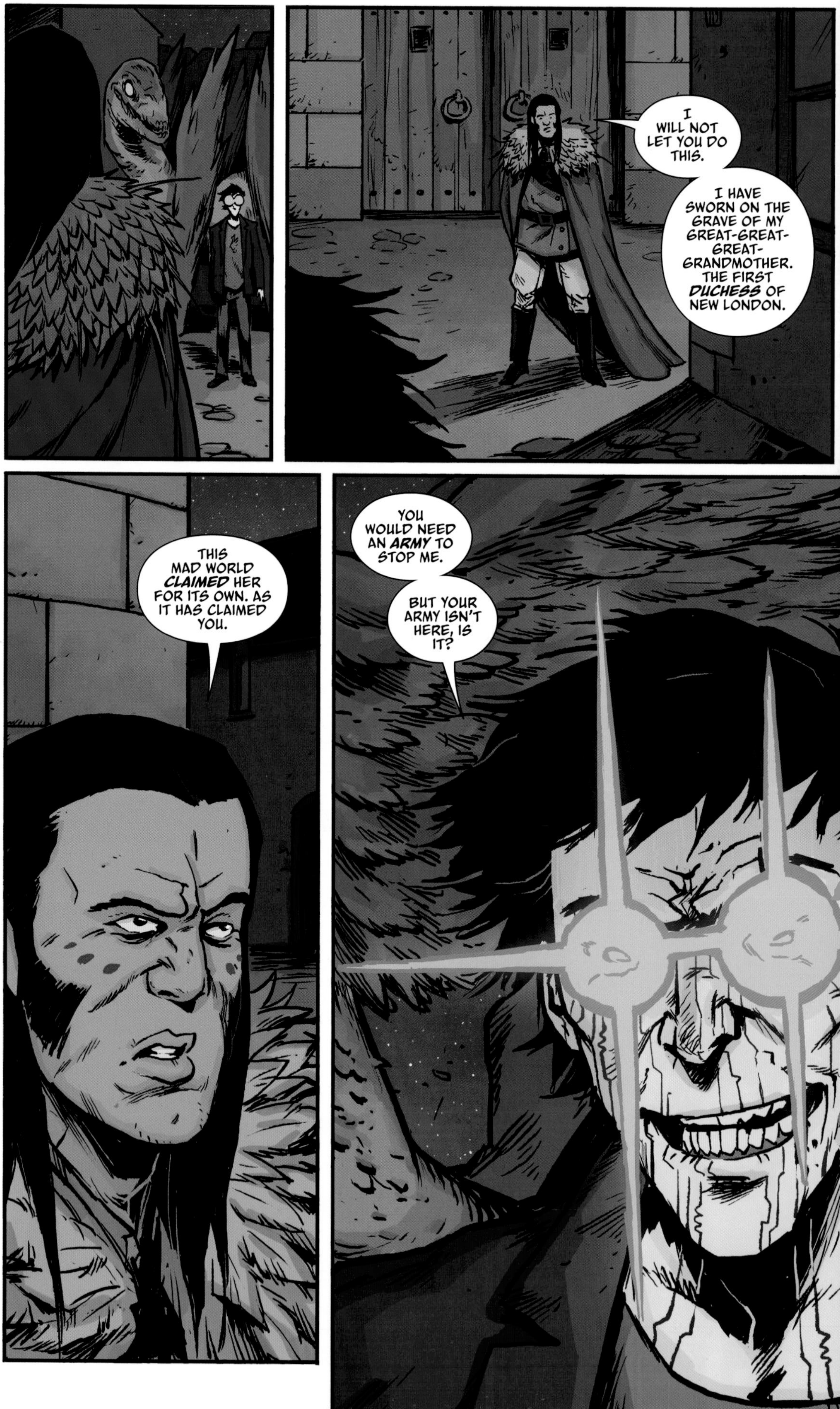

I WILL NOT LET YOU DO THIS.
I HAVE SWORN ON THE GRAVE OF MY GREAT-GREAT-GREAT-GRANDMOTHER. THE FIRST DUCHESS OF NEW LONDON.
THIS MAD WORLD CLAIMED HER FOR ITS OWN. AS IT HAS CLAIMED YOU.
YOU WOULD NEED AN ARMY TO STOP ME.
BUT YOUR ARMY ISN'T HERE, IS IT?

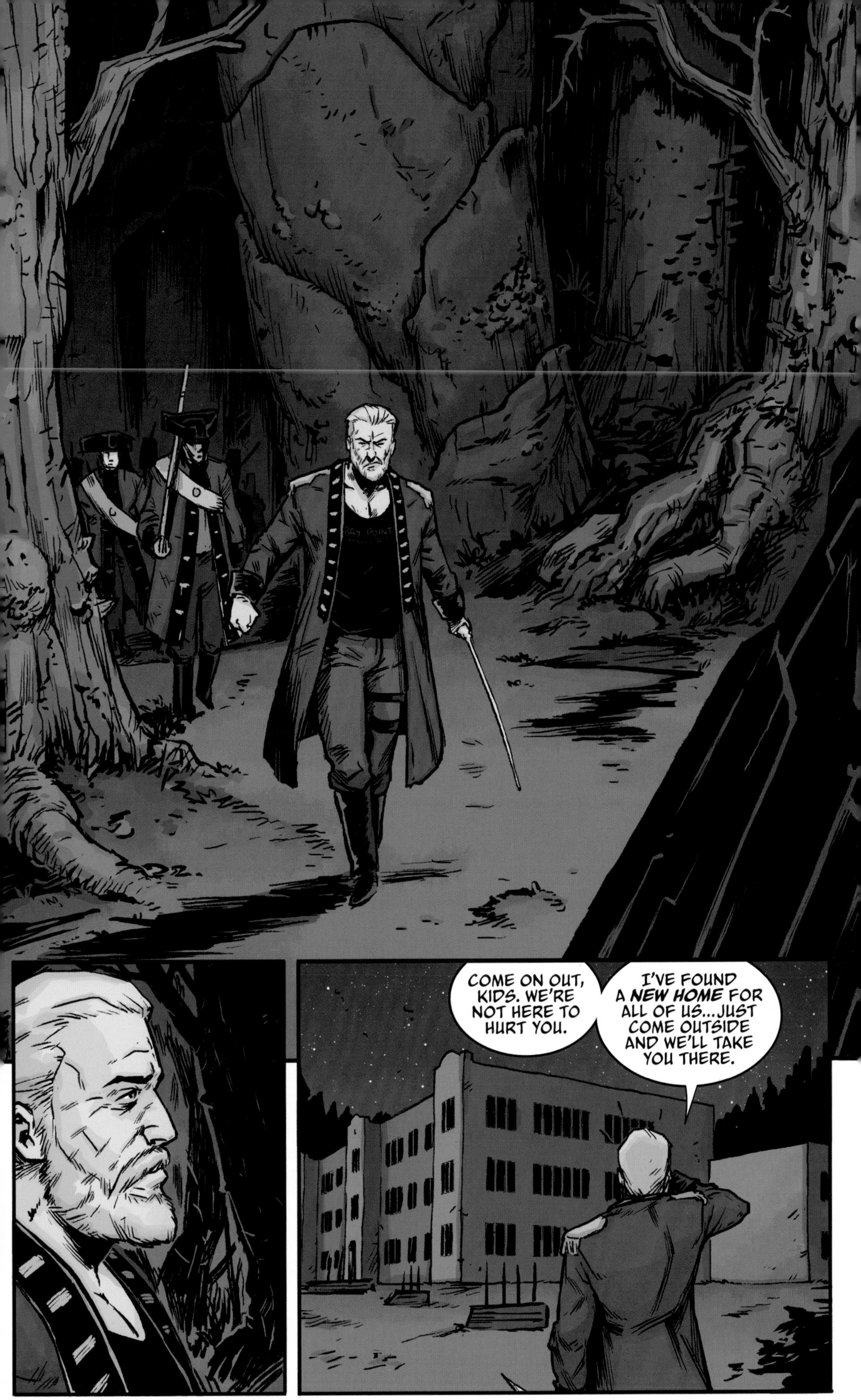
COME ON OUT, KIDS. WE'RE NOT HERE TO HURT YOU.
I'VE FOUND A NEW HOME FOR ALL OF US...JUST COME OUTSIDE AND WE'LL TAKE YOU THERE.

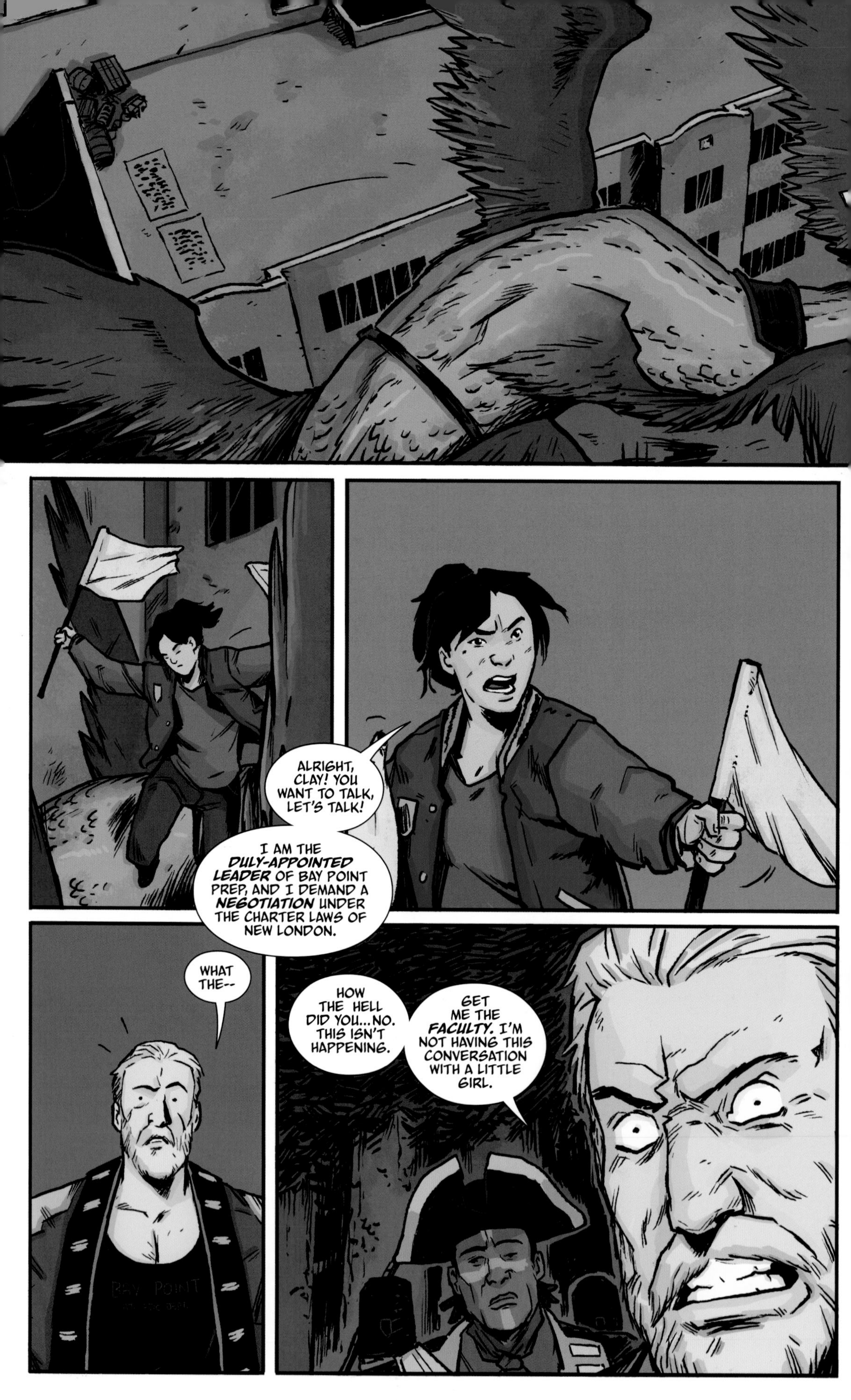
ALRIGHT, CLAY! YOU WANT TO TALK, LET'S TALK!
I AM THE ***DULY-APPOINTED LEADER*** OF BAY POINT PREP, AND I DEMAND A ***NEGOTIATION*** UNDER THE CHARTER LAWS OF NEW LONDON.
WHAT THE--
HOW THE HELL DID YOU...NO. THIS ISN'T HAPPENING.
GET ME THE ***FACULTY.*** I'M NOT HAVING THIS CONVERSATION WITH A LITTLE GIRL.

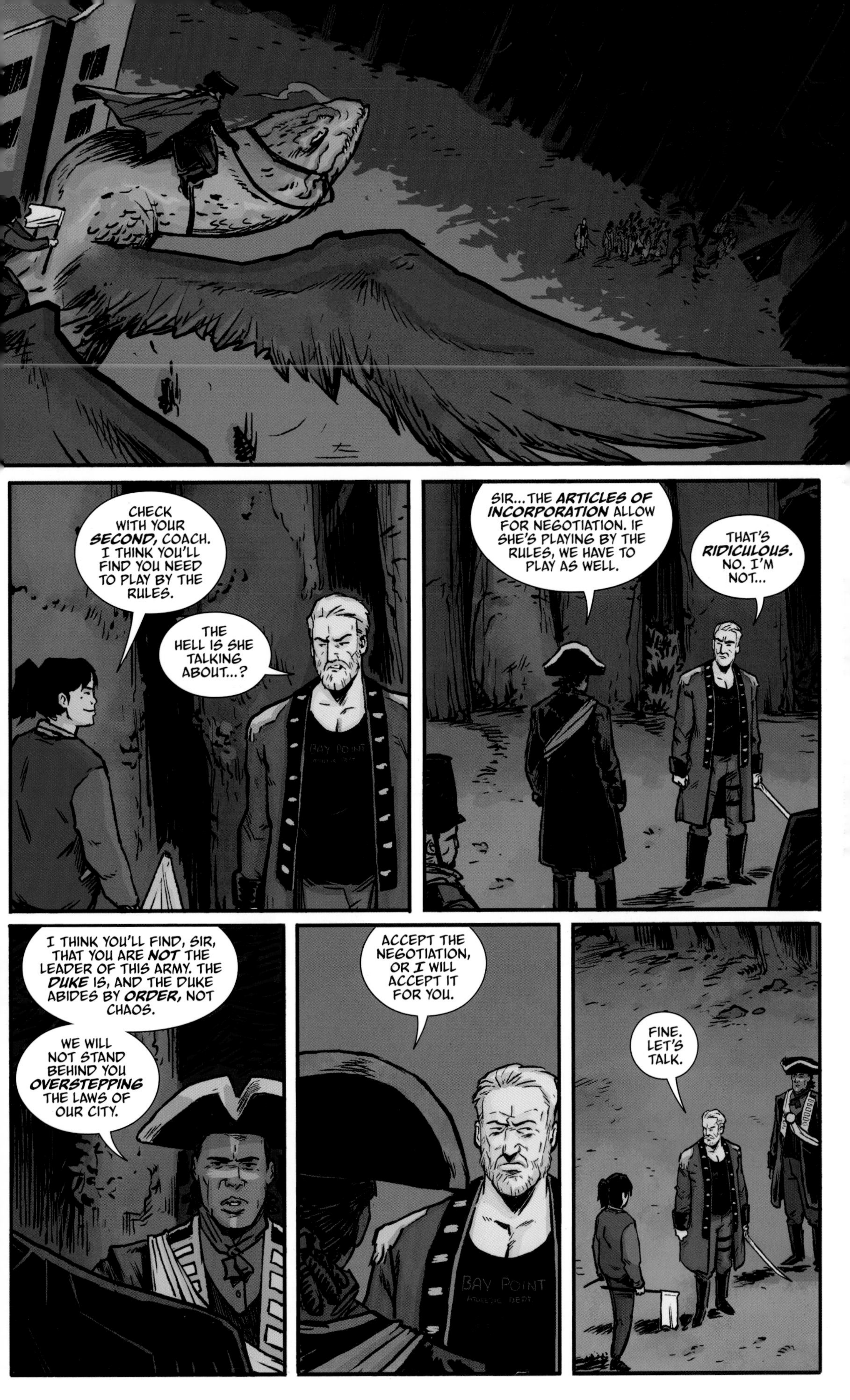
CHECK WITH YOUR SECOND, COACH. I THINK YOU'LL FIND YOU NEED TO PLAY BY THE RULES.
THE HELL IS SHE TALKING ABOUT...?
BAY POINT
SIR... THE ARTICLES OF INCORPORATION ALLOW FOR NEGOTIATION. IF SHE'S PLAYING BY THE RULES, WE HAVE TO PLAY AS WELL.
THAT'S RIDICULOUS. NO. I'M NOT...
I THINK YOU'LL FIND, SIR, THAT YOU ARE NOT THE LEADER OF THIS ARMY. THE DUKE IS, AND THE DUKE ABIDES BY ORDER, NOT CHAOS.
WE WILL NOT STAND BEHIND YOU OVERSTEPPING THE LAWS OF OUR CITY.
ACCEPT THE NEGOTIATION, OR I WILL ACCEPT IT FOR YOU.
BAY POINT
FINE. LET'S TALK.

IS THIS REALLY GOING TO WORK?

IT'S A *BUREAUCRATIC* MOVE, BUT THE DUKE HAS ALWAYS FETISHIZED BUREAUCRACY.

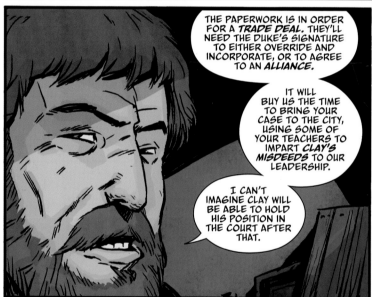

THE PAPERWORK IS IN ORDER FOR A *TRADE DEAL.* THEY'LL NEED THE DUKE'S SIGNATURE TO EITHER OVERRIDE AND INCORPORATE, OR TO AGREE TO AN *ALLIANCE.*

IT WILL BUY US THE TIME TO BRING YOUR CASE TO THE CITY, USING SOME OF YOUR TEACHERS TO IMPART *CLAY'S MISDEEDS* TO OUR LEADERSHIP.

I CAN'T IMAGINE CLAY WILL BE ABLE TO HOLD HIS POSITION IN THE COURT AFTER THAT.

SEE, KID, WE SAVED THE DAY.

WHOOPEE.

WHAT'S GOT YOU SO *TENSE?*

IT'S NOTHING... JUST GIVE ME A MINUTE, ALRIGHT?

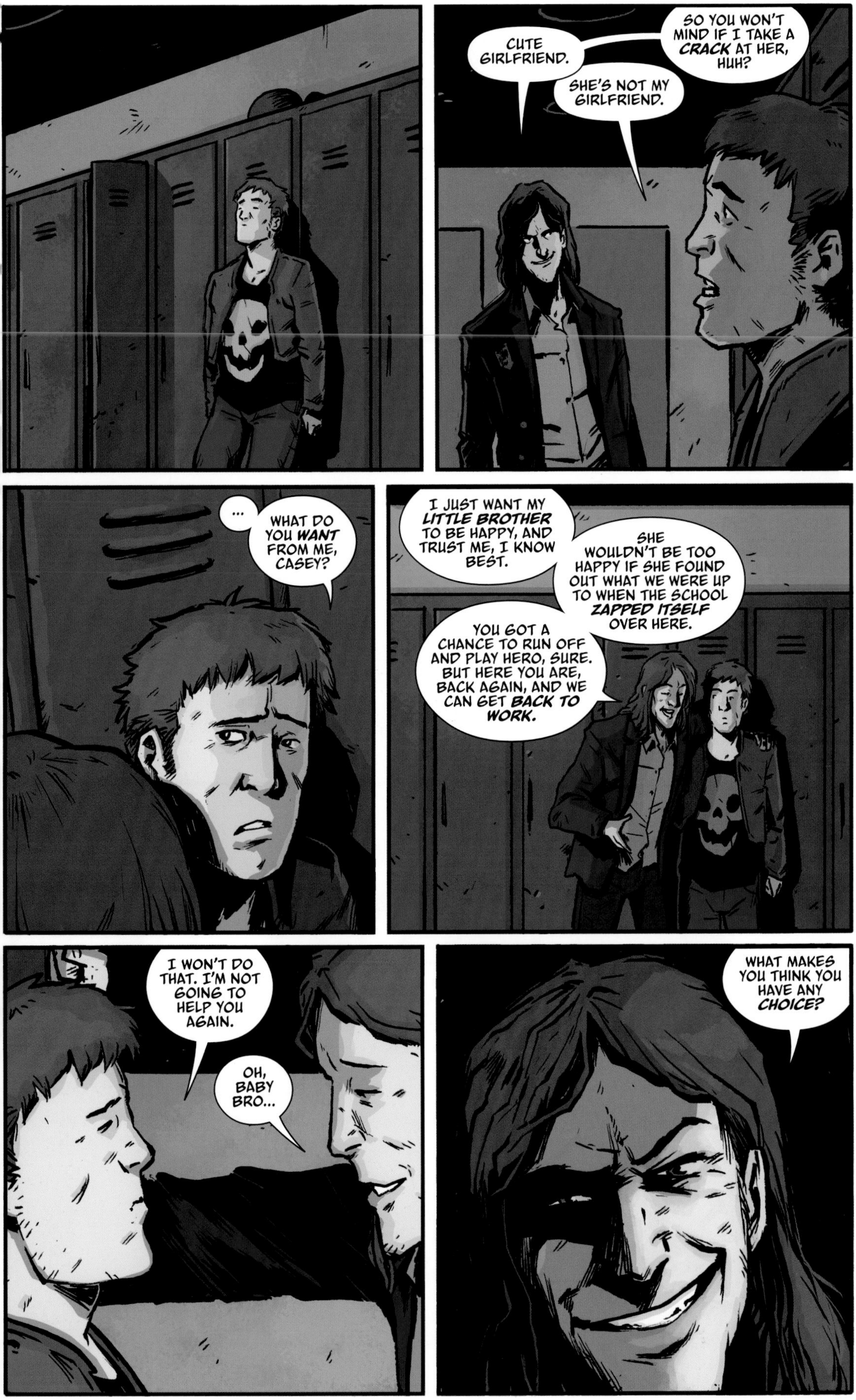
CUTE GIRLFRIEND.
SHE'S NOT MY GIRLFRIEND.
SO YOU WON'T MIND IF I TAKE A CRACK AT HER, HUH?
...
WHAT DO YOU WANT FROM ME, CASEY?
I JUST WANT MY LITTLE BROTHER TO BE HAPPY, AND TRUST ME, I KNOW BEST.
SHE WOULDN'T BE TOO HAPPY IF SHE FOUND OUT WHAT WE WERE UP TO WHEN THE SCHOOL ZAPPED ITSELF OVER HERE.
YOU GOT A CHANCE TO RUN OFF AND PLAY HERO, SURE. BUT HERE YOU ARE, BACK AGAIN, AND WE CAN GET BACK TO WORK.
I WON'T DO THAT. I'M NOT GOING TO HELP YOU AGAIN.
OH, BABY BRO...
WHAT MAKES YOU THINK YOU HAVE ANY CHOICE?

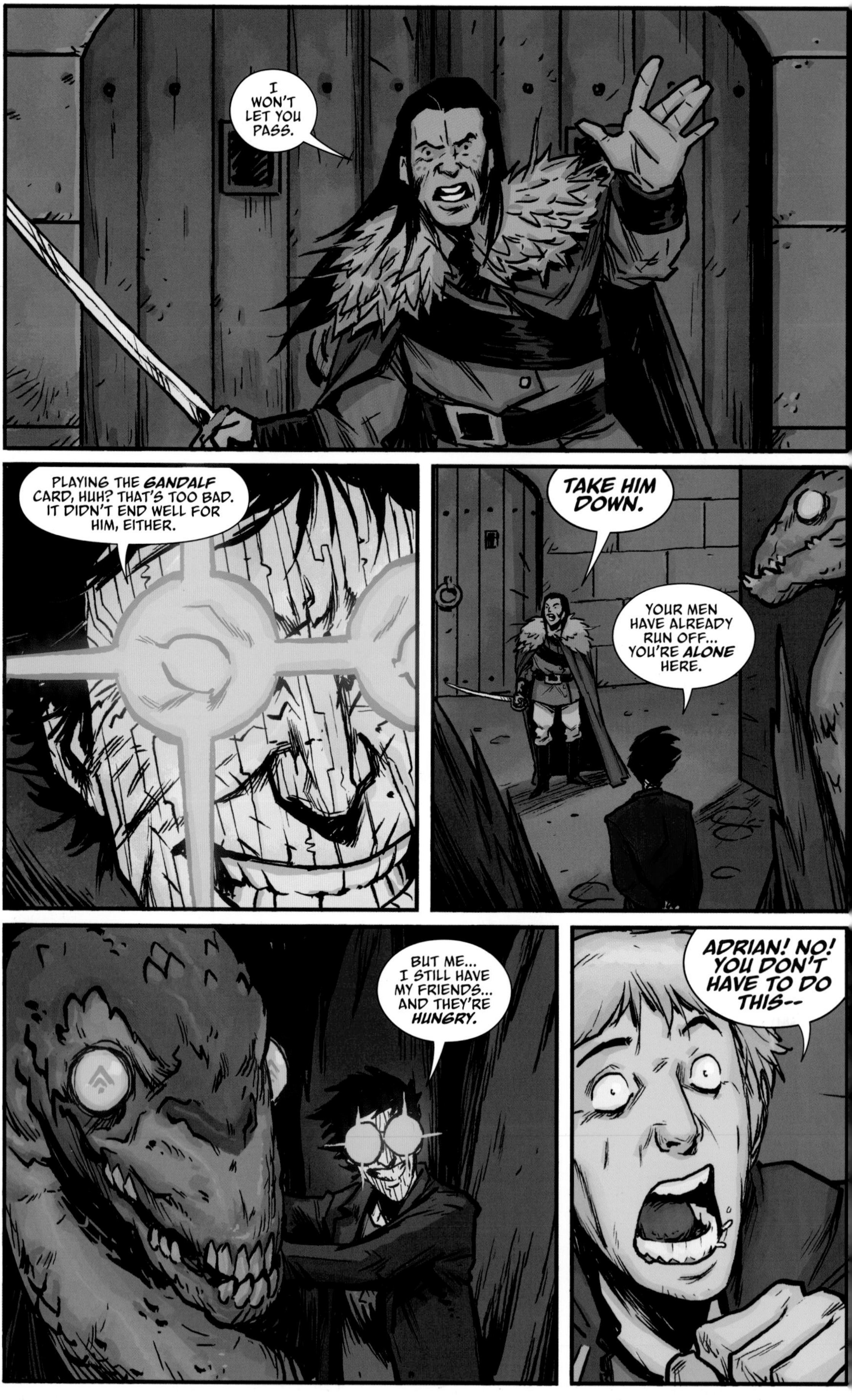
I WON'T LET YOU PASS.
PLAYING THE GANDALF CARD, HUH? THAT'S TOO BAD. IT DIDN'T END WELL FOR HIM, EITHER.
TAKE HIM DOWN.
YOUR MEN HAVE ALREADY RUN OFF... YOU'RE ALONE HERE.
BUT ME... I STILL HAVE MY FRIENDS... AND THEY'RE HUNGRY.
ADRIAN! NO! YOU DON'T HAVE TO DO THIS--

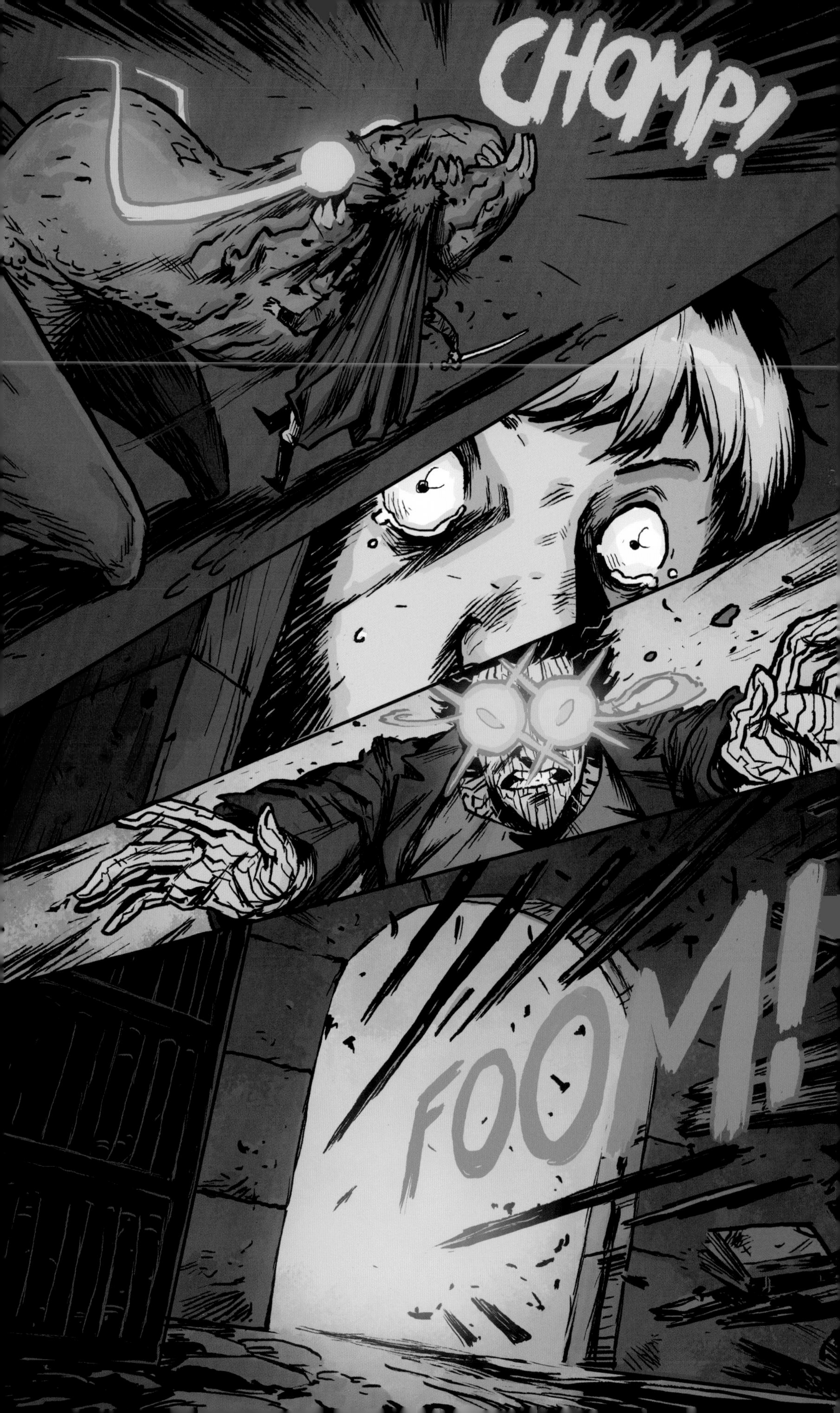
CHOMP!
FOOM!

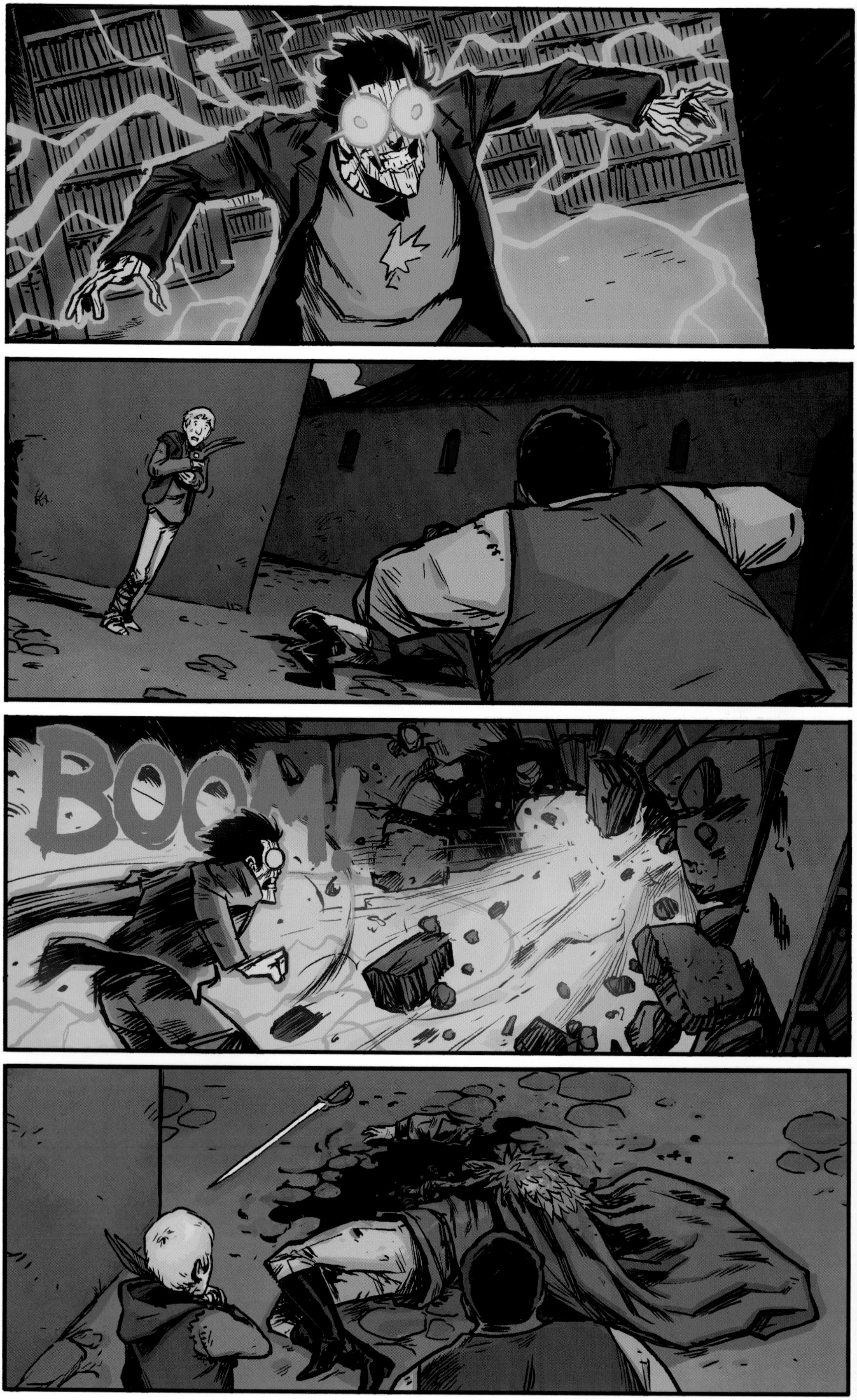
BOOM!

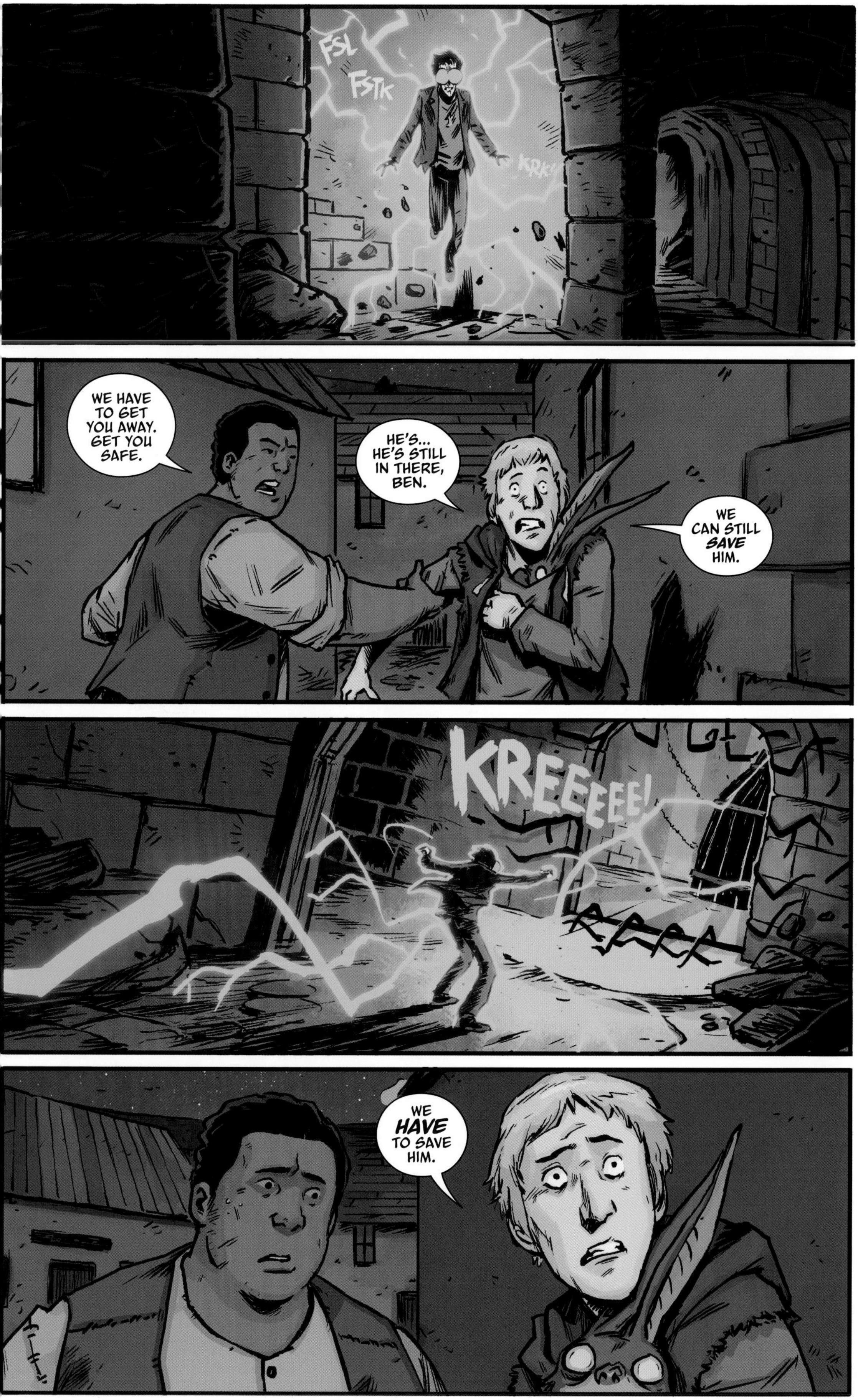
FSL
FSTK
KRK!
WE HAVE TO GET YOU AWAY. GET YOU SAFE.
HE'S... HE'S STILL IN THERE, BEN.
WE CAN STILL SAVE HIM.
KREEEEEE!
WE HAVE TO SAVE HIM.

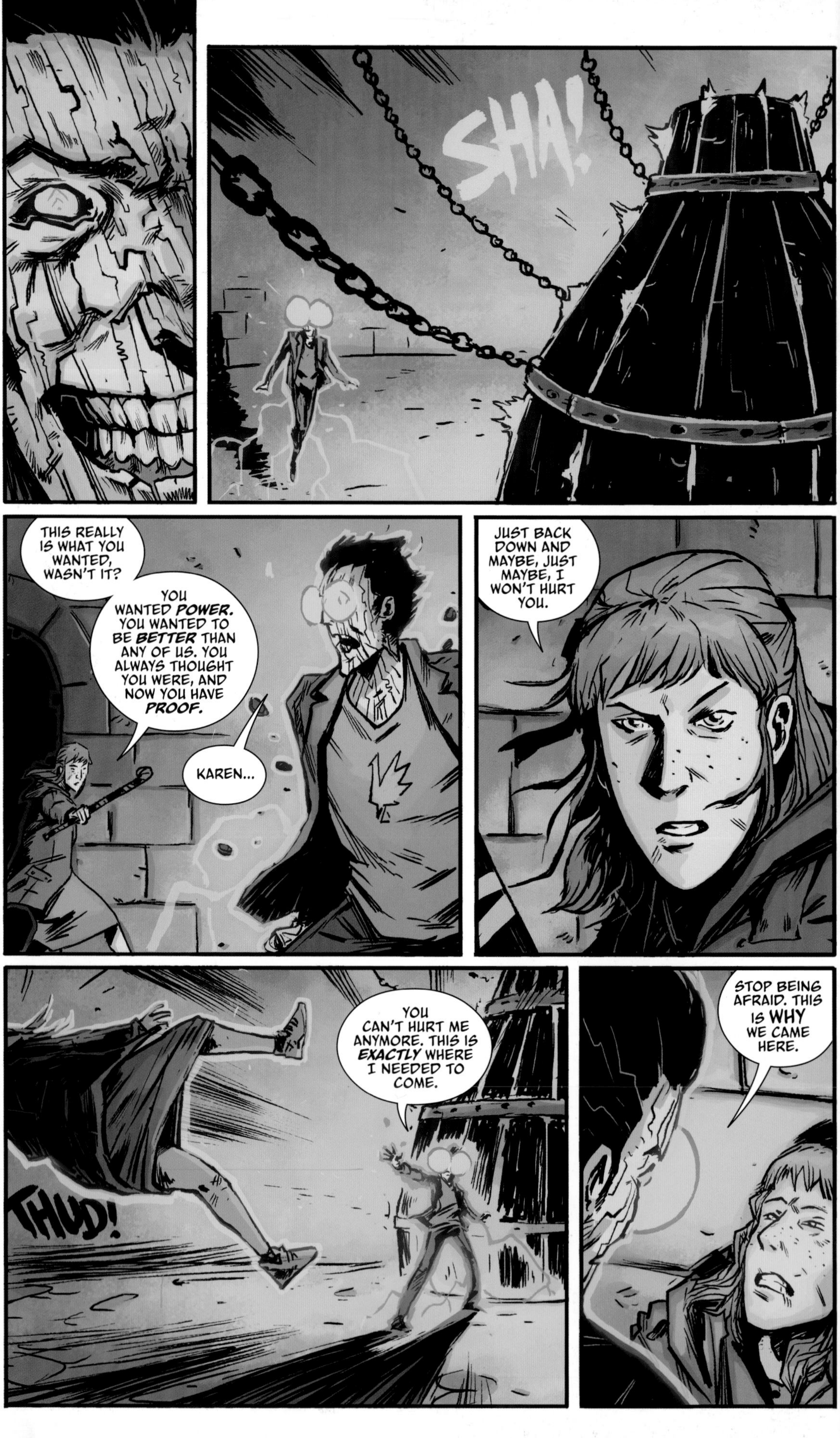
SHA!
THIS REALLY IS WHAT YOU WANTED, WASN'T IT?
YOU WANTED POWER. YOU WANTED TO BE BETTER THAN ANY OF US. YOU ALWAYS THOUGHT YOU WERE, AND NOW YOU HAVE PROOF.
KAREN...
JUST BACK DOWN AND MAYBE, JUST MAYBE, I WON'T HURT YOU.
YOU CAN'T HURT ME ANYMORE. THIS IS EXACTLY WHERE I NEEDED TO COME.
THUD!
STOP BEING AFRAID. THIS IS WHY WE CAME HERE.

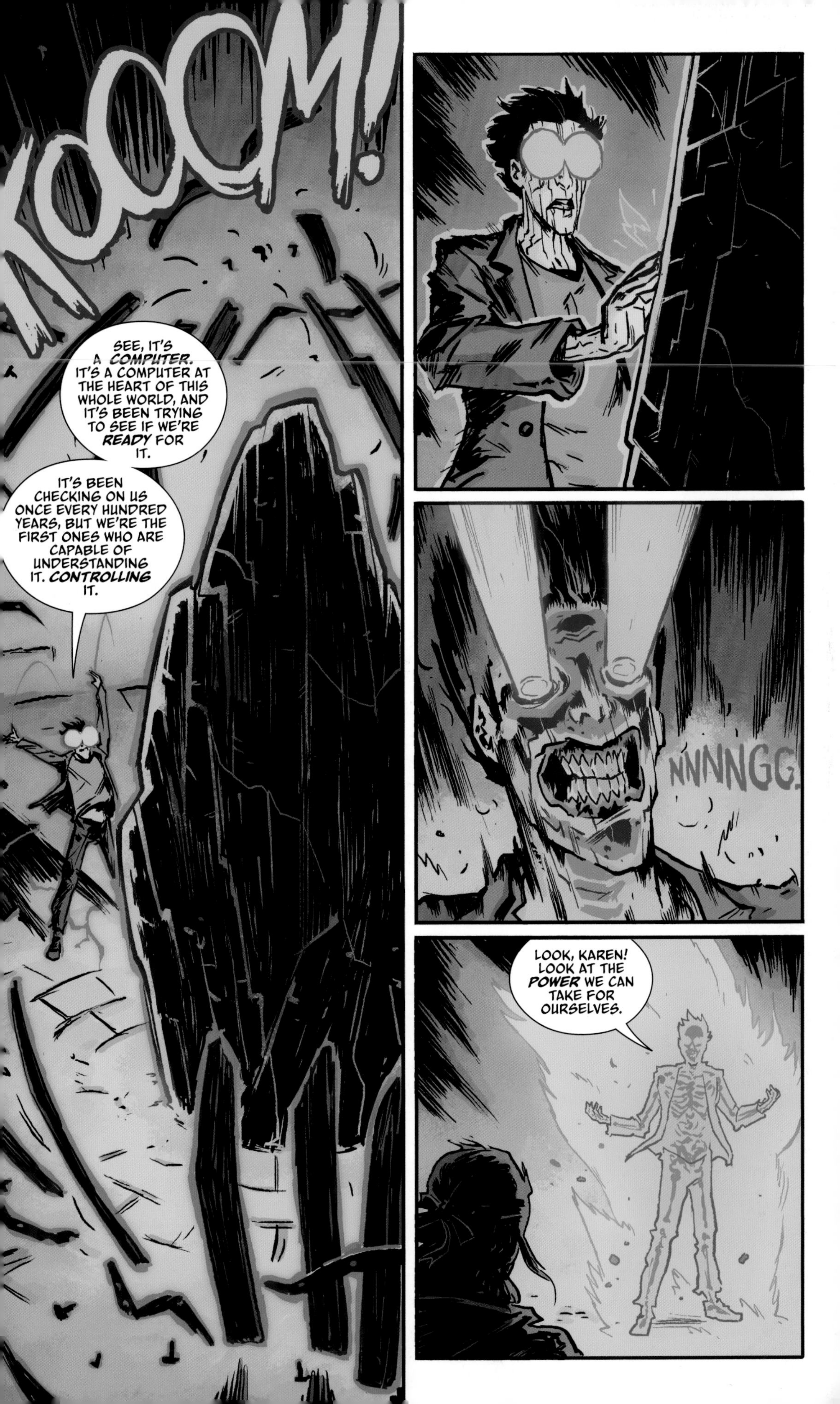

OOOM!
SEE, IT'S A COMPUTER. IT'S A COMPUTER AT THE HEART OF THIS WHOLE WORLD, AND IT'S BEEN TRYING TO SEE IF WE'RE READY FOR IT.
IT'S BEEN CHECKING ON US ONCE EVERY HUNDRED YEARS, BUT WE'RE THE FIRST ONES WHO ARE CAPABLE OF UNDERSTANDING IT. CONTROLLING IT.
NNNNGG.
LOOK, KAREN! LOOK AT THE POWER WE CAN TAKE FOR OURSELVES.

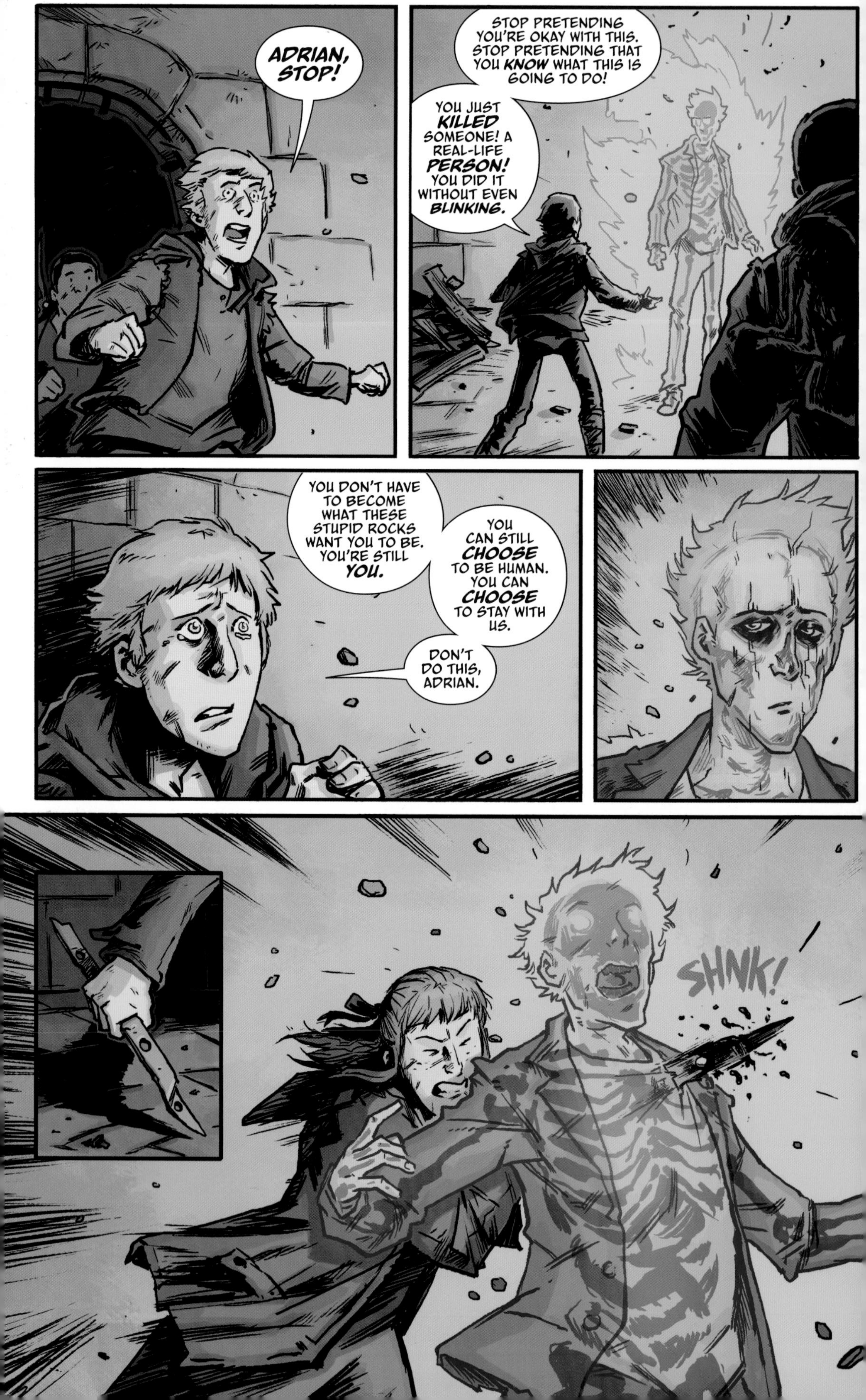
ADRIAN, STOP!
STOP PRETENDING YOU'RE OKAY WITH THIS. STOP PRETENDING THAT YOU KNOW WHAT THIS IS GOING TO DO!
YOU JUST KILLED SOMEONE! A REAL-LIFE PERSON! YOU DID IT WITHOUT EVEN BLINKING.
YOU DON'T HAVE TO BECOME WHAT THESE STUPID ROCKS WANT YOU TO BE. YOU'RE STILL YOU.
YOU CAN STILL CHOOSE TO BE HUMAN. YOU CAN CHOOSE TO STAY WITH US.
DON'T DO THIS, ADRIAN.
SHNK!

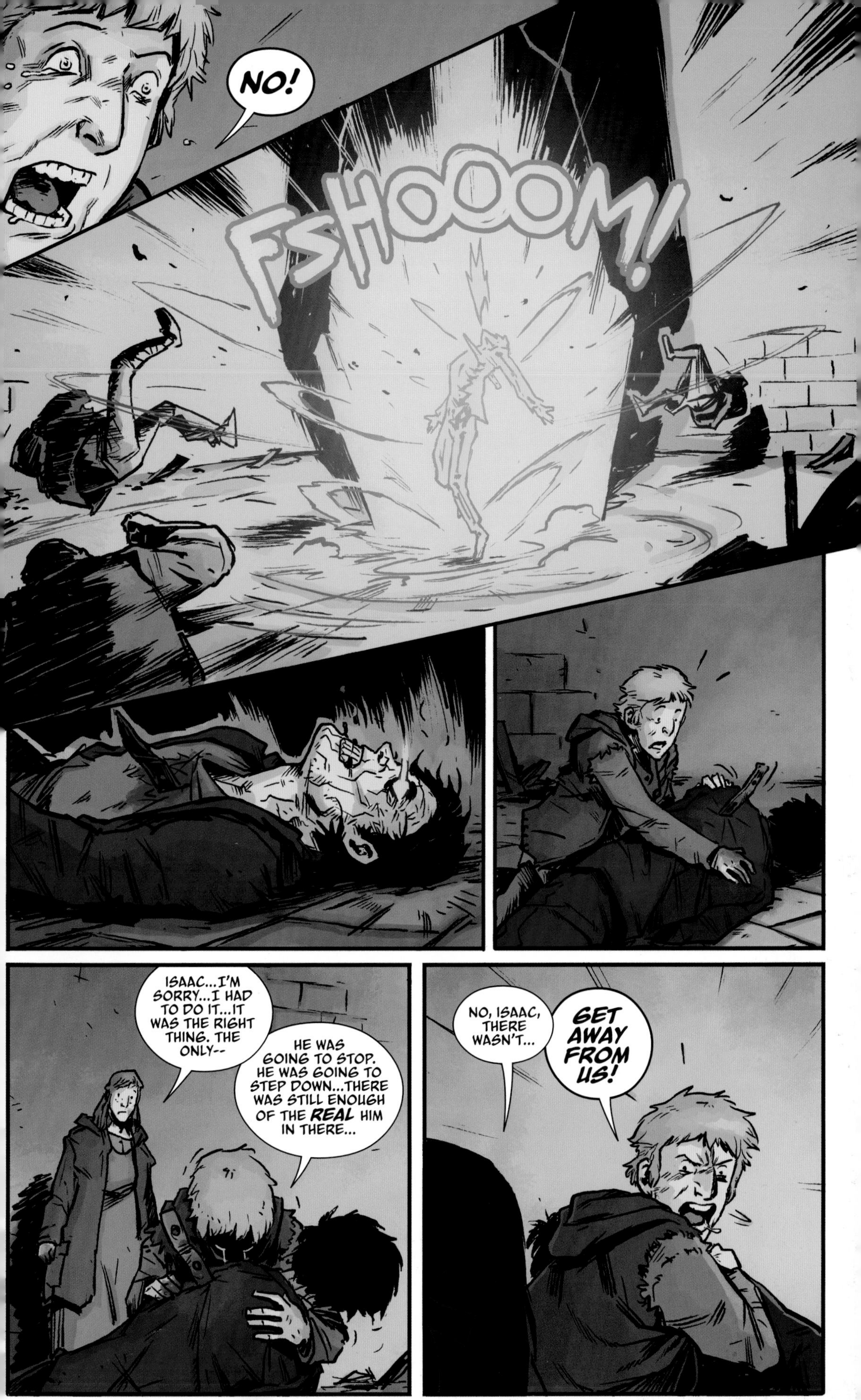
NO!
FSHOOOM!
ISAAC...I'M SORRY...I HAD TO DO IT...IT WAS THE RIGHT THING. THE ONLY--
HE WAS GOING TO STOP. HE WAS GOING TO STEP DOWN...THERE WAS STILL ENOUGH OF THE REAL HIM IN THERE...
NO, ISAAC, THERE WASN'T...
GET AWAY FROM US!

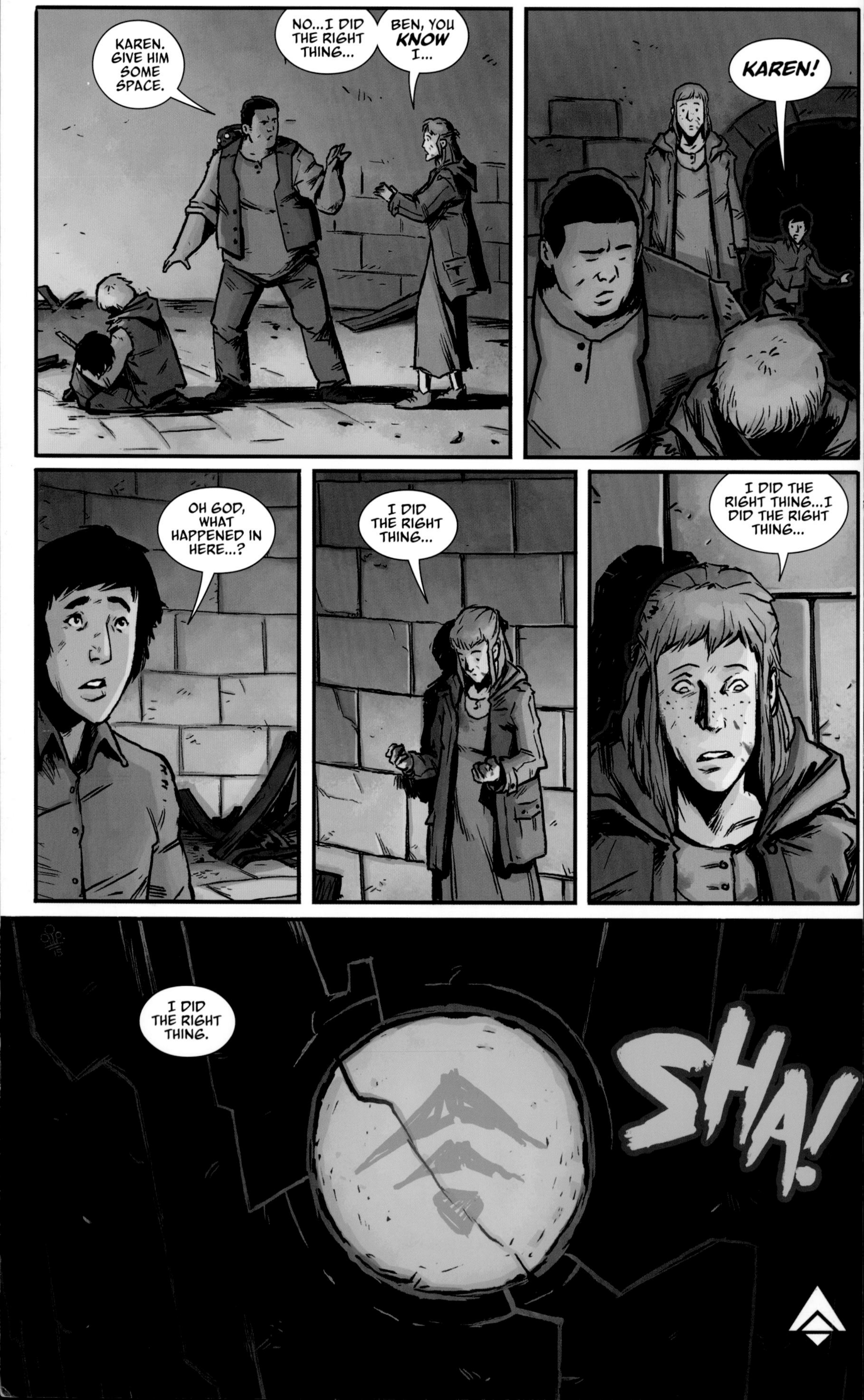
KAREN. GIVE HIM SOME SPACE.
NO...I DID THE RIGHT THING...
BEN, YOU KNOW I...
KAREN!
OH GOD, WHAT HAPPENED IN HERE...?
I DID THE RIGHT THING...
I DID THE RIGHT THING...I DID THE RIGHT THING...
I DID THE RIGHT THING.
SHA!

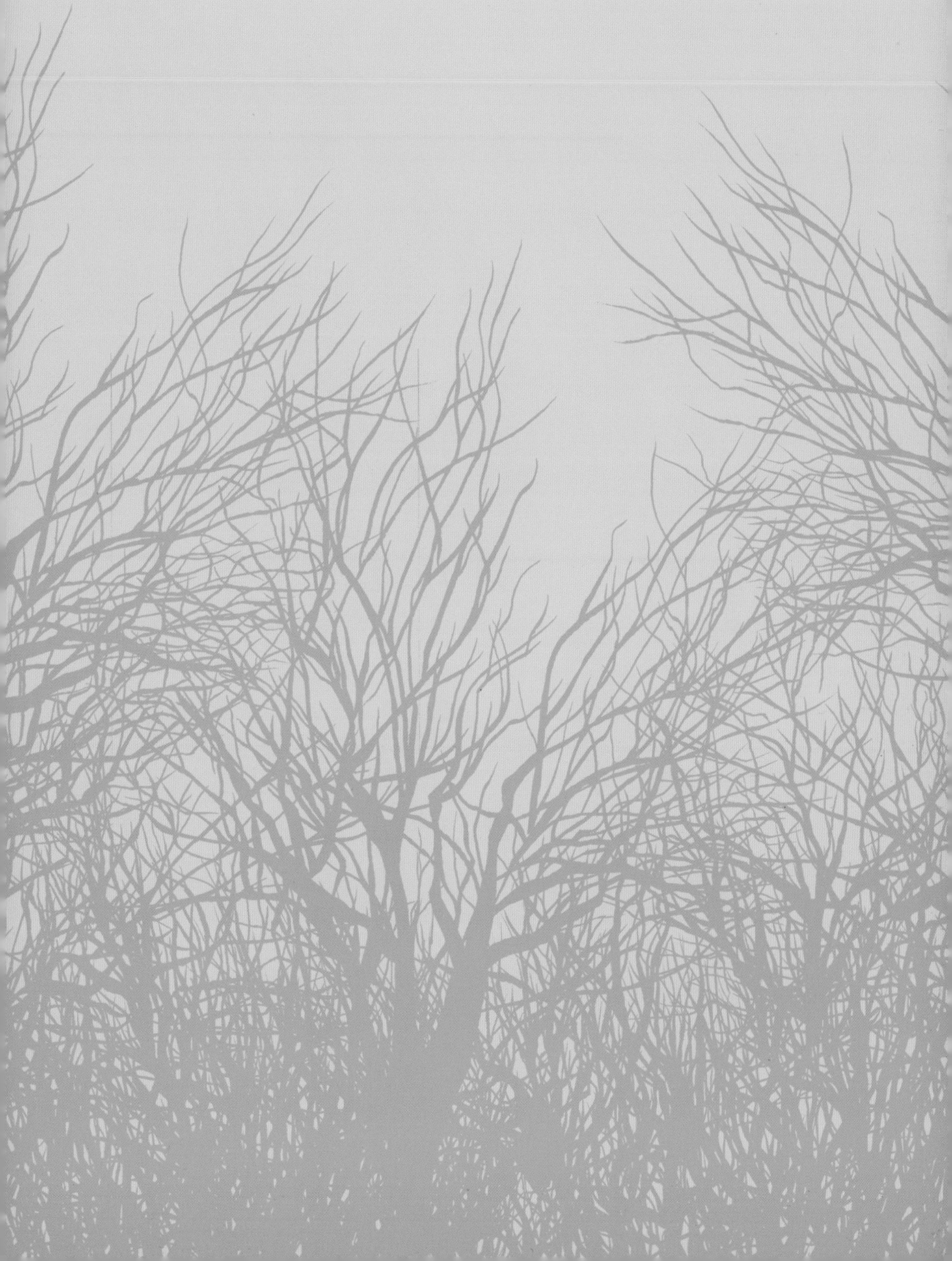

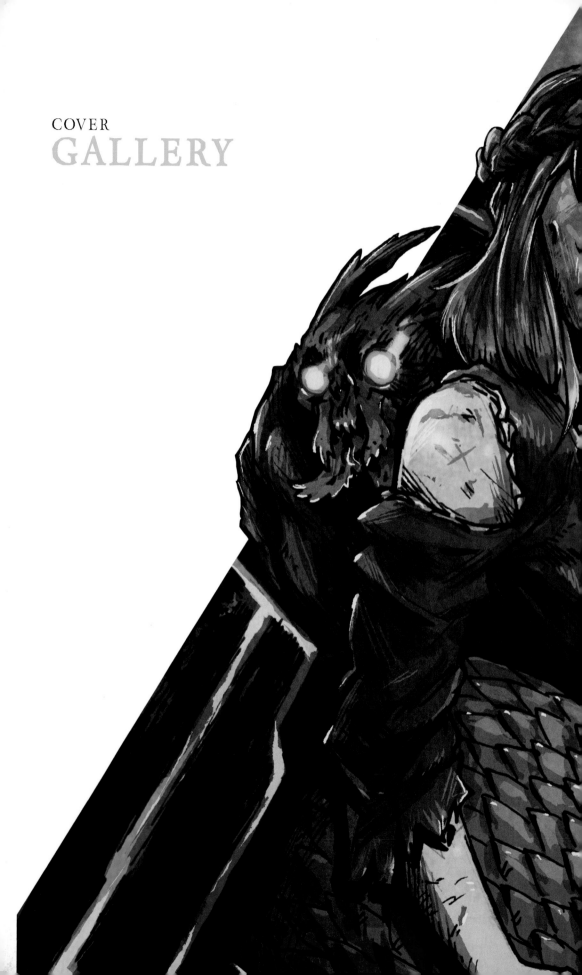

COVER
GALLERY

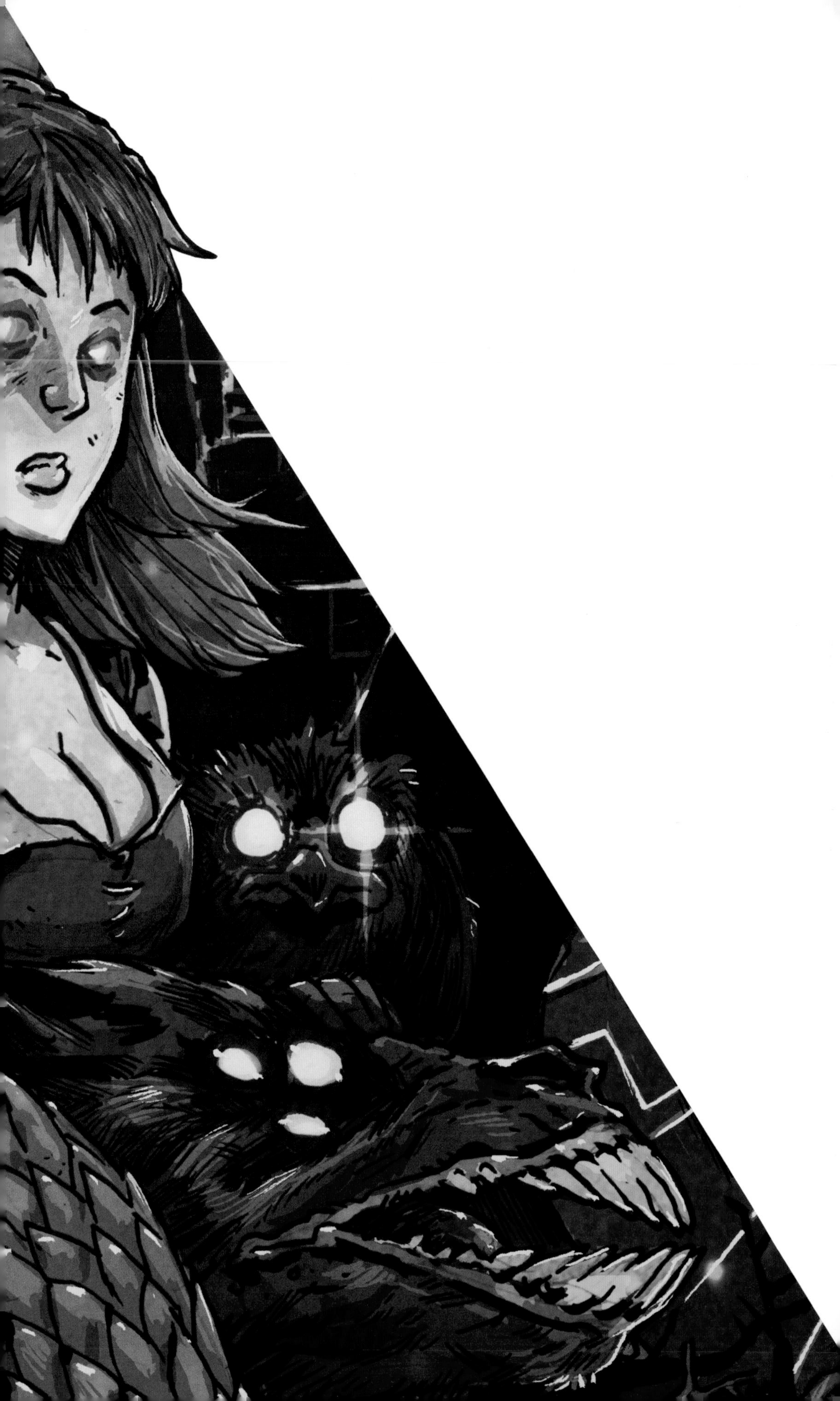

ISSUE NINE COVER **MICHAEL DIALYNAS**

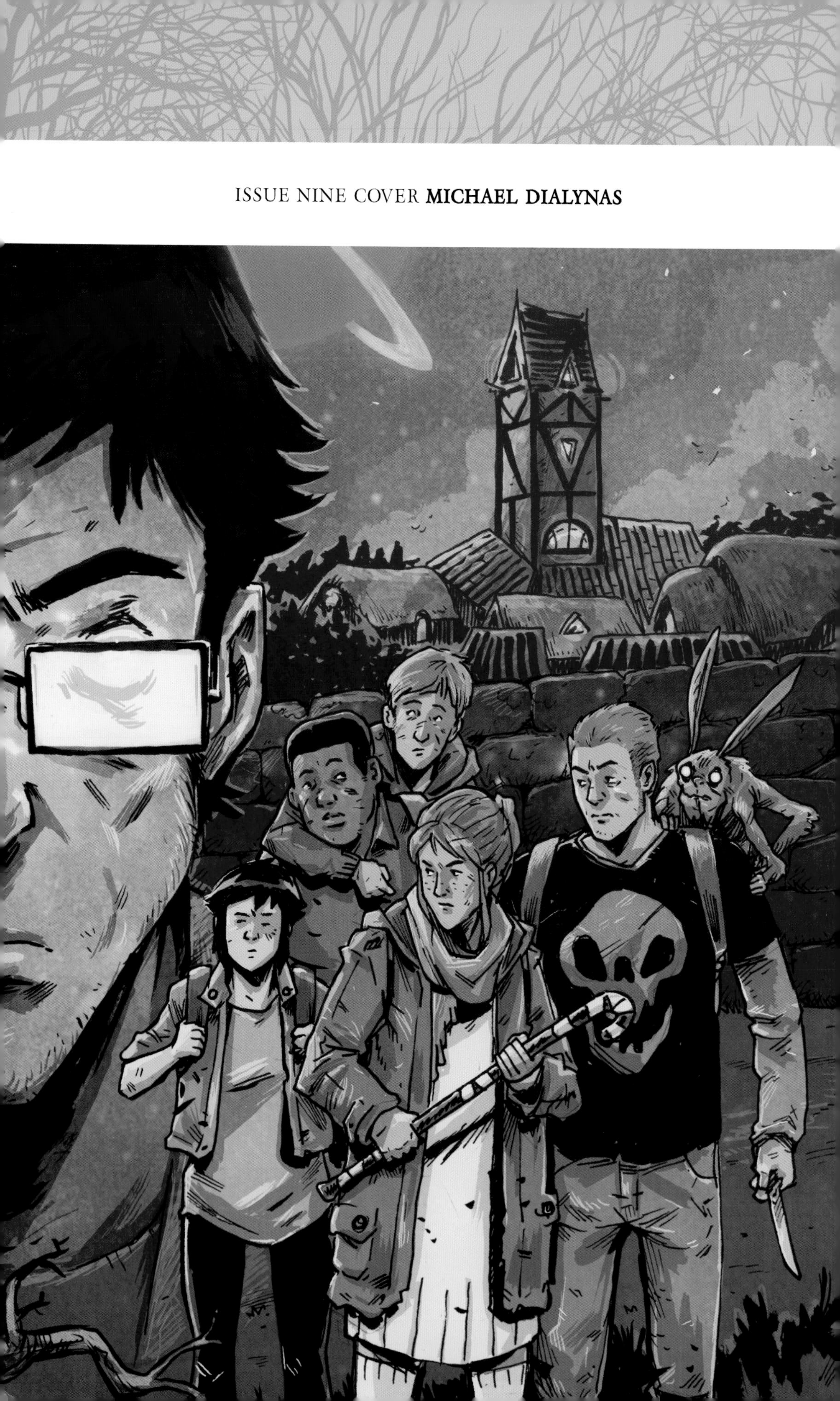

ISSUE TEN COVER **MICHAEL DIALYNAS**

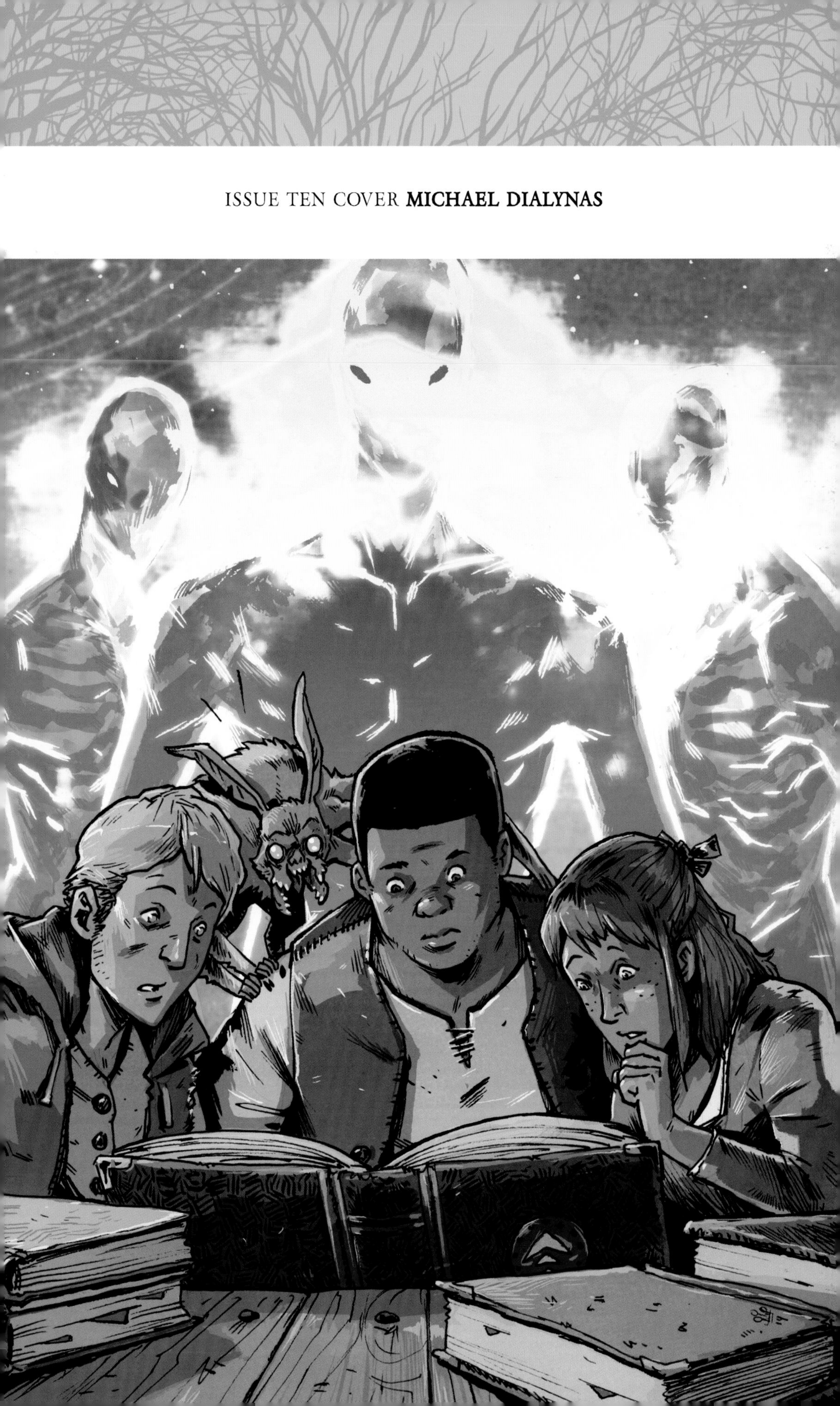

ISSUE ELEVEN COVER **MICHAEL DIALYNAS**

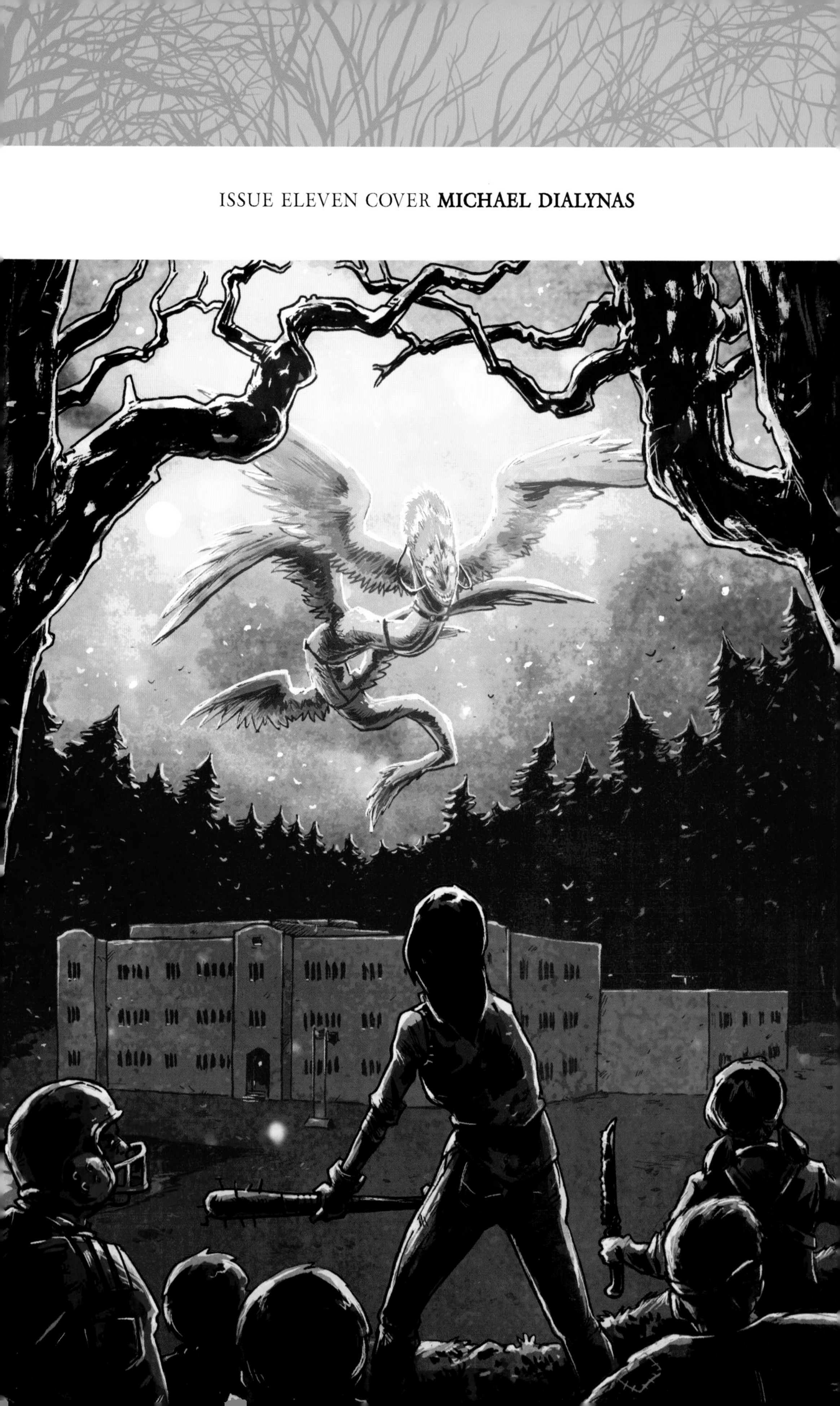

ISSUE TWELVE COVER **MICHAEL DIALYNAS**

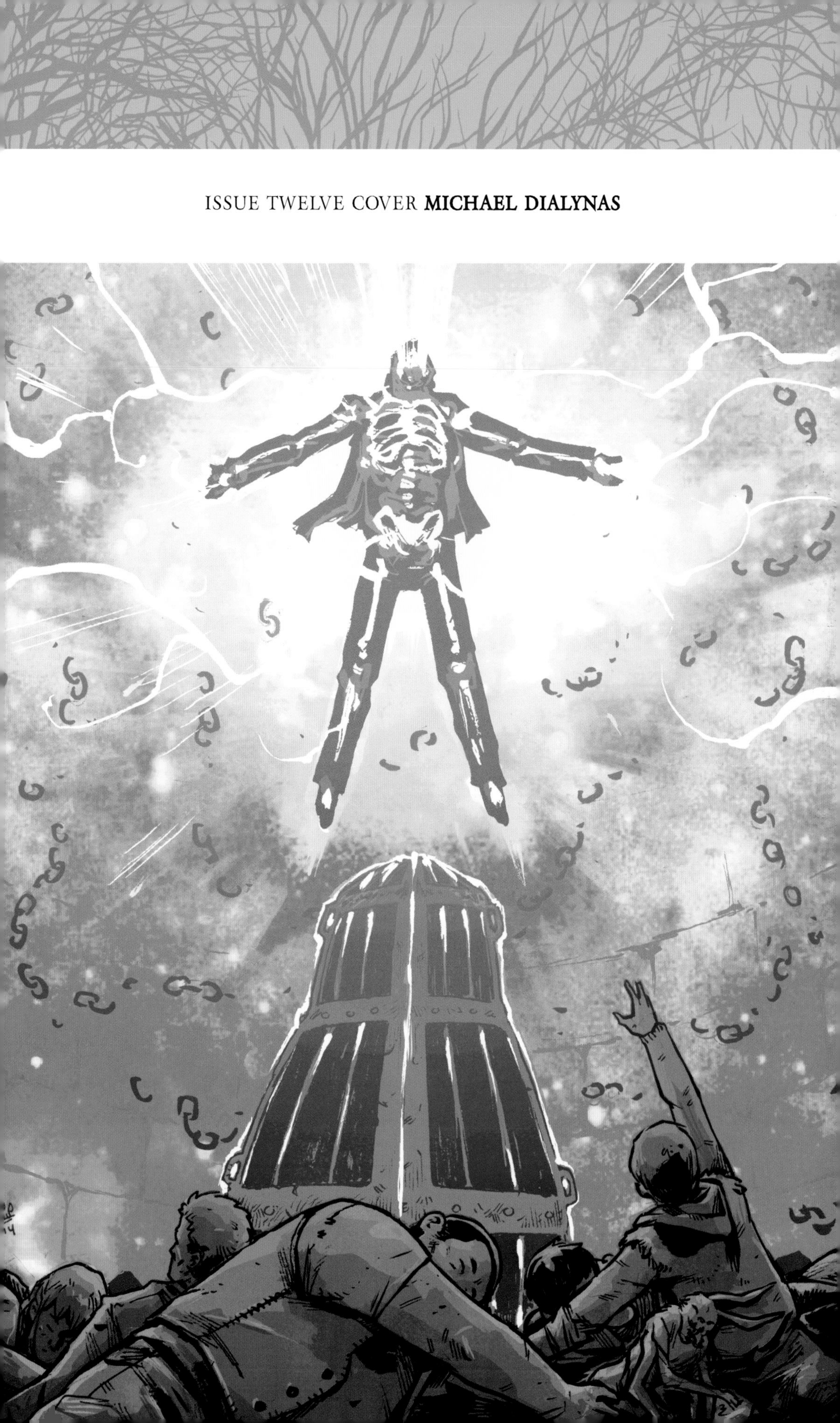

MICHAEL DIALYNAS

SKETCHBOOK

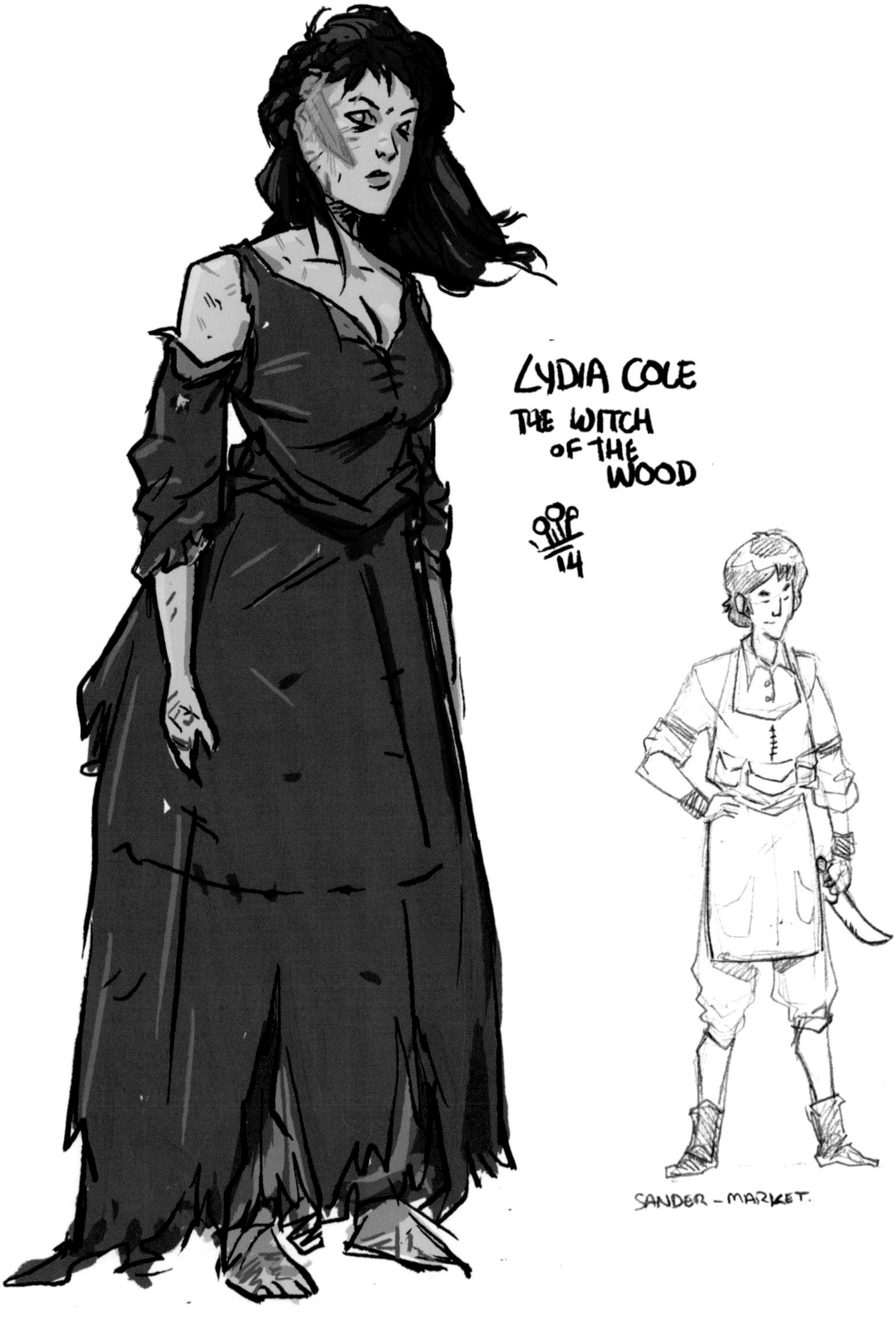
LYDIA COLE
THE WITCH OF THE WOOD
14
SANDER - MARKET.

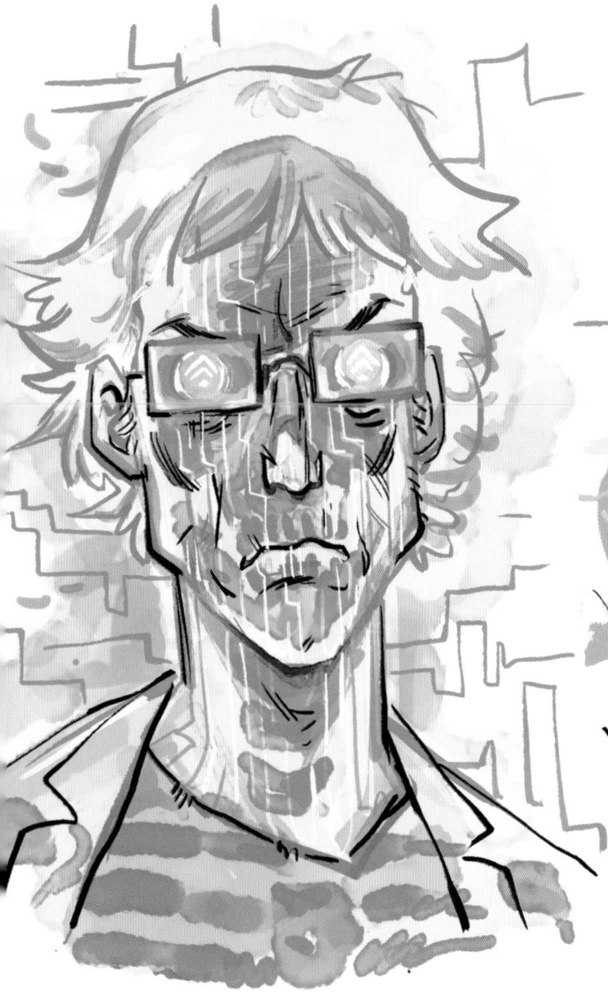

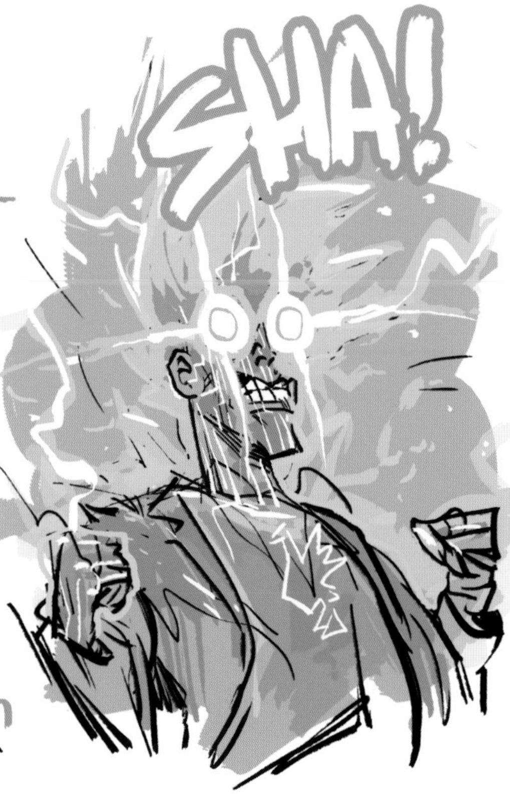
SHA!

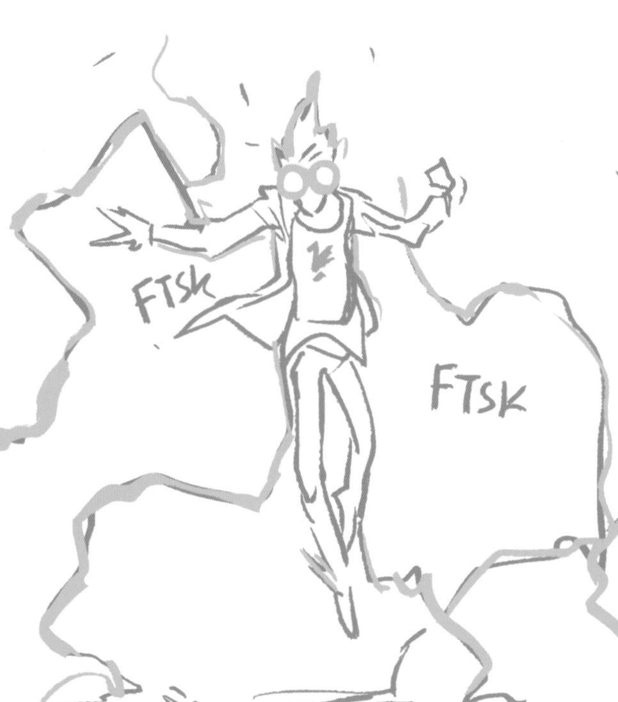
FTSK
FTSK

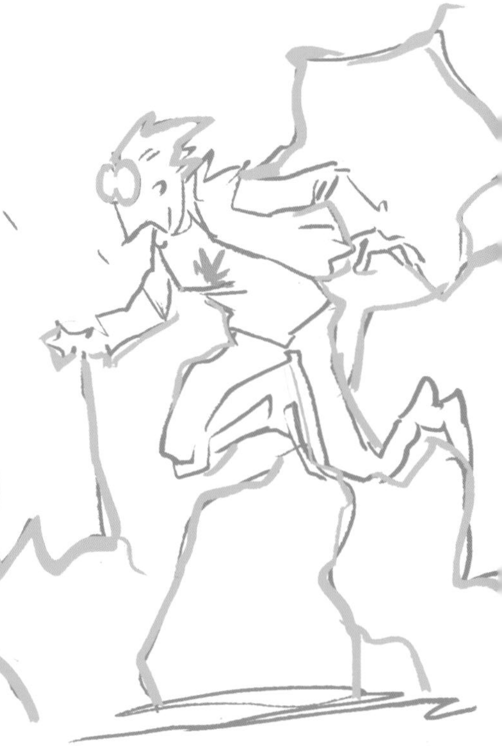

CASSIUS

NIGEL

GIDEON

FLORENCE

⑪
DRAGONS
SCHOOL
MARIA
BATTLE-READY

⑫
ADRIAN
STONE - NL

KIDS DEFEATED
'SAAC
REACHING

CORRINE

MISSY + MARIE

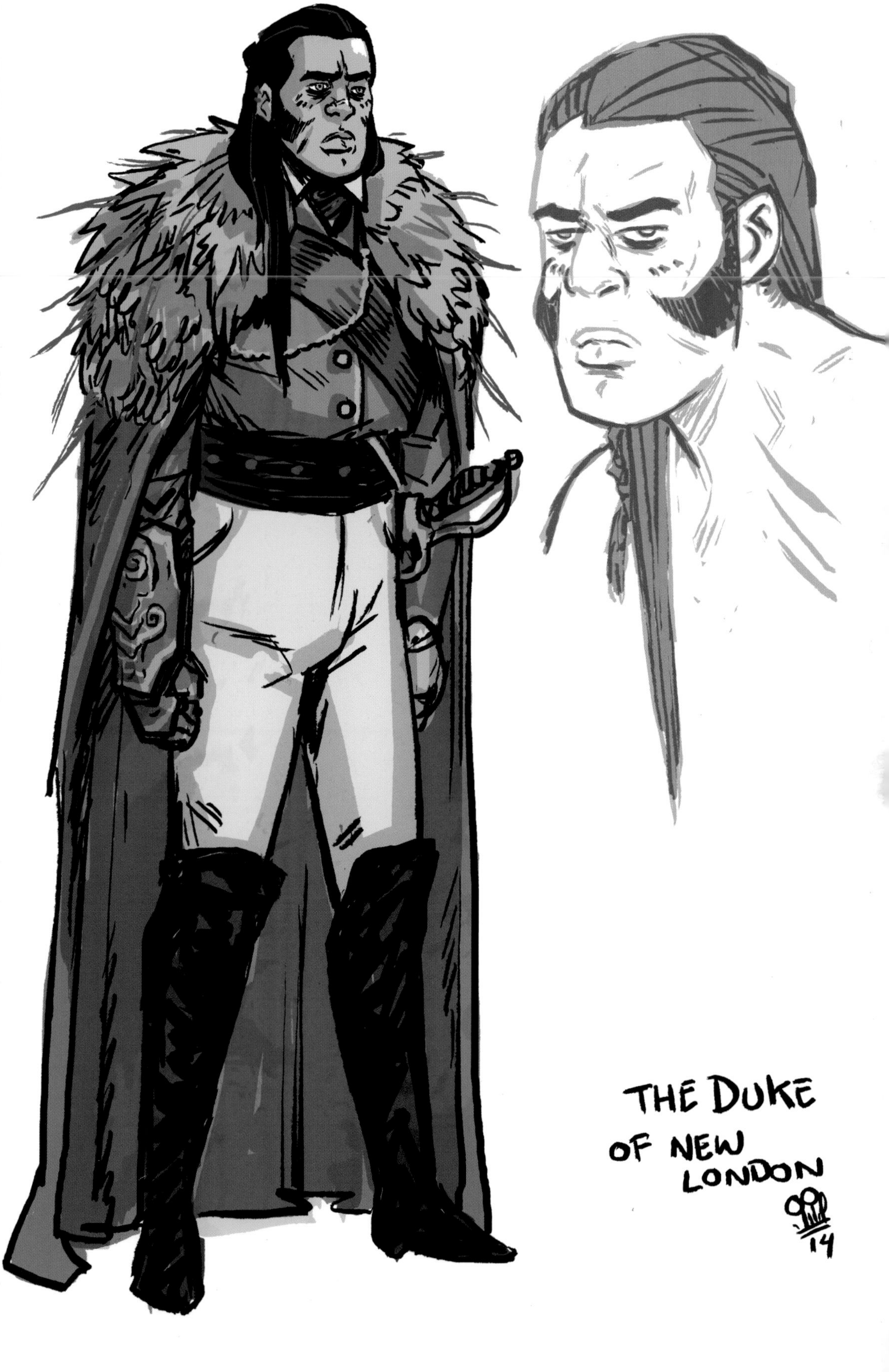
THE DUKE
OF NEW
LONDON
'14

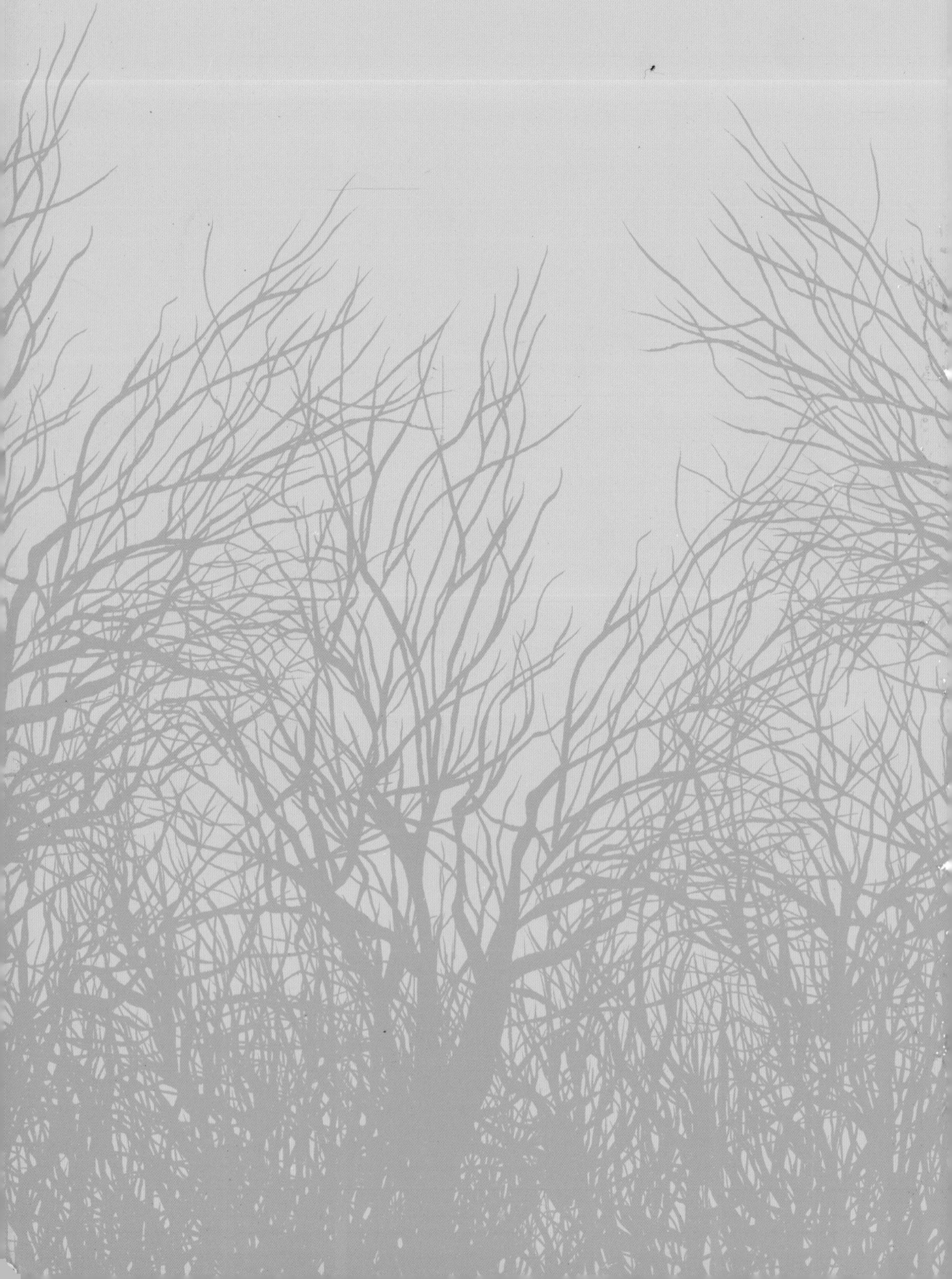